AMERICAN ORIENTAL SERIES

VOLUME 94

YANG XIONG AND THE PLEASURES OF READING AND CLASSICAL LEARNING IN CHINA

AMERICAN ORIENTAL
SERIES

VOLUME 94

AMERICAN ORIENTAL SOCIETY

NEW HAVEN, CONNECTICUT

2011

YANG XIONG AND THE PLEASURES OF READING AND CLASSICAL LEARNING IN CHINA

By

MICHAEL NYLAN

AMERICAN ORIENTAL SOCIETY
NEW HAVEN, CONNECTICUT
2011

Library of Congress Cataloging-in-Publication Data

Nylan, Michael.
Yang Xiong and the pleasures of reading and classical learning in China / By Michael Nylan.
p. cm. — (American oriental series ; v. 94)
Includes bibliographical references.
ISBN 978-0-940490-32-1 (alk. paper)
1. Yang, Xiong, 53 B.C.-18 A.D.—Books and reading. 2. Yang, Xiong, 53 B.C.-18 A.D.—Knowledge and learning. 3. Books and reading—China—History. 4. Learning and scholarship—China—History. I. Title.

PL2663.Y35Z79 2011
895.1'12—dc22

2011007622

The paper used in this publication meets the minimum requirements of the American National Standard for Information Sciences—Permanence of Paper for Printed Library Materials, ANSI Z39.48-1984. ♾™

To David Knechtges and Paul Kroll
Daniel Boyarin and Ramona Naddaff
Nathan Sivin and Henry Rosemont
Michael Loewe and Naomi Richard
Jamie Fuller and Gerry Boswell

Contents

What thou lovest well remains,
the rest is dross
What thou lov'st well shall not be reft from
thee
What thou lov'st well is thy true heritage
Pound, "Pisan Cantos"

Do not the archaic script forms and writings seem better to you than the non-standard? (*guwen buyou yu ye hu* 古文不猶愈於野乎)
Liu Xin, Yang's peer and rival

Acknowledgments

Several people helped during various stages in the preparation of this manuscript. Bill Boltz answered queries, as did Miranda Brown and Bill Baxter. Jianye He, reference librarian for Chinese studies at the East Asian Library at Berkeley, was invariably generous with her time, as were the two anonymous readers chosen by the American Oriental Society. Susan Stone gave me sound advice about computers and camera-ready copy, not to mention life. Phyllis Granoff and Koichi Shinohara provided sounding boards at crucial times.

This book is dedicated, with great pleasure, to those whose evident love of reading has quickened my own: David Knechtges and Paul Kroll, Daniel Boyarin and Ramona Naddaff, Nathan Sivin and Henry Rosemont, Michael Loewe and Naomi Richard, Jamie Fuller and Gerry Boswell.

The probable site of the Tianluge Library outside modern Xi'an

Introduction

Yang Xiong 揚雄 (53 BC-AD 18), the Han philosophical master, remarks at one point in his *Exemplary Figures* (*Fayan* 法言), "Books are as sexy as women."[1] Modern readers may frown at a comparison they regard as less than apt. Yang was supremely aware, however, of longstanding traditions, ascribed both to the sages and to the Classics, contrasting the unusual strength of the basic drives for food and sex with the general weakness of the acquired inclinations toward moral behavior.[2] To say that "books are as sexy as women" was to make bold to add to those traditions, adopting the manner of a sage; also to elevate the value of certain texts, at least, to the level of morality itself, insofar as they represented acquired tastes leading to the most desirable aspects of civilized life. Yang's statement is all the more intriguing when placed in the Western Han context, for in his era, as the *Fayan* shows, texts were frequently dismissed as the "mere dregs" of the sage's teachings, to be resorted to in the absence of living masters while training for careers in government.[3] One early figure spoke for many when he complained with a sigh, "Reading books makes me sleepy."[4] Another equated the composition

---

[1] *Fayan* 2/5. More literally, "as alluring as women," with "alluring" implying "sexual appeal" and the "ability to captivate." All refs. for *Fayan* are to the Han Jing 韓敬 1992 edition, hereafter FY. The title is usually rendered *Model Sayings* or *Exemplary Sayings*. I have chosen "figures," not only because it connotes "figures of speech," "emblems," "designs, and "images," but also because the *Fayan* contains many passages that cast the speech, conduct, and writings of famous people as examples for good or ill.

[2] See *Analects* 9/18, 15/13; *Mencius* 6A/4, 6B/1; also the preface to the Mao Ode (no. 143) "Yue chu" 月出. For newly excavated materials, see Riegel 1977.

[3] Significantly, Zhuangzi's famous story about Wheelwright Bian is repeated in HSWZ 5/6 (Hightower, 167) with no objection registered, which suggests that it is not merely a "proto-Daoist" story. See below. Kongzi in *Analects* 11/2b spoke of the necessity of reading, but for edification, rather than for pleasure. For Yang's detailed refutation of the conventional ideas that study and learning are "useless," unless they lead to an official career, see Nylan 2008.

[4] See *Zhanguo ce* 40/14/3, for the phrase *dushu yushui* 讀書欲睡. Cf. the complaint registered in SJ 24.1221 ("Whenever I listen to ancient music, I am afraid I will fall asleep."), and *Liji* 19.24/102/22 ("Yueji" 樂記).

of original texts with "torturing oneself."[5] Those conventions notwithstanding, Yang thought exquisitely refined writing – defined as compositions preserved in pre-Qin script or the latter-day productions that captured the spirit of the true pre-Qin masters – as alluring in its forms as any natural beauty: "With women, one hates it when paints interfere with their feminine graces. And with writings, one hates it when over-elaborate phrasing sullies or confounds the model and measure."[6]

Many readers before Yang Xiong must have *experienced* the pleasures of reading, as an idle comment in the *Huainanzi* suggests.[7] But to experience a pleasure is hardly the same as to write or theorize about it.[8] It was Yang Xiong and several of his contemporaries – especially Liu Xiang 劉向 (79-8 BC) and Liu Xin 劉歆 (53 BC-AD 23) – who constructed the first serious, sustained, and systematic case for the keen pleasures to be had from reading the Classics.[9] In building this case, Yang and his contemporaries started a trend, fashioning parts of pre-existing arguments into a distinctively new mix, which they traced back, on tenuous grounds, as we now know, to the Duke of Zhou and Kongzi, centuries earlier.[10] This new mix, which I dub *haogu* 好古 ("love of antiquity") for the sake of convenience, was championed by the most famous writers in the centuries after Yang Xiong, so much so that later

---

5 *Xijing zaji* 2.89, using the term *zi ku* 自苦, in connection with Yang Xiong's composing texts.

6 FY 2/5.

7 See HNZ 21.706 ("Yao lue" 要略) speaks of writings being enough to "make oneself happy" (*zile* 自樂).

8 Two illustrations should suffice to clarify the distinction between experiencing something and theorizing about it: (1) No accounts of urban city life in China prior to the twelfth-century *Dongjing meng Hua lu* (comp. 1148), supply a vision of a city that is "horizontal" (i.e., embracing all classes) and "integrated" (in the sense of crossing wards); and (2) W. G. Sebald 2003 has noted that nearly no Germans living in the immediate post-World War II cities commented, even in their private diaries, on the destruction of the cities that they witnessed every day.

9 HS 8.272; 36.1929, says that Liu Xiang "focused all his thoughts on Classics and the arts" (*jing shu* 經術).

10 See *Liezi* 4 20/18-21/8, especially the last line's description of Zhongni as one who "would strum and sing, and intone texts, until the end of his life, without stopping." The origins of the *haogu* movement can be traced to the Shiqu Pavilion conference in 51 BC. Elements that would come together in the movement can be found, for example, in a memorial by Yi Feng 翼奉 in 48 BC, two decades or so before Yang's arrival at court, but there is no sign that before Yang and his contemporaries that this movement in any way represented a strong challenge to the status quo.

literary convention virtually required learned members of the governing elite to express their unbounded delight in reading about antiquity.[11] Echoes of Yang, then, resound in Tao Yuanming's 陶淵明 (365-427) "There's pleasure to be had in it [the text],/ Pleasure reaching unto the utmost limits," as in Ge Hong's 葛洪 (280- ca. 343) line about the Ancients: "They ... diverted themselves with the Classics."[12] This monograph aims to provide a plausible explanation why Yang's particular style of assessing the distant past proved of such enduring appeal to readers over the centuries. To this end, it will survey the biographical information that we have for Yang and the state of manuscript culture in Yang's world in relation to authors and authority before turning to consider the close ties between the prevailing pleasure discourse and Yang's distinctive mode of writing, and Yang's leading role as classical master at a classicizing court.

Yang expended minimal effort on justifying classical learning for its benefits to family and state, presumably because he felt his readers were readily convinced of learning's utility in those areas. Instead, he argued that reading was critically important to the cultivation of that refined "taste" which underpins all well-informed and elegant writing – and this at a time when no author (as opposed to teacher) could hope to make a living from his writings. How fitting, then, that Yang is one of the few early masters to receive a substantive biography that adequately conveys a sense of psychological development.[13] Already in that biography, purportedly based on Yang's autobiography, two competing portraits of Yang contend for supremacy, just as they would in late imperial China.[14] The first depicts the poor, earnest scribbler, abused or ignored by inattentive or obtuse rulers, who is nonetheless hailed as a great poet and thinker by a small band of

---

11 The phrase *haogu*, of course, comes from *Analects* 7/1, where Kongzi describes his own love of antiquity.

12 For Tao, see Tian Xiaofei 2005: 148ff. For Ge, see *Waipian* 50/199/10 (*yi dianji ziwu* 以典籍自娛).

13 Yang's *Hanshu* biography (comp. ca. AD 92) is based heavily on his own autobiography (see below). In this Yang was unlike the Zhanguo thinkers and most Han writers. Sima Qian participates in the "family enterprise" of learning. Qu Yuan 屈原 (3rd c. BC) and Jia Yi 賈誼 (200-127) are two other figures thought to merit full-scale biographies, but both accounts are very brief, if we subtract their writings from their biographies.

14 Of course, the modern world, even in China, chiefly consigns Yang to oblivion. For example, Victor Mair 1997: 147-52, once (mis)characterized Yang Xiong as a minor figure in the Han; cf. Mair 1994. See also Willard Peterson 1989, who argued that Yang Xiong was hardly an innovative or original thinker.

dedicated followers who recognize his genius. (Yang's writings express his profound dissatisfaction that some at court thought him little better than an entertainer for hire.) The second depicts Yang-the-traitor, slavish supporter of the usurper Wang Mang 王莽 (d. 23), the consort clan (*waiqi* 外戚) regent who seized the throne in AD 9 while posing as a second Duke of Zhou.[15] A third portrayal that can be pieced together from Yang's biography is more likely to be true. That third portrait shows Yang enjoying considerable prestige as an authority regularly consulted on important affairs of state, including omen interpretation and foreign policy, despite the elegantly phrased yet forthright stances he used to skewer the Han emperors and his fellow courtiers, annoying powerful factions at the late Western Han court.[16]

Yang Xiong's first taste of court life came during the reign of Chengdi (r. 33-7 BC), a classically trained ruler then in thrall to two seductive beauties, Flying Swallow Zhao 趙飛燕 and her younger sister.[17] Perhaps the sex-drenched atmosphere at court plus the emperor's considerable interest in book learning prompted Yang's little joke about the sexiness of books.[18] (That Yang deplored the emperor's sexual indulgence is evident from a *fu* dated to 11 BC.)[19] Long before his arrival at court, however, Yang had immersed himself in the study of arcane vocabulary and phrasing, and his lifelong passion for rarified and refined language led him to cast the potentials of writing and classical learning in novel yet pleasing ways. Yang's writing, in contrast to the "subtle wording" ascribed in Han times to Confucius, supposed author of the *Annals* (*Chunqiu* 春秋), does not lay claim

---

[15] For Yang Xiong as a craven sycophant whose success at court was bought at the price of his integrity, see Su Shi's (1037-1101) "matching poem" to Tao Qian's "Imitating the Ancients," in no. 2 of 9 in the series, line 6 [慎勿從楊雄], Yuan Xingpei ed., 4.342; and Hightower 1970, Poem 48, then matched in a poem by Su Shi recorded in Lin Yixun 2008, 1258-61.

[16] Yang lambasted the war party of a previous era, in a thinly veiled attack against the expansionists of his own day. He argued in FY 13/29-30 that if the hawks had gotten their way, the Central States civilization would have been ruined. Today, Yang is seldom considered an omen expert, but HS 27B(c).1429, has Yang identifying a "drum omen."

[17] For Chengdi as a generally good ruler who could boast superb classical training, as well as an interest in historical precedents, see Ying Shao, *Fengsu tongyi* 2.6/14/26-2.6/17/6, a lengthy entry entitled "Han Wendi" 文帝.

[18] FY 2/5. I am indebted to Stephen Owen for this observation, but Paul Kroll (private communication, July, 2010) rightly queries whether Chengdi's court was more sex-drenched than other courts. The Zhao sisters, Chengdi's preferred consorts, may have seemed more dangerous than highborn empresses, however. But this is speculation.

[19] See Knechtges 1976: 55-56; Wu Fusheng 2007: 49.

to a systematic adherence to specific rules of composition. Yang, as will become clear below, is more inclined to play with the rules.[20] The extent of his unconventionality was matched only by the single-mindedness of purpose that he brought to his chosen pursuits, in particular to his proposed revision of classical learning.

Fortunately for those who would study him, Yang Xiong and his associates and admirers left an impressive paper trail. For Yang alone there exist two early accounts: the biography/autobiography preserved in Ban Gu's 班固 *Writings on the Han* (*Hanshu* 漢書 (completed ca. AD 92), and a second biographical notice recorded in Chang Qu's 常璩 (active. 265–316) *Record of the Lands South of Mount Hua* (*Huayang guozhi* 華陽國志) that strings together anecdotes collected by Yang's friends, acquaintances, and critics, including his disciple Huan Tan 桓譚 (43 BC-AD 28). There are the two philosophical masterworks, the *Fayan* and the *Canon of Supreme Mystery* (*Taixuan jing* 太玄), designed to update and expand the *Analects* and the *Changes* respectively, not to mention Yang's corpus of long epideictic *fu*, and two spirited defenses of Yang's decision to compose para-canonical masterworks after he became disgusted with the display *fu*. The *Correct Words* (*Fangyan* 方言),[21] Yang's third masterwork, may be the sole survivor among his several lexicographical works,[22] yet to this already impressive list can be added Yang 's reminiscences about his original intentions when composing court *fu* and a set of letters supposedly exchanged between Yang and Liu Xin in connection with the compilation of an early version of the *Fangyan*,[23] as well as the semi-hagiographic sketches offered by Yang's later admirers, including Tao Yuanming and Liu Xie 劉勰 (ca. 465-ca. 522).[24] Probably there survived in the first centuries AD many more pieces of Yang's writing, not to mention traditions about him, since the entire curriculum of the late second-century AD Jingzhou 荊州 Academy was supposedly organized around Yang's

[20] See Joachim Gentz 2008: 817. For the role of the "uncrowned king" and the place of "subtle wording" in Han, see van Ess (unpublished).

[21] This title is usually rendered *Dialect Expressions*, but, as will be argued below, it was far more than the earliest wordlist for dialect words and phrases.

[22] See below.

[23] Paul L-M Serruys and David R. Knecthges concur on the authenticity of these letters (see below), despite a few anachronisms, which were presumably entered during transmission.

[24] For Tao Yuanming, see Nylan forthcoming-a, chapter 6. For Liu Xie, see Wang Ping 2010: 201-22.

masterworks. Unfortunately, few details have survived, although early reports suggest that Yang's work most likely provided the inspiration for Wang Bi 王弼 (226-49) and the Mystery Learning (*xuanxue* 玄學) of the Six Dynasties.[25] Still, the extant sources provide abundant confirmation of Yang's uninterrupted influence in the centuries spanning Eastern Han through Northern Song. The modern scholar Yan Lingfeng 嚴靈峰 (1904-?) has found enough commentaries upon Yang's philosophical works for brief notices on those works to occupy some eighty printed pages.[26]

The various sources reiterate Yang Xiong's propensity to combine irony with self-valorization. Yang even supplied one of his philosophical *tours de force*, the *Taixuan*, with autocommentaries written in two distinct styles, one of them in the Han style that he was known to despise.[27] In the *Fayan*, some 16,000 characters in length, Yang strung together a series of snappy dialogues slyly mocking all manner of puerile propositions that passed for common sense. Clearly, Yang took immense pleasure throughout his life in deliberately deconstructing and reconstructing his public persona, as his autobiography, his *fu*, and his other philosophical masterworks attest. Yang

---

[25] Jingzhou was overseen by or known to such scholarly giants as Song Zhong 宋衷 (f. AD 192), Yu Fan 虞翻 (164-233), and Wang Su 王肅 (d. 256). The Jingzhou Academy scholars seem mainly to have opposed the readings of Ma Rong and Zheng Xuan. One apocryphal tale has Wang Bi dying after the ghost of Zheng Xuan appears to him and complains of his disrespectful treatment in Wang's writings. Still, so much has been lost that we cannot tell much at this remove. See Quan Hou Hanwen 91/5b-6a; Nylan 2001: 315-21; Wagner (2000), 45-51. The best secondary literature on Jingzhou includes Chittick 2003; Jin Ke 2001; Jin Renyi 2002; Liu Moshu 2006; and Wang Yongping 2005.

[26] See Yan Lingfeng 1975-79: vol. 5, 319-99. Zhu Xi, however, severely criticized Yang Xiong in particular and Han classical learning in general. For a brief reception history of the *Fayan*, see the Introduction to Nylan (forthcoming-b).

[27] The three neoclassics are Yang's FY, *Fangyan*, and *Taixuan*, modeled on the *Lunyu*, the *Erya*, and the *Yijing* respectively. The *Taixuan* was provided with two sets of commentaries, "Wings" written in imitation of the "Ten Wings" of the *Yijiing* ascribed to Kongzi; and *zhangju* 章句 written in imitation of the Han-dynasty commentaries that Yang typically excoriated. The latter autocommentaries have been lost, unfortunately. For Yang's disdain for "chapter and verse" commentaries, see Pokora 1963: 18, n. 11, citing HHS 28A.955, 40A.1330, 49.1429; cf. Dull 1966: 340-50. According to Serruys 1959: 98, the scholars who preferred, as Yang did, the "glosses and explanations" (*xungu* 訓詁) method "stressed the study of separate words in the original meanings and their relations with modern words," which led to an interest in old word forms and regional dialects. Note that the *Taixuan* hardly figures in the discussion below, because it is seems to raise and address other issues than those being raised in this monograph, though nothing in the *Taixuan* contradicts the picture we get of Yang's ideas from the *Fayan*.

also conveyed the delight he took in playing the classical master, playing with words and scripts, roaming through manuscripts, and competing with his preferred Ancients. Indeed, for his admirers Yang epitomized the ability to *wan* 玩 ("play"), a word denoting the tactile pleasure experienced when rolling something smooth around in the hand or the mental pleasure to be had from rolling something over in the mind or communicating one's thoughts to like-minded people of comparable taste and refinement.[28] Several cross-cultural comparisons spring to mind – Yang Xiong as counterpart to Callimachus (ca. 305-240 BC), the famous poet-librarian, or to Aulus Gellius (d. ca 180), "whose nightly joy lay in sucking out the meanings of words and the origins of customs."[29]

So skillfully executed was each of Yang's turns at playing that, for over a millennium after his death, he remained *the* master *par excellence* to emulate when basing one's life on the allied pleasures of reading and classical learning. Arguably, it was Yang who made one source of play – classical learning acquired through reading – the very definition of Chinese culture.[30] This monograph therefore seeks to recapture the sense of playfulness that superb stylists of the Han, beginning with Yang Xiong and his peers, brought to morally serious ideas about reading and classical learning. It focuses on the banter found in the *Fayan* dialogues, insofar as these tell us most about Yang's clever conflation of himself-as-writer with the character he constructed as Master Yang-the-classical master.

---

[28] The oils from a person's skin were thought to persist on books, marking them indelibly with the "moisture," "character" or "grace" (*ze* 澤), and smell of the person. A woman's saliva remained on the cups she used; a man's residue on his books, according to *Liji* 13.24/83-85 ("Yuzao" 玉藻). Cf. *Mencius* 8/22. It is important to realize that the senses, especially sight, were typically cast as responses to touch in early China, as in early Greece. For more on this, see Nylan 2008-b.

[29] For Callimachus, see Alan Cameron 1995; for Aulus Gellius, see Erik Gunderson 2009. According to Emily Gowers 2009: 13, "Aulus is rarely credited with any meaningful direction or design today," though "his freewheeling cleverness made him an important figure during the Second Sophistic's ruthless battles over points of grammar and classical allusions," which endowed him with intellectual and linguistic supremacy among bookish Romans who claimed to love learning for its own sake.

[30] Johan Huizinga 2000, Foreword.

I
Yang's Life from the Early Sources

THE EARLY BIOGRAPHIES

Unlike the great thinkers before him, Yang Xiong has two early biographies that supplement the view of the man and his activities to be gleaned from a selection of his writings. The first impression created by the *Hanshu* biography is of a powerless figure at court, too timid to broach awkward subjects in a hostile atmosphere, lest he endanger himself and his family. Yet this purported timidity is difficult to square with Yang's harsh criticisms of Chengdi and his predecessors.[1] Of course, the *Hanshu* biography, compiled nearly a century after Yang's death, has been purposely crafted to defend Yang against posthumous charges that he served as an insidious propagandist for the usurper Wang Mang, in the role of Wang's dupe or co-conspirator.[2] The stories circulating in Yang's time and shortly afterward lend credence to a more complex picture of Yang as a thinker increasingly preoccupied with subjects outside officialdom who was nonetheless well-regarded and well-rewarded at court – so much so that Chengdi even went to the considerable trouble of staging Yang's rather prosaic inscriptions at court.[3] According to one Han source,

---

[1] For several examples, see Wu Fusheng 2007: passim. Yang, for example, compared his ruler to the archetypal tyrants Jie and Zhou (see below).

[2] The very presence of this defense raises warning flags about the conventional attribution of large parts of the biography to Yang himself, since Yang died fully five years before Wang Mang's downfall. Yang, as an extraordinarily valued imperial servant, was buried at Anling 安陵, the imperial mausoleum town for Huidi (r. 195-188 BC). To be buried in the vicinity of such a mausoleum town was usually considered a signal honor. However, since at least the eighteenth century, Pi 郫 county in Sichuan has claimed to be the site of "Yang's tomb." I thank Mark Pitner for bringing this to my attention.

[3] Qian Yi 1984: 13.53.

> 孝成玩弄眾書之多, 善楊子雲, 出入遊獵, 子雲乘從. 使長卿, 桓君山, 子雲作吏，書所不能盈牘，文所不能成句，則武帝何貪? 成帝何欲? 故曰：玩楊子雲之篇, 樂於居千石之官。 挾桓君山之書, 富於積猗頓之財。
>
> Chengdi thought it great fun to play around with a broad array of texts. He was so fond of Yang Xiong that when he went in and out of the palace on excursions or hunts, he had Yang follow him in a carriage. Had [the two emperors, Wudi and Chengdi] employed Zhangqing, Huan Tan, and Yang Xiong as [regular] officers, then their writings would never have filled a single wooden board, or their compositions even a single complete line. How would Wudi have lusted after them, then? And how would Chengdi have desired them? As the saying goes, "To play around with bundles of Yang Xiong's writings is a greater pleasure than being a high-ranking official. To have Huan Tan's writings in one's possession is to be richer than Yidun [the Chinese Croesus]!"[4]

Yang's fearless advocacy of the learning and the literary style he traced to antiquity – despite the explicit challenge that his views posed to powerful factions at court, especially the state-sponsored Academicians – reflects the secure place he enjoyed at court, thanks to the continued patronage of several emperors and of Liu Xiang, his bureaucratic superior.[5]

For a biography to occupy two chapters (*juan* 卷) in Ban Gu's sweeping *Hanshu* narrative is a rare distinction that Ban conferred upon only two figures besides Yang, Sima Xiangru 司馬相如 (179-117 BC) and Wang Mang (d. AD 23). This convergence gains added significance from the close

---

[4] *Lunheng* 61/265/8ff. ("Yiwen" 佚文). The text, in mentioning Sima Xiangru 司馬相如 (Zhangqing), refers first to Wudi's era; Sima Xiangru died long before Chengdi came to the throne.

[5] See below. Note, however, that the "Warnings for Academicians" attributed to Yang Xiong in most editions (but to Cui Yuan 崔瑗 in some commentaries to *Guwen yuan* 古文苑), mainly discusses the post of the Academicians from two angles: (1) noting that the dynasty rises and falls on the excellence of its Academicians, and (2) warning the emperor not to follow the example of Qin, in its supposed over-reliance on technical theories, and a consequent neglect of ritual and ritual teachings encapsulated in the Classics. See Zhang Zhenze 1993: 393, citing *Yiwen leiju*, 46.831.

intertwining of Yang's story with those of both Sima and Wang. As readers will recall, it was the epideictic *fu* 賦 of Sima Xiangru, a fellow native of Sichuan, that initially inspired Yang's own efforts at composition in that genre,[6] and ultimately it was Yang's apparent acquiescence in Wang Mang's designs on the throne that sullied Yang's reputation, though no extant piece of Yang's writing bespeaks unqualified enthusiasm for Wang.[7] Weaving together Yang's own autobiography or "self-introduction"[8] with Ban's defense, the *Hanshu* biography predictably showcases Yang at his affable, disarming best.[9] Yang first appears as a poet and wordsmith of marvelous inventiveness, and only later as a serious thinker earning the plaudits of his more discerning peers. True, Yang's famous declaration of impatience with mere verbal virtuosity appears in this life, but only after a series of stunningly beautiful *fu* have been cited in full, whereas the contents of his three philosophical masterworks are briefly summarized – again, often in Yang's words – in a few pages of text near the end of Ban's account.

Yang's biography conveys an impression of his utter dedication in light of his poverty and low rank. Yang famously celebrated his own state of detached contentment in a passage repeated by Ban and later admirers:

---

[6] Some have argued, with Paul W. Kroll 2010 and Martin Kern 2003: 401, that, strictly speaking, no genre categories exist before the fourth century AD, but obviously *fu* writing would not have been confused with prose. The relation between Sima Xiangru and Yang Xiong is well known. See Kern 2003: 390, for example: "While he [Yang] first regarded Sima's work as the foremost model to follow, he later used his forerunner's compositions as the prime example to illustrate the serious shortcomings and ultimate failure of the genre." However, few scholars have noted that Sima Xiangru, like Yang Xiong, was known in his own day for compiling a word list (HS 30.1721). Note that some scholars, beginning with Liu Zhiji 劉知幾 (661-721), have argued that the *Shiji* biography of Sima Xiangru is also based on the poet's autobiography. I thank David Knechtges (private communication) for this information.

[7] See Knechtges 1978. Nylan (forthcoming-c) shows that FY chapter 13 cannot reasonably be read as praise for Wang. Bielenstein 1954-67, in all three volumes, makes the point repeatedly that Han officials did not generally give up office or commit suicide upon the change of dynasties, either from Western Han to Wang Mang's dynasty or from Wang Mang's dynasty to Eastern Han.

[8] On this, see Knechtges 1982: 3.

[9] This may be why Ban Gu omits several pieces from Yang's autobiography, including, as he tells us, three long poems about Qu Yuan. Certainly, Yang's extant "Fan sao" 反騷 displays Yang's cantankerous and self-confident side, in a work composed even before he left Shu for the Han capital.

不汲汲於富貴。不戚戚於貧賤。不修廉隅以徼名當世。
家產不過十金。乏無儋石之儲晏如也。

I do not scurry after wealth and honor,
Nor am I troubled by poverty and low position.
Although my family wealth does not exceed ten catties of
gold,[10]
And I lack stores of grain beyond a bushel or even a half,
I am content.[11]

Yang would have others see him as a person of paltry means who is nonetheless impervious to death, though not to overt or covert attacks upon his thinking. Yang seems to have risen from relatively humble origins because of his extraordinary talents in reading, transcribing, and composition, possibly thanks to a government scholarship in his home commandery of Shu.[12] And there was Yang's "stutter," most likely attributable to his arrival at court at the age of "over forty," which may have prevented mastery of the local patois in Chang'an.[13] Still, there are reasons to be suspicious of Yang's parading of his "poverty and low position."[14] After all, the *Huayang guozhi*

---

[10] The phrase *shi jin* 十金 (= 100,000 cash, or average farmland of 100 *mu*) is the standard (legal?) phrase used of the entire assets of an "average peasant farmer" in the Juyan documents. See Ōkushi Atsuhiro 1985: 49. Yang is pleading extreme poverty here – no better than the average farmer. The *Yantie lun* 4.1/23/4-5, speaks of "counselors amassing 1000 units, and *shi* (gentlemen?) amassing 100 units [of metal]. Yoshinami Takeshi 1976: 69, argues that 100 *jin* is the grant given to those at the rank of *guanneihou* ("noble within the passes").

[11] Knechtges 1982: 4 (slightly mod.).

[12] It is possible that he attended the famous school in Chengdu started by Wen Weng. But see J. Michael Farmer 2000. Yang speaks of the relative poverty of his family, perhaps because only a single son was born to each generation for several generations; his family owned "no more than ten catties of gold," and his personal assets supposedly "lacked reserves of even a bushel of grain."

[13] HS 87A.3514. Cf. the stutter of Han Feizi. (Notably two of the best writers in the early period seem to have been mocked for their inability to express themselves in speeches at court.)

[14] First, Tsuruma Kayazuki 1978: 15, refers to a very prominent Yang family from Chengdu, although it cannot be proven whether Yang Xiong was related to them. (The seventh-century commentator Yan Shigu 嚴師古 says Yang is no relation, but Yan is sometimes wrong, especially in his apologies. For the conflation of the characters 揚 and 楊, see Ren Naiqiang's annotations, 241, n. 3. And for a Yang Ban 楊班, also of Pi, Yang's home town, see *Huayang guozhi* 10A.537. (This may be pure coincidence, however.) Second,

describes Yang as poor "[only?] when young";[15] he had steady income from his mid-ranking appointment at court; and we know that he was given a hefty reward after submitting a memorial on the Xiongnu. In any case, Yang's auto-narrative recommends itself as a prime example of Han-era humilifics, that complex rhetorical style wherein the speaker ostentatiously discounts his own abilities and resources in the very phrases designed to demonstrate his artistic virtuosity and seriousness of purpose. For example, in Yang's telling, his *Taixuan* 太玄 is "subtle and deep" enough to plumb the subterranean worlds and to scale the empyrean heights, his relatively humble court rank notwithstanding.[16] A "wide reader," with a decided preference for the more demanding sort of glosses and explications,[17] Yang is endowed with "his own grand scheme of things."[18] That he aspired to a reputation for greatness is obvious, not only because he devised for himself a sacred lineage from a collateral branch of the Zhou ruling house (not coincidentally the dynasty he prefers!), but also because he freely compared his own poetic efforts with those of the sages who composed the Odes, as well as with Qu Yuan 屈原 and Sima Xiangru, the latter pair being monumental talents whom Yang emulated even as he criticized ("How unrestrained their pattern and narrow their substance!").[19]

A more attentive reading of Yang's self-portrait, the alleged basis for Ban Gu's later defense, shows the man to be a bundle of contradictions. He is by turns "easygoing and relaxed" and "taciturn and fond of deep contemplation."[20] While professedly a poor rustic whose family owned but a few acres, he nevertheless managed to study long years with the most eminent teachers in the cosmopolitan city of Chengdu, Yan Junping 嚴君平, Linlü Wengru 林閭翁孺, and Li Hong 李弘.[21] No "seeker after fame in his

---

Yang's rank as Courtier was on a par with those of Liu Xiang and Wang Mang, two of the best connected individuals at court.

[15] *Huayang guozhi* 10A.533. For more on the memorial, see below.

[16] HS 87B.3566; DRK 46-47.

[17] HS 87A.3513; DRK 12.

[18] HS 87A.3514; DRK 13.

[19] For Qu Yuan and Sima Xiangru, see HS 87A.3514; DRK 13; and for the quotation, see HS 87A.3516; DRK 14. For a further critique of Sima Xiangru, see HS 87B.3575; DRK 53, where Yang says that Sima's "persuasions" only made matters worse with Han Wudi.

[20] HS 87A.3514; DRK 12.

[21] For Yang's teachers, see *Huayang guozhi* 10A.532-34. Ren Naiqiang's notes suggest that marriage ties bound Linlü Wengru and Yang Xiong, but no specifics are given (p. 543). See also FY 11/23, for Yang's teachers. The identification of Li Hong is tentative,

own time," he unaccountably in middle age ventured forth from Chengdu to the Han court to make his fortune.[22] The *fu* being the literary style most favored at the Han court, his facility in composing display *fu* on demand quickly gained him an important patron, after which the emperor asked him to try serving as court poet.[23] He was soon appointed to a 600 bushel rank post, that of Courtier at the Yellow Gate 黃門侍郎 – the same post given to Wang Mang, Liu Xin, and an imperial favorite. And while this is generally regarded as the bottom of the top-tier of the bureaucracy, this was no inconsequential post, since scions of the imperial and *waiqi* clans served in the same office, which afforded direct access to the emperor's person. Once he became a fixture at court, Yang wrote dazzling occasional pieces depicting his emperor as a paragon of virtue, "equal in merit to that of the legendary Five Lords" of antiquity[24] – when he was not criticizing him! Ostensibly extolling the incredible luxury and brilliance of the court, Yang's poems suggest the degree to which the very splendors enveloping the members of the governing elite distort their perceptions of reality.[25] As those at court sometimes exaggerated their own powers, it is small wonder that the Son of Heaven, who "sedately stands in the midst of precious terraces, leisure lodges, jade finials and petals," found it damnably difficult to "purify His soul, gather His vitality, or concentrate His thoughts."[26]

Such *fu* pieces, written during Yang's first years at court, no less than Yang's later condemnations of the genre, illustrate the profound ambivalence that he felt as an onlooker and participant in court spectacles. On the one hand, he was awestruck by the court's magnificence; on the other, he was

---

since it is difficult to ascertain the dates for Li Hong's life, and perhaps Yang meant only that he modeled himself after Li, not that he was a pupil of Li's.

[22] For the first quotation, see HS 87A. 3514; DRK 12. Yang was supposedly "over forty" when he travelled from Shu to the capital, where he found an early patron in Wang Yin 王音, the Commander-in-Chief. Yang was appointed to the same rank as Wang Mang and Liu Xin, two men who clearly remained allies after their service in the 600-bushel post, but we do not know whether Yang was a part of their circle. I suspect that he was on the margins of their faction. See below.

[23] For the importance of the *fu* at the Han court, see Kern 2003: 383. But Kern 2003: 397, notes the "virtual absence of the genre in Sima Qian's *Shiji*" and in the "elaborate *Hanshu* account of literary activities at the Emperor Wu court [sic]."

[24] HS 87A.3523; DRK 17.

[25] For example, HS 87A.3526; DRK 19: When they raise their heads and look on high,/ Their vision is blurred and they see nothing/... They are simply dazed and confused;/ Their souls perplexed and befuddled."

[26] HS 87A.3530; DRK 21.

appalled by extravagance and waste.[27] Supremely aware of the force of precedents ("Because they were long in existence...."), Yang presents himself as a force mindful of tradition who nevertheless urges the court to undertake major reforms. Called to task for these multiple contradictions by imaginary interlocutors (the voices in his own head?), Yang supplied an astonishing hermeneutical key to his *fu*, wherein the more overwrought and exaggerated his praise of a given phenomenon, the more profound his actual rejection of it.[28] Only absolute inversions could highlight the ludicrous topsy-turviness of things occasioned by the moral benightedness of Yang's superiors – or so he says. Despite his disgust, Yang tried hard to "go back and weave a net"[29] of such surpassing beauty and strength that the emperor's regard – compared by Yang to a fish he is angling for – may yet be caught and thereby drawn into sober reflection. Yang's growing disappointment at his failure to bring this feat off becomes evident in the increasing boldness with which he proclaims the subtext of his relentlessly gorgeous rhymes to be the massive disparities between the wealth of the court and the poverty of farmers and weavers, made more grotesque by the court performances that feed an ugly addiction to destructive or demeaning spectacles.[30]

As Yang matured as a poet, he struggled to break free of *fu* conventions altogether. Eventually, in set pieces outwardly glorifying the august presence of the reigning Son of Heaven, he substituted for the usual sustained focus on the imperial person a dialogue pitting "Plume Grove" 翰林 against "Ink Guest" 墨客 nudging the figure of the ruler, unobtrusively yet firmly, off center stage.[31] As Yang confesses ca. 10 BC, some eight years after his arrival at court, he prefers to allow the Ink Guest (a stand-in for the

---

[27] For example, he describes "the excursion lodges so unique and rare"), Ma Jigao submits that the tension between eulogy and admonition was not resolved in the Han *fu*. See Ma Jiagao 1987: 138-41.

[28] HS 87A.3535; DRK 24.

[29] HS 87A.3534; DRK 25.

[30] For example, the "Hedong *fu*" contains a passage describing the glorious "good ole days," when the emperors "took nothing from the people's rich and fertile grain lands or mulberry and silkworm thorn areas" (HS 87A.3539; DRK 28) and the "Tall Poplars Palace *fu*" inserts in a description of a lavish hunt scene the sentence, "At this time, the farmers were unable to harvest their own crops." See HS 87B.A.3557; DRK 39. One of the few studies to take Yang seriously as a political thinker is He Lingxu 1988: 411-54.

[31] This exchange begins on HS 87A.3557; DRK 39. For similar sentiments, cf. FY 6/22, for example. One wonders whether the phrase "Zimo keqing" 子墨客卿 (usually translated as "Master Ink as Guest") is not an oblique allusion to Kongzi and Mozi, whose names are linked in many Han texts as the ultimate wise men.

reader liable to Yang's persuasions) "to examine the salient points" for himself.[32] His most salient point seems to be that the Han leaders, having witnessed more than enough bloodshed, should no longer think costly successes in battle more valuable than achievements through quiet diplomacy. Wars and hunts should not become the "regular endeavor of state."[33] Only a fierce determination to conserve men and material will insure that "farmers do not cease their harrowing,/ Nor weavers leave their looms/.... and [both empire and emperor] Truly earn their reward from the spirits."[34]

Fed up with navigating court life during the six years of Aidi's reign (7-1 BC), when the court was pullulating with intrigues among the consort clans and male favorites with few or no claims to special dignity,[35] Yang trumpeted his retreat to his study to draft the *Taixuan*, his neoclassic modeled upon the *Changes* and its "Ten Wings." His mock defense of that decision declared that he preferred to abandon the rough-and-tumble of court life, lest further engagement fail to "vermilion his wheel hubs" (i.e., elevate his official rank) and instead "turn his entire clan blood-red" (i.e., leave him liable to criminal prosecution as a traitor).[36] He meanwhile lambasted those in charge of classical learning in his time. It is only when the empire

> .... 不能安當其亡事也。
> 章句之徒相與坐而守之。亦亡所患。
> Is faced with no momentous problems,
> That chapter-and-verse commentators
> May sit together and claim to "protect it,"
> Without creating cause for concern.[37]

In Yang's estimation, the court Academicians of his time were of little use, with "the empire facing momentous problems."[38] But how were true

---

32 HS 87B.3559; DRK 40.

33 For the first mistake, see HS 87B.2564; DRK 45; for the second, HS 87B.3563; DRK 44.

34 HS 87B.3563; DRK 44.

35 I speak here of the Ding 丁 and Fu 傅 *waiqi* consort clans, as well as of Dong Xian 董賢, reputedly the male lover of Aidi (r. 6-1 BC), who at least had the signal virtue, from the Eastern Han historians' point of view, of slowing the seemingly inexorable rise of Wang Mang at court.

36 HS 87B.3565; DRK 46.

37 HS 87B.3569; DRK 49 (mod.).

38 HS 87B.3569; DRK 49.

scholars such as he to advise the court, knowing that the wisest men in antiquity had to scramble to save their skins in equally troubled times?[39] Even such paragons as Confucius 孔子 and Guan Zhong 管仲 would be forced to lie low at the Han court, were they to come back from the dead, since they would doubtless fail the Grade A examinations administered by the Academicians to fill the bureaucratic ranks. Only "when the timing and opportunity are right"[40] can the best sort of man enter the fray without fear for his life. Yang's distaste for many of his fellow classicists always related to his strident criticisms of the court and the throne. At one point he went so far as to compare Emperor Cheng to the archetypically evil last emperors of the Xia and Shang dynasties[41] – and he was lucky to escape with his life.

Twice Yang insists, once in his autobiography and once in the *Fayan*, that he eventually quit writing *fu* altogether ("I stopped and never again engaged in writing them."),[42] around the time of Pingdi's accession in 1 BC. As Yang tells it,

> 賦者將以風之。必推類而言。...既迺歸之於正然覽者已過矣。
> The *fu* is for the purpose of persuasion. It must speak by adducing examples, [but] by the time it gets around to the moral message, the reader has lost the point.[43]

Despite his ostensible renunciation, it is hard to see how Yang could have resisted entreaties and orders coming from the court, given his dependence on the court for his salary, and, indeed, the received traditions have Yang marshaling his energies to write several more display *fu* – with disastrous results for his later reputation. The most egregious example of Yang's employment of inflated praise as ruthless satire is his "Excoriating Qin while

39 HS 87B.3570; DRK 49.

40 Translating *shi* 時 as both "timing" and "opportunity," since it has both these senses.

41 In his "Sweet Springs *fu*," Yang compares the building projects at Sweet Springs to the building projects of those bad rulers. See HS 87A3528; Wu Fusheng 2007: 48. Similarly, once Liu Xiang compared Emperor Cheng to the "tyrants of the Qin in pursuing wasteful luxury," saying, "I am ashamed of your majesty." Chengdi did not punish Liu Xiang, which is amazing. See HS 10.330; 36.1956-57.

42 HS 87B.3575; DRK 53. Cf. FY 2/1: "Grown men do not engage in such activities."

43 HS 87B.3575; DRK 53.

Praising Xin," in which a single line of the poem offers over-the-top support for Wang Mang.[44] If the received traditions are correct (a big if!), Yang continued to write occasional pieces for the court, including three "inscription poems" (*ming shi* 銘詩) on luxury items, a eulogy for the dowager empress Wang, and a group of formal "warnings" that catalogue the duties and characteristic lapses of the major officers in the Han bureaucracy, beginning with the Provincial Shepherds with responsibility over the outlying regions and the Three Lords at the capital.[45]

Yang Xiong's posthumous reputation rested primarily on the *Fayan* and *Taixuan*, in that order. Aside from linguists, few care to mention his work (no longer extant) dramatically expanding the *Cang Jie* 倉頡 word list or the *Fangyan* (which may originally have been compiled at least partly in pre-Qin or unusual scripts).[46] Yang's position at court as resident "wisdom bag" or man of encyclopedic knowledge meant that learned men of every persuasion came to him with difficult questions about omens and "strange scripts."[47] "From time to time there were men who asked me questions, and I always used examples to answer them,"[48] and these historical and literary allusions became the core around which Yang supposedly built his *Fayan*. Most striking about the *Fayan*, especially the last four chapters, is Yang Xiong's willingness to assume the role of a second Confucius, acting as a "praise and blame" historian, weighing the merits of controversial policies under discussion at the Han court.

---

44 See Knechtges 1978.

45 The titles of the three "inscription poems" are given below. The eulogy probably dates to AD 13, when the dowager empress Wang died at the age of 84; at that point, Yang would have been around 66 *sui*. This eulogy is not preserved in the early sources, but it appears in *Guwen yuan* 古文苑, *juan* 5, and *Yiwen leiju*, 15.282-83. A eulogy in commemoration for General Zhao Chongguo 趙充國 (d. 51 BC), who defeated the Qiang, is preserved in HS 69.2995, but dated imprecisely to the reign of Chengdi. The various "warnings" can be found in Zhang Zhenze 1993: 313-400. As the twelve provinces were an administrative innovation under Wang Mang's government, these pieces should date to Yang's final years. For strange scripts, see below.

46 *Huayang guozhi* 10A.533 says the *Fangyan* is modeled on the *Erya*, in a passage that otherwise matches HS 87B3582, but here diverges. The *Erya* contained "old script." See the fourth chapter of this monograph.

47 My reading of the term "strange script" (*qi zi* 奇字) will be justified in the fourth chapter of this monograph. HS 87B.3585; DRK 60, presents some of these questioners as curiosity-seekers, since Yang had survived the charge of possible treason.

48 DRK 57. Readers may wish to compare my translation with that of Wu Fusheng 2007, as there are some differences.

Despite the fact that the lion's share of readers' attention has for centuries gone to the *Fayan*, it may well be that Yang considered the *Taixuan* or even the *Fangyan* to be his best writing. After all, Yang defended the *Taixuan* at considerable length in a mature *fu*, "Justification Against Objection"; the *Fangyan* represented the methodological foundation for Yang's classical turn; and the compilation of the early *Fangyan* recension preoccupied him for nearly three times longer than either the *Taixuan* or *Fayan*.[49] Han classicists after Yang Xiong repeatedly remarked upon the innovative quality of the *Fangyan*, and Yang's unwillingness to let Liu Xin appropriate it may account for Yang's coolness towards Liu Xin, as much as Liu Xin's unswerving adherence to Wang Mang's cause (see below).[50] In his "Justification," however, Yang admits that most of his contemporaries think his attempts to capture in writing the unseen patterns of the universe (not to mention his research into ancient scripts) "simply wasted his energy, on the one hand/ And annoyed scholars on the other," making him like "the painter who tries to paint the formless,/ Or a zither player who strums to the soundless."

Most historians think Ban Gu appended little to Yang's autobiography except the exculpatory tale of Yang's arrest and attempted suicide under Wang Mang and an admiring appraisal composed by one of Yang's most famous disciples, Huan Tan. As the narrative in the addendum goes, Yang was quietly collating documents in the Tianlu Gallery 天祿閣,

---

[49] On the first two works, Yang supposedly labored for some ten years each, but the early records say he was preoccupied with the *Fangyan* compilation for a total of twenty-seven years. For that figure, see *Fengsu tongyi* 風俗通義, *xu* 序, which also compares the *Fangyan* directly to the *Erya* 爾雅. In his entry in *Early Chinese Texts*, Knechtges (p. 101) writes that he believes that the *Fayan* was written probably in AD 8 or 9, before Wang's takeover in AD 9. Knechtges says, "The *Fa yen* was not composed all at one time, but represents Yang Hsiung's random jottings written over a decade or more." While I would query Knechtges' use of the word "random," he is undoubtedly correct in his other assessments about the book.

[50] Yang does not explicitly mention the *Fangyan* in his autobiography, but we cannot at this remove tell whether the autobiography was truncated, as some allege, or whether he had not yet finished the work. The *Hanshu* biography does mention what is presumably another piece of Yang's epigraphical research: "Of the works for scribes, he [Yang] thought none better than the *Cang Jie* 倉頡, and thus he compiled the *Compilation of Annotations*," a "product of a conference convened by Wang Mang [as regent] in AD 5." See HS 87B.583; DRK 59, 143, n. 496. Fragments of this work have been collected by Ma Guohan 1883: *ce* 冊 74, 66/6a-7a. For the astronomical and musical aspects of this conference, see Christopher Cullen 2010: 329-30.

one of several imperial libraries,[51] when the authorities barged in to interrogate him about his ties to Liu Fen 棻, son of Liu Xin, who was reportedly discovered engaged in a plot to remove Wang Mang.[52] Their reason: Yang had been teaching "strange scripts," the pre-Qin and regional character forms that often figured in apocryphal revelations "from on high" pronouncing on questions of legitimacy. Yang in terror threw himself off the upper storey or top of the building, nearly killing himself. Upon hearing of the affair, Wang Mang issued an edict to the officers proclaiming Yang's innocence.[53] This event occurred in AD 10, when Yang was already a senior figure.[54]

Huan Tan 桓譚 a disciple of Yang Xiong, has the last word on Yang's life in the *Hanshu* biography, for Ban Gu cites Huan's remarks that Yang's work compares favorably to Laozi's *Way and its Power* (*Daode jing*), a short work that generations have deemed "superior to the Five Classics," according to Huan. By implication, Yang's work deserves all the more admiration, since it is consistent with the Five Classics he so loved. At the time of Ban's compilation, put some "forty years" after Yang's death (?),[55] Ban notes that the *Fayan* is in wide circulation, but the *Taixuan* "is still not well known."

The Letters Exchanged between Yang Xiong and Liu Xin

Additional information about Yang and his contemporaries comes from an exchange of letters between Yang and Liu Xin, spurred by Yang's compilation of a word list related to today's *Fangyan*. While some scholars

---

[51] One text puts Yang at work in the Stone Chamber 石室 imperial library, which probably refers to the Shiqu ge 石渠閣 (Stone Canal Tower). (Some editions read "Shiqu" for "Shishi.") See Liu Rulin 1935, entry for AD 15.

[52] For details, see HS 99B.4123; Dubs 1938, vol. 3, 307-11; cf. HS 87B.2584. The Tianlu Gallery 天鹿閣 [but also 天祿, as above], built by Xiao He 蕭何 to store the imperial book collection, had statues of "heavenly deer" (hence the name) at the site, supposedly to ward off evil influences. See HS 96A.3889, n. 2; *Sanfu huangtu* 6.97.

[53] HS 87B.3584; DRK 60.

[54] HS 99B.4123.

[55] One wonders if there is not a misprint in HS 87B.3585. If not, Ban Gu must have written the concluding appraisal to the chapter around AD 60, or very early in his career, unless he is again quoting a third party here, perhaps Huan Tan (?), his senior.

have impugned the authenticity of these letters because of a few anachronisms, the eminent linguist Paul Serruys has proved beyond a reasonable doubt that the letters are genuine. David R. Knechtges, the leading expert on Yang's work, concurs. The gossipy letters refer to a sex scandal at court involving another courtier who hailed from Yang's home commandery of Shu 蜀 (in present-day Sichuan).[56] Liu Xin's reference to the affair seems calculated to apply none too subtle pressure on Yang, so that he would hand over to Liu his documents and notes. The details are unclear, but Yang was apparently feeling some heat in connection with the case, either because he had once recommended the courtier or just was known to have been on friendly terms with him. At the very least, the letters vividly illustrate the dangers attending life in the late Western Han court. Meanwhile, the letters show the emperor making conscientious inquiries about the "light carriages" of earlier dynasties, in which envoys to distant regions journeyed to inquire about the state of local customs. Liu Xin continues in one of the letters:

> 歆先君數為孝成皇帝言，當使諸儒共集訓詁爾雅所及，
> 五經所詁不合爾雅者，詁・為病....博士至以窮世之博學者....
>
> "My late father often told Chengdi that he ought to have all scholars collect explanations and glosses, those cited in the *Erya* 爾雅 and those glossed in the Five Classics. Those that did not agree with the *Erya* would be judged defective. For when the various masters for the Classics lack [sufficient] evidence, the Academicians end up being considered the most widely learned scholars of the age."[57]

No fewer than four conclusions may probably be drawn on the basis of this short passage: (1) that the *Erya* – then a relatively recent compilation, if the modern scholar Zhou Zumo is correct – had already achieved the status of a

---

[56] This courtier engaged in illicit sex with one or more female bondservants in government employ, after which he stole a sackcloth towel from the palace, perhaps as a memento of the dalliance.

[57] For the letter, see *Fangyan*, cited in *Siku quanshu* [e-Siku], 13/26b. For Han commentaries on the *Erya*, see *Erya Han zhu* 1968. Important secondary material includes von Rosthorn 1942; Coblin 1972; Carr 1979; and Xu Chaohua 1987.

canonical text,[58] presumably because it contained pre-Qin characters and phrases; (2) that Chengdi himself evinced considerable interest in classical learning, an idea underscored by his decision to have the contents of the imperial libraries organized and catalogued by a team of handpicked specialists headed by Liu Xiang, head of the Liu clan affairs;[59] (3) that Chengdi nonetheless hesitated about the controversial proposal to collect and evaluate all glosses, in keeping with his tendency to dither over major policy proposals; and (4) that Liu Xin was apt to heap scorn on the court Academicians, whose interpretation of the Classics trusted to cumulative "tradition" rather than to early usage (words and phrases in the "strange," often pre-Qin script).[60] (Liu, in writing this way, might well have been angling for Yang to become his ally.) Liu Xin's letter then proceeds to the most monumental of Yang's lexicographical works, saying that Yang in the *Fangyan* has gathered "obsolete words from former dynasties and unusual expressions from strange lands, which you have put into 15 *juan*. The explanations are rather numerous.... "

The letters also mention that Chengdi had generously granted Yang three year's leave, in which to "improve his mind," perusing documents in yet another of the imperial libraries, the so-called Stone Chamber. The decree generously allowed him to retain his regular salary, while the Palace Secretariat (*Shangshu* 尚書) supplied him with "brushes, ink, and sixty thousand cash." In gratitude, Yang crafted three ornamental poems in the

---

[58] See Zhou Zumo 1984. Ye Mengde 葉夢德 (1077-1148) was the first student of the *Erya* to point out that insofar as the book often refers to the Mao school of the *Odes*, which dates to Western Han, the present recension of the *Erya* cannot predate the Han dynasty. Zhu Xi 朱熹 (1130-1200) showed that the *Erya*, rather than being a source for the *Odes* commentators, had evolved from it. The *Erya* also contains quotations from the *Lüshi chunqiu* and *Shanhai jing*. See von Rosthorn 1942.

[59] See Homer Dubs 1938: vol. 2, 355, which lists two teachers of Chengdi's teacher as Zhen Guanzhong and Zhang Yu. NB: it was under Chengdi's reign (33-7 BC), towards the end of it – i.e., when Yang Xiong was active – that the number of Academicians' disciples or clients supposedly rose dramatically, from 1,000 to 3,000. See HS 9.285, 291; HS 88.3596.

[60] Liu Xin is probably best known today for his letter of complaint about the Academicians, which is often cited in connection with *Zuozhuan* studies. I doubt that the term *qi zi* 奇字 (rendered in this monograph consistently as "strange script") can refer to one of the six ornamental scripts studied by small children, since grown men like Liu Fen, Linlü Wengru, and Yang Xiong made this their life's study. See the fourth chapter in this monograph for details, including the arguments for the term *xiao xue* 小學, in this context meaning "philological studies" that prepared men to assess and edit old texts.

yongwu 詠物 mode on luxury items and intricate technical devices: "Embroidered Patches," on a type of mat; "Numinous Knots," on a "longevity cane"; and "Dragon Bone," on a water wheel.[61] None of the three are extant, but we are told that Chengdi liked them all. Continuing imperial favor allowed Yang the freedom to continue with what he regarded as his real business:

> 故天下上計、孝廉及內郡衛卒會者，雄常把三寸弱翰，齎油素四尺，以問其異語，歸即以鉛摘次之于槧，二十七歲于今矣。而語言或交錯相反，方覆論思詳悉集之，燕其疑。
>
> "Whenever officers presented the annual accounts or the *xiaolian* 孝廉 nominees came from various parts of the empire, or the interior commandery military officers came to the capital, I took out my three-inch soft brush, provided myself with a four-foot piece of oiled white silk, and quizzed them. As soon as I got home, I then used lead powder [used to write comments on texts] to make extracts and arrange them on tablets."[62]

This passage – presumably genuine, with echoes in contemporaneous works – has Yang Xiong eagerly jotting down in note form any peculiar expressions that he could glean from travelers from distant parts, then transcribing the characters (probably many in obsolete forms, given the frequency with which local and earlier variants appear in archaeologically excavated Han texts) on the equivalent of file cards, which he then arranged and rearranged, reordering and double-checking the information until such time as this sort of play helped him arrive at an improved picture of word usage over long stretches of time and space. "Occasionally expressions and words were mixed up or they contradicted one another and then I repeatedly discussed them, mulled them over, and collected all I could in great detail, in order to

---

[61] These poems were probably of the sort that we now associate with the *yong wu* 詠物 poems of the post-Han period.

[62] See *Fangyan*, in *Siku quanshu* [e-Siku] 13/30b. This language echoes Yang's talk of his annotations to the *Cang Jie* 蒼頡, as does Liu Xin's rhetorical question in "Memorial on the Academicians" (HS 36.1971), cited as epigram to this essay.

settle any doubts."[63] Swearing that his final aim would be to show experts his results, Yang nonetheless demurred at Liu Xin's request that he submit his notes to the throne or its representatives before they were well and truly finished. Only a more mature version, said Yang, would finally allow his ruler to "sit behind his curtains" and yet know how things are said across extreme distances and in out-of-the-way places, let alone transmit the texts of the Classics intact to posterity, along with the "words entered into the Han [official] records."

THE TESTIMONY OF PEERS AND LATER FOLLOWERS

Given Huan Tan's dual status as a devoted disciple of Yang and a recognized authority on Yang's early standing as classical master, it is understandable that historians through the ages have probably relied more upon Huan's anecdotal evidence for Yang's portrait than upon any other single source, aside from Yang Xiong's own autobiography and Ban Gu's assessment of Yang's career in the *Hanshu*.[64] Huan Tan was a prolific writer, the author of a much-consulted work known as the *Xinlun* 新論 (New Treatises)[65] in 29 *pian* (bamboo bundles), supplemented by an additional 26

---

[63] A comparable passage in *Xijing zaji* 3.66 says, "Yang Xiong was curious about everything. He often carried a lead 懷鉛 (pencil?) so that he might write things down. And he would follow around those who had come [to court] from the commanderies and kingdoms, asking them where they had come from, if they knew anything about the border areas; and what local expressions there were, so that he could increase his own knowledge."

[64] Huan Tan apparently came to the court when he was a mere seventeen years old, and he was given the very junior post guarding the Western Gate 西門 of the palace at the Small Park 小苑. See Li Fang 李昉, et al., compilers, *Taiping yulan* [hereafter TPYL] 215/9a. Much of the following is drawn from Pokora 1975, though a recent critical edition of *Xin lun* now supersedes earlier works: Zhu Qianzhi 2009. The *Xinlun* is now known from fragments preserved in Song collectanea. The date when it disappeared is a matter of some dispute, but in 1091-92 Emperor Zhezong of Northern Song sought a copy of the by-then rare work from some Koreans. Note that some confusion about its textual history has been generated by the existence of multiple works by this same title.

[65] Although Huan said his work presented "actions that should be taken," which might suggest that the title means "Treatises on the New" [i.e., on current events], the "new" in the title might equally well refer to "new editions," as it does with many other famous prose works in Han. In any case, the text presents anecdotes about recent events and people as tools to help in the analysis of contemporary problems. Most traditional accounts assume that the work was presented to Guangwu (r. 25-57), founder of Eastern Han, shortly after

pian of *fu*, eulogies, letters, and memorials. In his era, it was not unusual to combine skill in writing with skill in the martial arts, so Huan came to Chang'an to study with acknowledged masters in these two endeavors. He appealed to Yang, the leading court master of the *fu*, to school him in that literary form. Yang's advice: read a thousand *fu*, and you will become skilled at writing them.[66] That was perhaps one of the lesser trials along the way to producing the appropriate rhetorical flourishes on command, for Yang supposedly told the following story to Huan about his own experience.

> 成帝時，趙昭儀方大幸，每上甘泉，詔令作賦，為之卒暴，思精苦。賦成，遂困倦小臥，夢其五藏出在地，以手收而內之。及覺，病喘悸，大少氣，病一歲。
>
> When sacrificing at the Sweet Springs Palace, Emperor Cheng ordered me to write a *fu* in commemoration. I put my whole mind and soul into the task, with the result that I became utterly exhausted. Then I took a little nap, during which I dreamt that my viscera spilled out onto the floor, and so I stuffed them back in with my hands. When I later woke up, my store of vital *qi* 氣 was greatly depleted, and I was ill for a year.[67]

Huan Tan's biography in the *Hou Hanshu* says of him, "In general, he followed Liu Xin and Yang Xiong when analyzing doubtful or strange occurrences."[68] And since it was Huan who compiled the record of their

---

his accession to the throne, since the official Song Hong 宋弘/宏 presented Huan Tan to the throne in AD 26. Guangwu particularly appreciated Huan Tan's zither performances, but he was annoyed by Huan's critique of the apocryphal traditions attached to the Classics, which Guangwu tended to revere.

66 *Xijing zaji* 2.89. For this trope, compare *Sanguo zhi* 13.420.

67 Huan Tan, cited in TPYL 75/8b, 587/7a, 739/2a. One version has Yang Xiong dying within a year of this dream. *Wenxin diaolong* 6.1/66/24 also refers to this passage, saying, "Yang Xiong had nightmares because of his writer's block."

68 Not that Huan slavishly followed everything his masters said. Huan considered his own understanding of astronomy and music to be far superior to that of Yang, for example, as shown in an anecdote recorded in TPYL 2/11a-b, with strong echoes of the Wheelwright Bian story in the *Zhuangzi*. Huan Tan also took full credit for persuading Yang to abandon one astronomical theory, that of the "Canopy Heaven" (*gaitian* 蓋天), in favor of a second, the "Spherical Heaven" (*huntian* 渾天) theory. Huan Tan and Yang Xiong also

friendship, he had the last word, and though they disagreed about astronomy and music, Huan's remarks generally convey nearly boundless admiration for his master. Huan Tuan's insistence that few people manage to discern a true sage was surely intended for Yang's ears,[69] for Yang feared that his contemporaries at court would never get past his comparative poverty to recognize his monumental achievements. And when a certain Zhang Zihou complimented Yang Xiong, calling him a virtual "Kongzi of the West," Huan Tan retorted, "Ziyun [i.e., Yang] is also a Kongzi of the East. Was Zhongni [Confucius] only a Confucius for Lu? He was also a sage for Qi and Chu!"[70] Yang Xiong's influence pervaded the entire civilized world, in other words, for in Huan's view, "Yang had had no equal since the founding of the Han!"[71] Huan particularly praised Yang's *Taixuan*, saying that it would doubtless be transmitted to later generations, even if his owncontemporaries undervalued it.[72]

Huan's high regard for Yang Xiong did not deter him from offering a mixed assessment of Yang's character. Huan suggested, for example, that Yang was a "recluse in wine," "hiding in the crowd" – a person who straddled officialdom and reclusion while juggling moral seriousness with indulgence in sensual pleasure. This portrayal would figure largely in the later imaginary of Yang.[73] And when speaking of Yang Xiong's poverty, Huan Tan insisted, "Had Yang Xiong not been so very poor, he could never have written his *Taixuan* (Canon of Supreme Mystery)."[74] Remarks ascribed to Huan Tan supply one plausible explanation for Yang's supposed poverty late in life: when Yang's two sons died about the same time, he was determined to have their bodies carried back to his home district in Sichuan for burial.

---

disagreed about musical theory. Because Huan greatly preferred the "new music" to the solemn strains of the court music, Yang berated him for having only a modicum of cultivation: "It is very easy to be pleased by shallow things, whereas something profound can only be understood with great difficulty. Naturally, you dislike the court odes and prefer the tunes of Zheng instead!" See TPYL 565/5b.

[69] *Quan Hou Han wen* 13/6a.

[70] *Yilin* 3/9a. Zhang Zihou is otherwise unknown. Of course, the "West" refers to Yang Xiong's birthplace, in Sichuan, in southwestern China. It is very relevant that it takes a sage to recognize a sage, so Huan's praise of his master was hardly disinterested.

[71] *Quan Hou Han wen* 15/8b.

[72] Ibid.

[73] See Tao Qian's "Twenty Drinking Poems," poem 18 of 20 in the series; Yuan Xingpei, 3.276. On the image of the recluse, see Aat Vervoorn 1990; and Alan Berkowitz 2000. Vervoorn tends to read the recluse stories as historical accounts, and Berkowitz, as literary archetypes.

[74] *Yilin* 3/7b, saying attributed to Huan Tan.

"As a result, he bankrupted himself, harming himself through his excessive fondness for his boys and his lack of restraint" in mourning their untimely deaths,[75] depriving himself of money for his own funeral expenses.[76] For this reason, Huan Tan repeatedly characterized Yang's utter "disregard for material possessions" as a paradoxical "blind spot in an otherwise intelligent man."[77]

YANG'S BIOGRAPHY FROM CHANG QU'S *HUAYANG GUOZHI*

According to the *Basic Annals of the Shu Kings* traditionally ascribed to Yang Xiong, Yizhou in the Chengdu Plain was once an idyllic land enjoying the fruits of Central States civilization, until suddenly, in the eighth century BC, it was abruptly "cut off" and relegated to the status of cultural backwater by the decisions of Kings You and Li to abandon their original Western Zhou stronghold not far from Shu and build a new capital hundreds of miles to the east, the better to avoid attacks by nomads.[78] For native sons of Shu, positing such a scenario may have been one way to claim a centuries-old allegiance to the Zhou ruling house. In his autobiography, Yang claimed descent from a collateral branch of the Zhou ruling house,[79] and this may have led others to ascribe to Yang, on very poor grounds, the compilation of this chronicle.

---

75 TPYL 556/1b.

76 Soon after his sons' death, Yang Xiong fell ill and died, and there was then no money left to arrange for his own funeral, so he was buried near Chang'an, not "returned" to his home district in Sichuan. His wife left the capital after the funeral, returning home to her native Shu.

77 Kong Pingzhong 1990: 3.31, quoting Huan Tan's *Xin lun*. Kong was a poet who lived ca. 1040-1105. This appears to be based on a fragment from the TPYL 556/1b. FY 1/21 suggests that Yang would not have minded having no lavish burial.

78 See *Shuwang benji*, *juan* 1. The Han house then expanded the territory of Yizhou far beyond the Chengdu Plain, adding an additional eight commanderies to the four that had been subject to Qin rule. See Zhang Zhenze 1993: 334-36. These *Regional Admonitions*, twelve of which still exist, were intended to give advice to the governors of the various provinces (*zhou* 州). They can be found in various collectanea, including *Quan Han wen*, 54/1a-4a. As mention is made of them at the very end of Yang's *Hanshu* biography (HS 87B.3583), so they are generally taken to be genuine.

79 HS 87A.3513; DRK 12, says, "My forebears were descended from Boqiao 伯僑 of the Zhou ruling house."

Then, at the turn of the third century, Chang Qu, another native of Shu, compiled an important new source for Shu local history, the *Huayang guozhi*, which included eulogies for several in Yang Xiong's circle. Four out of the forty-three Shu residents whom Chang commemorated in a chapter devoted to "former worthies, male and female" related to Yang, three being his teachers in Chengdu and the fourth Yang himself. As earlier scholars have noted, Yang's three teachers probably owe their continued prominence in local memory to Yang's warm testimonials on their behalf.[80] In any case, Chang Qu paid the teachers respectful compliments, but for Yang he reserved the most glowing terms: "profound and accomplished/ showing clearly an immensity of wisdom." More importantly, for the purposes of this chapter, Chang Qu reports that Yang based his *Fangyan* on the *Erya*. (This may well be the first citation to make explicit reference to Yang's *Fangyan*, even though Ying Shao's *Fengsu tongyi*, compiled circa AD 204, seems to refer to that masterwork, also linking it with the *Erya*.)[81] Chang Qu's biography notes something else: Yang Xiong at the beginning of his career held the same post as Liu Xin, Wang Mang, and Dong Xian 董賢 (the male favorite of Aidi, a sycophant powerful enough to halt the seemingly inexorable rise of the Wang family to power),[82] and yet he saw three Han emperors come and go, without ever being raised to a higher official post. This tells us, first, that Yang's post as Courtier was hardly menial, as it gave direct access to the emperor, and second, that the posthumous defense of Yang would consist mainly of the assertion that the golden-tongued scholar had evidently exerted remarkably little influence over the rulers he served, given his failure to advance rapidly within the bureaucratic ranks. The *Huayang guozhi* biography ends with a long list of writers, thinkers, and scholars, who admired Yang's work extravagantly, including the renowned classicists, Song Zhong 宋衷 (fl. AD 192-218) and Wang Su 王肅 (195-256).

The *Huayang* encomia for Yang's three teachers suggest that aspects of Yang's writing can be traced back to Sichuan. From Yan Junping 嚴君平,

---

[80] Béatrice L'Haridon 2006: vol. 1, 38.

[81] See the preface to Ying's work. For further information, see Michael Nylan 1982, chap. 1.

[82] In this, Chang Qu repeats Ban Gu's defense of Yang, as recorded in HS 87B.3583. Ban said of Wang Mang and Dong Xian that the "power [of each] toppled [his] ruler" (*quan qing ren zhu* 權傾人主). For Dong Xian and his sway over the court of Aidi, see Loewe 2000: 67-69. At one point, Aidi in his cups suggested that he would abdicate in favor of Dong Xian; after Aidi's death, Dong was accused of treason; his body was exhumed and buried in the grounds of a prison; and his goods confiscated and sold at auction.

Yang would have received good training in recensions of the *Yijing*, *Laozi*, *Zhuangzi*, and possibly the *Analects*,[83] as well as the predilection for using divination texts to teach ethical behavior that reappears in the *Taixuan*. In Li Hong 李弘, Yang would have found a prime example of thoroughly incorruptible behavior while in office, given Li's allegedly "inflexible" attitude toward corruption and sycophancy. And from the reclusive Linlü Wengru 林呂翁儒 (working closely with Yan, according to Chang Qu), Yang would have gotten the idea that fundamental to any serious study of antiquity (*guxue* 古學) were "the sounds and rhymes of the imperium," as these served as good guides to local customs and airs (*feng* 風) as well as to more elevated and antique (*ya* 雅) practices.[84] Not surprisingly, Linlü Wengru is identified as philologist and as Yang's main inspiration for the *Fangyan*.[85] Finally, the *Huayang guozhi* conveys the idea that it was the *Taixuan* (Supreme Mystery) – and not the *Fayan* – that impressed leading scholars and thinkers of the second and third centuries, even if those of Ban Gu's time, a century earlier, had scoffed at it.

TALES FROM THE *XIJING ZAJI* 西京雜記 (*WESTERN CAPITAL ANECDOTES*)

The *Xijing zaji*, an early sixth-century compilation whose 132 entries impersonate the authorial voice of Liu Xin,[86] contains several anecdotes that feature Yang Xiong. One particularly interesting entry concerns the probable date of the *Erya* (see above), and it has Yang, in answer to a query from Liu Xin, his old sparring partner, affirming that the work is early and genuine:

---

83 Some traditions credit Yan with working on this text as well.

84 The definitions of *feng* and *ya* offered here are tentative, as *feng* and *ya* also refer to parts of the *Odes*.

85 *Huayang guozhi*, 10A.533.

86 Lao Gan 勞榦, one of the most respected of the modern Han historians, has identified a number of anachronisms in the *Xijing zaji* (comp. ca. AD 500). These and many other features of the work are discussed in David Knechtges' unpublished essay, "Secrets of the Western Han Court Exposed," which builds upon earlier work by William Nienhauser on the same subject. The term *prosopopeia*, meaning "literary impersonation," refers to a common genre or practice in the Six Dynasties period (and earlier).

> 余嘗以問楊子雲，子雲曰：「孔子門徒游、夏之儔所記，以解釋六藝者也」家君以為外戚傳稱「史佚教其子以爾雅，爾雅，小學也」 又記言孔子教魯哀公學爾雅。」爾雅之出遠矣。舊傳學者，皆云周公所記也，「張仲孝友」之類，後人所足耳。
>
> "I once asked Yang Xiong about this, and he said, "The *Erya* is a work recorded by Confucius' disciples, Ziyou and Zixia, in order to explain the Six Classics. My father believed as follows: The 'Memoirs of the Consort Clan' says, "The Scribe Yi taught his son the *Erya,*" and thus the *Erya* is a work of philology. Furthermore, the records say that Confucius encouraged Duke Ai of Lu to study the *Erya*. The origins of the *Erya* go far back in time, indeed! Those of old who transmitted learning all said that the *Erya* was compiled by the Duke of Zhou. Such passages as 'Zhang Zhong is filial and brotherly' were interpolated by later people."[87]

Other entries testify to the excruciating pains that the creative writer seeking inspiration may experience, regardless of his past mastery of a chosen genre.[88] In one passage, for example, Yang senses that all his hard work in composing the *Mystery* may come to naught:

> 楊雄讀書, 有人語之曰: 無為自苦. 玄故難傳. 忽然不見。雄著太玄經, 夢吐鳳凰集玄之上。 相而去。
>
> Yang Xiong was reading aloud when there came a man who said to him, "Do not make so much work for yourself! The Mystery/*Mystery* (i.e., the Dao or the *Taixuan*) will certainly be difficult to transmit." Suddenly, the man disappeared. When Yang wrote the *Taixuan* he dreamt that he spit out phoenixes, male and female, which proceeded to perch on his text, and *then suddenly they were gone.*[89]

---

[87] See *Xijing zaji* 3/96.

[88] Cf. TPYL 75/8b, 587/7a, 739/2a; and *Quan Hou Han wen* 14/6a.

[89] *Xijing zaji* 2.89. It is impossible to know whether the first reference to Xuan ("Mystery") refers to the *Mystery*, Yang's book, or to the Dao, since "Xuan" as the "Mystery" is an epithet for Dao.

This profligate spewing out of gorgeous living things – a physical evocation of Yang's marvelously inventive imagination and its flights of fancy – makes a second appearance in the hagiographic sketch given of Yang in Poem 18 of Tao Yuanming's "Drinking Poems," where Yang is portrayed as spewing out bits of information and advice to any comers in return for wine:

> 子雲性嗜酒，家貧無由得。時賴好事人，載醪祛所惑。
> 觴來為之盡，是諮無不塞；有時不肯言，豈不在伐國。
> 仁者用其心，何嘗失顯默。

> By nature, [Yang] Ziyun was fond of wine.
> His family, being poor, had no means to get it.
> At the time, he depended upon those interested in affairs
> To bring him wine so that he might resolve their doubts.
> When the goblets came, he always drained them dry.
> He then never left unanswered their queries.
> If, like Kongzi, he was, on occasion, unwilling to speak,[90]
> It was due to his reluctance to speak about attacking other states.
> Thus do humane men employ their minds.
> When did Yang ever err in verbal displays or silences?[91]

High praise indeed, from an admirer who saw Yang putting his vast store of erudition to good use. Through the only coin he had, Yang Xiong managed to bind friends and acquaintances to him, to give sound advice to seekers after the Way, and to make life just a bit more bearable with a goblet of good wine.

---

[90] According to the *Analects*, Kongzi, the Master, "refused to speak" about certain topics, including fate and feats of strength. HS 56.2523, the biography of Dong Zhongshu, cites a remark by Liuxia Hui 柳下慧: "I have heard that when attacking countries, one does not ask about benevolence" (吾聞伐國, 不問仁). Hence the following line.

[91] See Tao Qian's "Twenty Drinking Poems" (poem 18 of 20 in the series); Yuan Xingpei, 3.276 (Hightower 1970, Poem 42).

II
Playing with Manuscripts

A serene belief in the capacity of some texts to give infinite pleasure – and not merely to improve one's chances of office-holding or promotion – shines through an anecdote told about an older contemporary of Yang named Kuang Heng 匡衡 (active ca. 31 BC). As a young man Kuang dedicated himself to book learning, but he could ill afford to pay for a fire to read by at night. His neighbor's house being well lit, Kuang bore a small hole in the common wall, so as to "borrow" a bit of light. (Note the implicit pun on "light" and "enlightenment.") Inevitably, the hole in the wall was discovered, but the master of the adjacent house, far from being angry, was so delighted with Kuang's dedication to learning that he lent him a great many manuscripts to read.[1] In most pre-Han and Han stories, the motive for boring a hole through a neighbor's wall is the kind of voyeurism that more typically ends in an assignation with the neighbor's daughter. Thus the anecdote about Kuang Heng alludes to his sensual longings for and delight in book learning, which set men like Kuang apart from the common run.[2]

However difficult they were to read, interpret, and imitate, the writings of Yang Xiong became the standard for writing that was both brilliant and lucid (*ming* 明 embraces both connotations), a standard against which authors compared themselves and were compared until at least the twelfth century.[3] Therefore, this chapter uses Yang's writings as a departure

---

[1] *Yiwen leiju* 55.990. This episode is told in the *Mengqiu*, trans. Watson, 23. Jiao Guimei 2009: 87-88, gives many examples from the Six Dynasties period, long after Yang's era, demonstrating the continuing difficulties of procuring good manuscript copies.

[2] See Riegel 1997, on the Fuyang version of the *Odes*; and Nylan and Huang, 2007.

[3] See, e.g., Cao Pi, "Lun wen," trans. in Owen 1992: 62. Xie Yiwu 謝夷吾, an Eastern Han figure (fl. 55-84?), in recommending Wang Chong 王充, said that "not even Yang Xiong, Liu Xiang, or Sima Qian could surpass him [in talent and erudition]," which makes Yang a standard against which writing and genius were compared. Cf. Wang Wentai 1972: 2/14a (p. 75), citing Xie Cheng 謝承 and *Wenxin diaolong* (see below), which frequently singles out Yang's writings for praise. Already in the eighth century, woodblock printing may have been commonly in use for the mass printing of religious tracts. The tenth century saw a dramatic expansion of the uses to which woodblock printing (i.e., xylography) was put.

point for discussing two topics that are too seldom brought to bear upon discussions of Han philosophy: early manuscript culture in China and the pleasures of reading the past. Clearly, neither Master Yang nor his contemporaries could have foreseen the book culture of the Wei-Jin through Northern Song periods that they helped to foster, as neither paper nor woodblock printing existed in their day. Writing paper, invented a century after Yang's death, came to rival silk in quality only in the fourth century AD, and woodblock printing became common only in the late tenth century, judging from the available evidence.[4] In Yang Xiong's world, then, manuscripts worth saving and transmitting were mainly inscribed on bamboo strips or on silk scrolls, the former being bulky and cumbersome to prepare and store, and the latter quite expensive.[5] Neither format facilitated "roaming through a manuscript" in the sense of reading at leisure and dipping back into earlier passages to savor them anew. Format alone made it difficult to produce tables or locate the contents and themes of a manuscript once read.[6] Conventions of punctuation, script, and format had yet to be regularized.[7] Reference works were either unknown or in their infancy.[8] A

By the end of the twelfth century, Yang Xiong began to come under severe attack, as moral and literary exemplar.

[4] After woodblock printing becomes common, the number of private libraries grows substantially. See Drège 1991:167, citing Pan Meiyue's *Songdai cangshujia kao*.

[5] "Killing the green" (*shaqing* 殺青), getting rid of the excess moisture in bamboo, was a laborious but necessary process, if the bamboo strips were not be destroyed by splitting and rotting, by decay, or by insects. Liu Xiang insisted on this, according to TPYL 606/2a. Bamboo, expensive enough, was used often for drafts, according to HHS 60B.1991-92, describing a second-century AD text. Bamboo and silk production were centered in Shandong and later in Sichuan as well. Perhaps that, along with the concentration of wealth in these two areas due to mining and agriculture, explains why so many classicists hailed from the northeast and southwest during the period.

[6] It would be interesting to know when the first index for an individual book was produced in China. I can find no reference regarding this, and none of the experts I've consulted seems to know. For the difficulty of producing tables (increased by the lack of a standardized numerical rendering for reign titles) in another manuscript culture, see Dennis Feeney 2007.

[7] As in Rome, punctuation initially was employed mainly to facilitate oral reading. By Eastern Han, conventions were set for the length of script for each type of manuscript (as Wang Chong notes), such that the longer the bamboo strip, the more authoritative the contents of the text. Other technical innovations, such as punctuation, because they were relatively new in Han, would also have shaped readers' perceptions and affected the readers' appreciation for texts. Both Roger Chartier and D.F. McKenzie would remind us how much the format, size, medium, and location of a piece of writing determine its reception and interpretations. Even in the pre-Qin era, a few kinds of punctuation marks had appeared,

few word lists were available, but no etymological dictionaries or lexicons of regional expressions.[9] (As we have seen, Yang dedicated three decades to remedying this lack, eventually producing the first word lists and glosses for regional languages and obsolete expressions.) So few private libraries existed that if Yang Xiong had not been fortunate enough to gain access to the imperial libraries, then closed to the vast majority of Han officials and aristocrats,[10] it is doubtful whether even he, a man of genius, could have come up with the "old finery" that adorns his most famous compilations. Yang himself conceded as much.[11] Between the post-Han and Northern Song, when expertise in Five Classics learning finally became the primary

---

most notably, a double parallel line to indicate the need to repeat a single character. But in Qin and Han manuscripts, filled dots and empty circles set off divisions in the text (e.g., the end of a sentence, a section or a paragraph); L-shaped marks work like parentheses; black oblongs set off one set of quotations from another; wedge-shaped inserts served as commas in lists; and so on. To set off special lines in the text, the margin could be filled with color or otherwise decorated. For the history of early punctuation, see Guan Xihua 2002; Giele 2005. Guan speculates that controversies over *zhangju* during Han often concerned punctuation.

[8] As Cherniack 1994:8, notes, "The use of apparatus changes the reading experience."

[9] Here I query part of the reconstruction proposed in Bagley 2004: 225ff. While Anyang scribes may well have had word lists to train scribes, it seems that Anyang is too early to have developed systematic word lists organized by category in the manner of the *Erya* or *Shiming* 釋名 types. Bagley assumes a stable script deposited in archives. He may be right, but to date the OBI found haven't been deposited in archives, but in waste pits.

[10] HS 30.1701; HS 36.1967. HHS 79A.2548 reminds us that many of the documents in the libraries were "secret texts."

[11] On the paucity of private libraries, I write contra Tsuen-hsuin Tsien 2004: 11-12, which argues, based on three possibly apocryphal stories about pre-Qin figures (Mozi, Su Qin, and Hui Shi), that "[it] was common" during Zhanguo for private scholars to possess collections of books relating to teaching and writing. For those stories, see Mei Yi-pao 1929: 140; *Zhanguoce* 3/3b; *Zhuangzi* 10/38a. (It need hardly be said what an achievement Tsien's book is, despite some questionable statements.) A few "private" (i.e., non-imperial) libraries are recorded for Han, but most of those belonged to members of the imperial Liu clan. See Appendix on book collecting.

Wenxin diaolong, 8.3/80/ (Shih, p. 289) says, "Ziyun [i.e., Yang], with all his talent, said of himself in a memorial that he was a man deficient in learning, and that his literary achievement was the result of the study he did in the [imperial or Chengdu?] Stone Chamber." This statement, first put in a memorial, according to *Wenxin diaolong*, now appears in a letter attributed to Yang in *Guwen yuan* 5/5b; see Knechtges 1977. We know also from HS 87B.3584 that Yang worked collating documents in the Tianlu Gallery. That the imperial libraries were closed to most Han officials is made clear by HS 80.3324.

qualification for office-holding, major shifts in the social practices of the text had to occur.[12]

Before sketching the precise pleasures of reading and classical learning in Yang Xiong's own era, modern scholars must pose the following questions, whose answers are not at all self-evident:

> How was the authority of authors construed and built during this time?
> What do we know about readers in the Han?
> What were their social practices and expectations when reading and reciting?
> What changes in reading habits occurred over the long centuries when manuscript culture predominated?
> How did Yang view his readers, current and future?
> What were the Classics, and what authority was invested in them?
> What did "the past" represent for Yang and his fellow thinkers?
> What, in Yang's view, were the connections between reading, writing, pleasure, and classical learning?

and finally,

> If both the materials and formats of manuscript culture made it impractical to roam through a manuscript, why is it that Yang's followers adopted the metaphors of *you* 遊 –"roaming," "wandering," or "sightseeing," and "playing" (*wan* 玩) – when describing the most significant activities of Kongzi and his true followers among the classicists?[13]

---

[12] Yang knew that erudition, while undeniably useful to the ruling house in the administration of its realm, did not automatically qualify a person for office-holding in Han (in stark contrast to later ages), though the mastery of written *and* oral texts was evidently a precondition for certain entry- or low-level jobs. For birth as the primary qualification for entry into the ranks of Han officialdom, see Nylan 2008.

[13] This metaphor of "roaming" is employed, for example, in describing the Ru 儒 texts in HS 30.1728; also in *Lunheng* 39/189/4 ("Chaoqi" 超奇); and that of "playing" in the Classics in HS 30.1723. Both Ban Gu, author of the *Hanshu* and Wang Chong, author of the *Lunheng*, were ardent admirers of Yang. Hsü Fu-kuan 1966: 60-64 attributed to the influence of Zhuangzi the idea of *you* as "play" and "disinterested contemplation"; the impracticality of "roaming through" a manuscript has little to do with the acts of reading, imagination, and contemplation (*you xin* 遊心).

Good reasons exist to see the following discussion not as a detour from the main topic of this chapter, the pleasure ensuing from reading and classical learning, but as the straightest path toward a better understanding of Yang Xiong's place in the history of reading and classical learning, for manuscript cultures rooted in different places or social strata exhibit huge variations among themselves. Millennia ago, astute thinkers in China had already noted the confusion engendered by innovations in writing technologies and practices and in the preferential treatment accorded certain types of texts.[14] The best classicists acknowledged their uneasiness at the likelihood of a severe break from earlier traditions.

Stages in an Evolving Manuscript Culture

This section gives modern readers the basic information needed to gauge the manuscript culture as it evolved during the first half of the classical era (323 BC-AD 316), the better to understand what denotations and connotations the "right people" would have assigned to authorial authority, to ideal readers, and to classical learning. Of course, in taking up such subjects, the usual caveats must be duly registered. As every sentence below rests on an analysis of the surviving texts (received and excavated), a single archaeological discovery could dramatically alter the chronology laid out here, though the prospect of such a major reversal diminishes with each new manuscript find.[15] Obviously, too, any chronological outline tends to over-standardize practices and attitudes within particular eras. Older ways of thinking about texts and textual authority do not simply disappear overnight, for older texts in circulation serve to keep older views alive before the mind's eye, so that novel ideas can be grafted onto the old, and contradictory

---

[14] Employing faulty logic, some scholars insist that China could not have witnessed massive changes in the social practices of the text, since the logographic script we call "Chinese" has "been passed on from father to son, and from master to disciple, over the long millennia." See Thern 1966: 15.

[15] The excavated texts have made some historians more careful readers of the received traditions, but they have not generally overturned historians' basic ideas about writing and manuscript culture. See Nylan 2008.

assertions happily coexist in the same manuscript, as Yang himself acknowledged.[16]

Stage 1, Zhanguo (475-222 BC), Before True Authorship

Prior to unification by Qin in 221 BC, there were no true "authors" in the modern sense of the word. Indeed, the very ease with which those in the pre-Qin era moved between oral and written transmission precluded the possibility of authorship in a strict sense.[17] If the word "author" is to have meaning at all, the word "authorship" must "claim that the particular words belong to a specific person and are not merely one possible articulation of a general truth."[18] Nor can authorship mean much if a weak concept of a fixed "original" text is combined with a strong expectation that divergent traditions – oral and written – will proliferate over time.[19] Above all, the modern word "authorship" implies intentional composition to achieve a particular end in a particular context. It denotes more than the mere transcription of spoken or imagined words into writing.[20] During the Zhanguo period, attribution of a piece or set of writings to a particular figure tended to be purely conventional. It signified a belief that the writing(s) somehow reflected the teachings or actions associated with a politically prominent person who nearly always was a sage-minister or sage-ruler, Mozi and Zhuangzi being notable exceptions.[21] By most accounts, the first person to put a personal stamp on his

---

16 FY 1/11.

17 Dirk Meyer 2008: 40, writes, "The interplay of the spoken and the written, but also the fusion of various traditions within one text, exclude the existence of a single identifiable author for the different texts."

18 Owen 2006: 214.

19 Jack Goody in many of his works argues that the concept of one, fixed "original" version is inappropriate when discussing oral cultures.

20 This task is often left to copyists and scribes.

21 Mozi and his followers seem to be exceptions to much of what follows, so historians can only fervently hope them to be the exception that proves the rule. A conference devoted to that very topic took place in Leuven, June, 2009, with Carine Defoort and Nicolas Standaert as hosts. I take Xunzi and Han Fei, who lived shortly before unification by Qin in 221 BC, to be transitional figures. On the one hand, they were authors well aware of the difficulties of persuasion. On the other, modern scholars, including Chen Qiyou 陳奇猷 and Liang Qixiong 梁啟雄, cannot agree which parts of the texts ascribed to Xunzi or Han Fei were authored by them. By contrast, no responsible scholar today argues which parts of the *Guanzi* were written by that sixth-century BC figure, since none of them were. Notably, in early times, Mencius is hardly mentioned as the author of a book, but applauded for his "sayings" (*shuo*). Cf. the FY 12/9, on Liu An, Prince of Huainan.

compilations was Kongzi (i.e., Confucius), but he, of course, was initially cast not as "author" but as "editor" of the *Chunqiu* or *Annals*, just as he was editor of the *Odes* and *Documents*.[22] Only when manuscript culture spawned true authors was the figure of Kongzi reconfigured as an author instead of an editor or compiler.

Before unification, governing elites generally deemed exemplary figures' ritual decorum, as expressed in heroic deeds and formal rhetorical speech, to be the most potent way to convey important lessons inherited from a distant past.[23] At the same time, in Yang Xiong's view, the accounts allowed to survive under the Qin ruling house (*jiayan* 家言) were preserved at the expense of the crucial ethical writings associated with the early sages.[24] A century before Yang Xiong, the Senior Archivist Sima Qian, to take one influential example, had Kongzi saying that he preferred to illustrate the efficacy of moral action not through "empty phrasing" (*kong yan* 空言), but through specific examples of extraordinary men and women making decisions and taking action.[25] The supposed limitations of "empty" words was a theme Yang Xiong and his peers were to address later.

---

[22] Only later, probably in Eastern Han (25-220), did Kongzi become the "author" of the *Annals*.Retrospectively, the Duke of Zhou is also made "author" of [some sections in] the *Odes* and *Documents*, as can be seen in the memorial sent by Yi Feng in 46 BC, requesting the Han dynasty to move its capital to Chengzhou. See Liu Rulin 1935: vol. 2, 13, citing *Han shu*.

[23] Yang himself began to promote the idea that writings – at least those by sages and worthies – can even serve as an adequate substitute for the sage himself. See FY 5/13. Exemplary figures in the pre-Qin and Qin period are cited not so much for their sayings as for their deeds or for the two-character slogans that encapsulate their main motivations and messages (e.g., Mozi's "universal love").

[24] See Zhang Zhenze 1993: 393, citing "Boshi jian." Yang speaks there of the "destruction of the Odes and Documents," saying, it was only the "sayings of the [Qin] line, these they [the Qin boshi] preserved." He continues, claiming that the Qin and its Academicians failed to set out ritual vessels, and they and/or the Qin "overturned the altars of grain and soil." This "warning" seems to imply that the Academicians have not always promoted the Confucian system of rites and music, as they should.

[25] Hence, Kongzi's rationale for compiling the *Chunqiu* (Annals), according to Sima Qian, as summarized in Durrant 1995. Judging from the *Analects*, Kongzi was hardly thinking of exemplary women, but the *Chunqiu* does contain references to such women, and certain female characters in the *Shiji* are certainly heroines, including one assassin-retainer's sister and Empress Dowager Lü herself.

Stage 2, Early to Mid-Western Han, Authors Emerge

Aside from the enigmatic and anomalous figure of Mozi,[26] the first identifiable "author" is the semi-legendary Qu Yuan (332-295 BC), who supposedly composed the lament "Encountering Sorrow" shortly before he committed suicide. In prose the first major author is Sima Qian (145-ca. 80 BC), whose monumental *Archival Records* (Shiji 史記) was produced circa 100 BC, centuries after Qu's "Li sao." Possibly poetry was linked to personal authors long before prose, given the official character of most prose writing at the time. But it is equally possible that Qu Yuan's "authorship" is itself an artifact of Sima Qian's powerful biography of the southern poet.[27] At this remove in time, it is hard to tell. Before Sima Qian, tantalizing hints suggest that writings represent specific persons, but only hints.[28]

In early to mid-Western Han, serious thinkers still argued that "those who understand speech do not hoard books."[29] Many conceived authorial intent as having less to do with the expression of personal, possibly idiosyncratic feelings cherished by an author than with "the historically situated, *public* responses" of a politically important agent to a specific set of political circumstances.[30] Quite possibly the first authors, like Sima Qian, were motivated to establish the authority of teachings tied to their own families or localities.[31] In any case, we know that Sima Qian is crucial to any story about self-conscious authorship.[32] But by Sima Qian's own account, political actors supposedly turned to authorship only after being forced out of the political arena. With and after Yang Xiong, however, highly personal

---

26 "Enigmatic" because we know so very little about Mozi, who is given a biography only twenty-four characters long in the *Shiji*, and none in the *Hanshu*. For this "biography," see Nylan (forthcoming in *Oriens Extremus*).

27 As Owen 1992: 214, notes, it is in Sima Qian's work that for the first time we see important figures principally as authors (e.g., Qu Yuan), so it may be that an earlier formulation of a notion of authorship does not predate Sima Qian.

28 *Mencius* 5B/8, for instance, spoke briefly of "finding friends in history," but we cannot be certain whether Mencius simply finds in historical writings an authoritative model for conduct or he means that the best sort of finder will immerse his thoughts in a piece of authoritative writing to ascertain and then emulate the underlying authorial intent. He seems to have referred to the latter when he spoke of exegesis of the *Odes*, using the phrase:以意逆志，是爲得之 (*Mencius* 5A/9).

29 HNZ 12.392; cf. Zhang Shuangdi 1997: 1249, n. 2. I am indebted to Sarah Queen for this citation.

30 Vankeerberghen 2010.

31 I.e., *cheng yi jia zhi yan* 成一家之言.

32 Li Wai-yee 1994 is probably the best account of this, along with Durrant 1995.

single authorship (some of it quite unrelated to dynastic fortunes) came to be considered the most desirable form of persuasion, thanks in large part to the success of Yang Xiong's manner of persuasion.[33] For example, Ge Hong (284-364) writes that his goal in composing his masterwork was to "establish the sayings of one single expert" (*li yijia zhi yan* 立一家之言),[34] apart from familial or state traditions. (Still, no author could hope to earn a living from his writing until the printing era, long centuries after Han.) Attributions to single authors gave readers two obvious hermeneutical advantages: readers could logically presume cohesiveness within a body of work ascribed to a single person, no matter how complex the personality of the author, and readers could better gauge the honesty and value of claims made in writing if a record of the same author's life choices was available.

Stage 3, Mid to Late Western Han, Archives to Libraries

A *haogu* 好古 classicizing movement was unlikely to have developed had it not been preceded by a series of changes in the social practices and attitudes associated with book learning in mid to late Western Han (206 BC-AD 8). Chief among these changes was the transition from archives to libraries, a major conceptual turn by which the once disparate items in palace archives came to be seen as part of integrated library collections. Rulers and advisers from the fourth through the second centuries BC valued documents, maps, and registers of land and population – the "charts and registers" (*tuji* 圖籍) or "charts and writings" (*tushu* 圖書) of the time – according to a single standard: each document's utility to the centralizing projects of the various powerful states contending for supreme power.[35]

---

[33] Some historians of the social practices of the text have also noted the inherent difficulty of cataloguing works by multiple authors. The reference to "dynastic fortunes" is occasioned by the fact that some of the *Odes* exegetes (most notably the Mao tradition) "identified" (in some cases, invented) the authors of individual odes as a necessary step in explicating those odes' intention.

[34] *Bao Puzi*, "Autobiography" [e-Siku 4/70a]; Ware trans., p. 17. Some believed that writings tended to get lost in the cataloguing process, if a set of writings had multiple authors. By contrast, when Sima Qian is quoted as using the same phrase in "Letter in Reply to Ren An" (HS 62.2735), he means to refer to a family's collected writings.

[35] Xiao He's (d. 193) possession of "charts and writings" (*tushu*) supposedly helped Liu Bang to defeat Xiang Yu for possession of the empire. As one persuader put it to his king, "If you take in hand the charts and registers,... in order to command all the empire, none in the empire will dare to disobey you." See *Zhanguo ce* 44/17/26; cf. SJ 70.2282, said by Zhang Yi to King Hui of Qin. From a series of such statements we may infer that maps

Items in archives, however, tended to be pitched when no longer of immediate use. Behind the Qin and early Western Han palace walls, then, we should imagine enormous refuse heaps of bundled bamboo accounts.[36] (Compare the discarded Shang oracle bones found in waste heaps at Anyang.). Items in full-fledged library collections, by contrast, acquire value in roughly inverse proportion to their practical use. Texts became prestige items, cultural capital for demanding connoisseurs, only when specific aspects of the manuscripts had acquired value: their age, fragility, relative rarity, place within the entire library collection, and the number and range of ritual activities entailed in their textual production and transmission.[37] It is libraries, not archives, that spark passions, even pathologies,[38] insofar as they are deemed more than the sum of their individual parts. It is they that are the brain-children of supreme intellectual ambition, since libraries combined aspects of palace, museum, and shrine to the hallowed past.[39]

One major step in the transition from archives to libraries was supposedly taken by Han Wudi's uncle, Liu De, the King of Hejian 河間 (active 155-129? BC), whose palace library became the envy of others in power. Hejian held an outstanding library collection because the king set about assembling not only the best textual experts that he could find (as had been done before),[40] but also the best editions of *older* texts from throughout

---

and books on strategy and registers were placed in palace archives long before unification took place in 221 BC.

36 In Han, some accounts were sent up to the throne from the localities in the tenth month of each calendar year. Joseph McDermott 2006: 25, says that, even in Song, paper was still expensive enough to warrant its regular recycling; the Song court offices even relied on the sale of used paper to finance a banquet or increase their revenue. The writing materials used before paper were harder to recycle, but the split ends of bamboo books might have been trimmed, the wooden boards planed, and the rag silk reused.

37 It is these sorts of texts that are used as talismans in the early histories and philosophical works, but our evidence is too limited to know how to interpret this fact.

38 Cf. Li Qingzhao's "Afterword" to the *Jinshi lu* which claims that a passion for anything – even "transmission of knowledge and commentary" – is a "disease" and a "delusion," regardless of one's reputation. See Ronald Egan 2004, contra Owen 1986: 66-79.

39 It may be no coincidence that the term *shi shi* 石室 (Stone Chamber) is associated with shrines, with libraries, with tombs, and, by early medieval times, the mountain hideaways of recluses; also, that there is confusion (to modern eyes) in the duties assigned the *taichang* 太常 (ritual master) as head of the library and its staff; and that *shi* (routinely translated as "historian") just as often means professional "diviner" and "invocator."

40 See, e.g., SJ 59.2093; 103.2769; and HS 30.1708, 1712, 1725-26, and 53.2410. Liu De's library holdings purportedly included rare editions of antique works that were curated and taught by specialists known as "Academicians" (*boshi* 博士). However, several sources

the realm. This investment of time and labor reportedly resulted in a set of well selected, ably culled, carefully collated, and finely executed editions, which were treasured as the epitome of the most sublime cultural values inherited from antiquity. Hejian's king united in his person a cachet attached to erudition, a notable preference for the antique, and a connoisseur's appreciation for the tactile pleasures associated with fine manuscripts. Surely he enjoyed pride of ownership as well, for tremendous social prestige accrued to the leading collectors of books, nearly all of whom, prior to Wudi's reign (r. 141-87 BC), were princes and rulers.

Once learned men and rulers began to tout their holdings as repositories of all wisdom and expertise that had been painfully acquired and transmitted over centuries, the idea of the library as cultural memory was born. It was then but a matter of time before an emperor would seek to capitalize on the new institution of libraries to manifest his superiority. Shortly after coming to the throne at age sixteen, Wudi had several libraries constructed inside and outside his main residential quarters at Chang'an. To stock these libraries, he recruited functionaries to copy texts, "going so far as to include the masterworks with their commentaries and explications," we are told.[41] Some of Wudi's successors continued to have copies of new writings deposited in the imperial libraries, with the result that "after a century, a veritable mountain of books had been gathered."

> In the outer court were the collections (*cang* 藏) of the Superintendent of Ceremonials (*taichang* 太常), the Senior Archivist (*taishi* 太史), and the writings of the Academicians. Inside the palace residences were the repositories of Yan'ge 延閣, Guangnei 廣內, and Mishi 秘室.[42]

---

about Liu De's library are very late (e.g., *Nan Qi shu* 南齊書 24.251). Supposedly Liu De housed his experts in great style.

41 HS 30.1701. Sometimes the lure of imperial rewards prompted the fabrication of "old" books.

42 TPYL 619/1a, citing "Qi lue"; cf. HS 30.1702, n. 10 (Ru Chun 如淳 commentary). Cf. "Qi lue" 七略 (T/Dunhuang 213), 108c. (It appears that Yang's works were not included in the "Qi lue" catalogue, and they were added by Ban Gu to his "Yiwen zhi" [HS 30]). If one accepts Ying Shao's preface to the FSTY, the books presented to the emperor were conserved in the Mishi. By Chengdi's reign, these efforts seem to have collapsed. HS 30.1701-2 suggests that the imperial efforts to build a set of libraries "without lacunae" were unsystematic, at best.

In 26 BC, sixty years after Wudi, Chengdi named the members of a commission whose members were to identify lacunae in the imperial collection, locate copies of the missing texts, produce better recensions through collation and editing, and classify all the versions produced for the official imperial collections. An imperial envoy, Chen Nong 陳農, was dispatched from the capital to scour the suburbs and countryside for lost books. Palace Superintendent Liu Xiang 劉向, as the official head of the imperial clan, was duly appointed to oversee the all-important task of revising the Classics and their commentaries, as well as the philosophical and the poetic works. He was well chosen. A distant member of the imperial family, descended from a King of Chu who was likewise a brilliant classical scholar and patron of scholars, Liu held the rank of minister in charge of the palace residences and their contents. Before Chengdi came to the throne, Liu had submitted a strongly worded memorial urging Chengdi's father, who was known to be in sympathy with the classicists at court, to restore the antique values espoused in the old texts as a way of shoring up the waning dynastic fortunes.[43] Ren Hong 任宏, an infantry colonel, was to superintend the acquisition and editing of military texts for the imperial collections; the Senior Archivist Yin Xian 尹咸, the technical manuals (*shushu* 數術);[44] and Li Zhuguo 李柱國, a court physician, the medical texts. Meanwhile, Liu Xiang, as head of the entire commission, set out to compile an annotated catalogue of the imperial collections that would serve as reference guide for the emperor and his staff. This library catalogue, so far as we know, was the first of its kind. An elegant persuasion piece dating a century later tries to capture the realities of Chengdi's era, when men of "great talent and vast erudition" were put to work "collating secret writings" in the four major libraries within the palaces.[45] Several early sources place Yang Xiong in those palace libraries, working under Liu Xiang's direction, which confirms the picture of Liu as Yang's patron.

Supervising the collation and editing and cataloguing of the imperial collections, including illustrated books, charts, and maps, occupied Liu Xiang for nearly twenty years. Shortly after Chengdi and Liu Xiang died in 7 BC, Liu Xin, Xiang's son, presented to the new boy emperor Aidi a catalogue

---

43 The memorial is dated to 42 BC.

44 Or, "quantitative arts" (?). *Shu* generally refers to "regular changes" that can be predicted and enumerated.

45 See Ban Gu, "Two Capitals" *fu*, in *Wenxuan* 1/12a-b; cf. HHS 40.1341. Ban Gu, of course, was related to the imperial family by marriage.

entitled *Qi lue* 七略 (Seven Summaries),[46] based on his father's work. The *Seven Summaries* groups under seven subject headings the total of 13,296 scrolls in the imperial library collections: (1) the "Six Arts" or Classics; (2) philosophical masterworks; (3) verse; (4) military works; (5) treatises on the technical and quantitative arts, including divination; (6) medicine; and (7) miscellaneous works.[47] For the first time, so far as we know, texts – not just masters – were treated as experts in their own right.[48] Yang Xiong's own philosophical works might resist easy classification under his patron's bibliographic categories,[49] but Yang's writings suggest his wholehearted support for Liu's decision – surely approved by Chengdi – to give pride of place to the Classics, above the masterworks, verse, and technical manuals.[50] Paradoxically, however, that decision may have been the first step on a road that led finally to later scholars' easy conflation of library catalogues with "national history," and thence to serious distortions of the classical past.[51]

---

46 HS 30.1701; HS 10.310. According to *Suishu* 32.905, such books were put in the "Warming Chamber" (*Wenshi* 溫室), built by Wudi, before being transferred to the Tianlu pavilion. Liu Xiang's death dates are given variously as 8 or as 7 BC. Notably, the Ru experts' writings are put in a separate bibliographic classification – that of the "Masters" (*zhuzi*) – from the Six Arts (i.e., the Classics).

47 See *Tongzhi*, 21.1825, whose premise is that "illustrations and texts.., when put together, make a complete text." This account of the "Summaries" varies from that given in Fu Yuzhang 2008: 46, which retains numbers 1-6, but makes the First Summary the catalogue list itself and omits "miscellaneous works." Fu also cites a figure of "more than 33,000 *juan* of books."

Cf. the work by Zhang Yanyuan, *Lidai minghua ji* (comp. 847), which speaks of painting and writing having the same origins. Acker trans., p. 64, speculates the two arts were not often distinguished in the pre-Song period.

48 See Queen 2001: 62.

49 As noted in *Tongzhi* 71/836a, Zheng Qiao applied the "suoxu" 所序 classification to the *Taixuan*, *Fayan*, and *Yuezhen* (Music Admonitions) by Yang Xiong. See Drège 1991: 102, n. 49.

50 The sevenfold classification scheme was replaced in the third century AD by a different bibliographical scheme that further privileged the Classics above philosophy, history, and literature, perhaps in response to the efforts spearheaded by the two Lius, father and son, with the assistance of Yang Xiong.

51 Here I repeat an observation made in Glen Dudbridge 2001: 4-6. Fashions in bibliography could work against collecting certain types of works. See *Tongzhi*, 21.1826, which gives an example: when Liu Xiang's Seven Summaries did not include a separate category for *tu* (charts, pictures), this diminished, according to Zheng, the impetus to collect them. We might argue that the social and economic value of that category of texts declined, though pictures were, of course, to rise in value as paintings and scrolls.

It is easy to overlook the sheer magnitude of the editorial changes wrought by the activist editors working under Liu Xiang's direction, massive changes that ended in the compilation of "new texts" (their term). To take just one example, the new edition of the *Liezi* 列子 in eight *juan* (scrolls or chapters) was produced after comparing and collating short works, only one of them a shorter *Liezi*, that once circulated under five separate titles in twenty *juan*. By Liu Xiang's own account, he found many incorrect characters and some duplication among the various recensions. Assuming the old palace editions to be more reliable than those circulating "among the people," Liu made a new edition, which he hoped showed more internal consistency within chapters (though Liu doubted whether the original chapters "were by the same hand").[52] Similarly, Liu Xiang made up a "revised and reduced" *Zhangguo ce* 戰國冊 in thirty-three bamboo bundles from six different manuscripts whose texts he described as a total mishmash.[53] More astonishing still, Liu Xiang rejected as "duplicates" all but thirty-two of 320 *pian* of the *Xunzi* 荀子, or one-tenth of the originals he had at his disposal, when making his new edition of that masterwork; that tenth he had transcribed in a fair hand on strips of properly seasoned bamboo, in order to minimize future damage.[54] Like father, like son. Liu Xin's labors in the imperial library reduced a *Shanhai jing* 山海經 in thirty-two *pian* to a mere eighteen.[55]

Perhaps it was an implicit faith in the authentic text's potential for perfect communication across great gaps of time and space (across "clouds and seas," as the poet Su Shi 蘇軾 would later put it) that allowed Liu Xiang, Yang Xiong, and the other activist editors to believe that the authentic (or "true" or "accurate") versions or portions of manuscripts would become evident to careful perusal, comparing, and judging. Yang Xiong asserted that the texts of the Five Classics had sustained "additions and subtractions" – losses and interpolations – however regrettable such emendations were in the

---

52 Liu Xiang, cited in *Quan Hanwen*, 37.6a-6b.

53 One of the titles was *Guo ce*, but none of the six titles match the title *Zhanguo ce*. See Liu Xiang, cited in *Quan Hanwen*, 37.1a-2b, which compares the texts to taros mashed together.

54 Activist editing did not begin with Liu Xiang and Liu Xin. The *Rites* expert Dai De 戴德, to take one example, excised all but eighty-five *pian* out of an original 214 *pian* to create the *Da Dai Liji* 大戴禮記; Dai Sheng 戴聖, his relative, expunged another forty-six *pian*.

55 ECT; cf. Liu Rulin 1935: vol. 2, 109.

case of authoritative works.[56] At the same time, Han legends countenanced, even celebrated, activist editing, styling the sage Kongzi as the first editor to take a hatchet to antique writings in order to distill and refine their moral message.[57] Plenty of later examples of drastic editing were known within the circles of Han classical scholars.[58] Evidently, manuscripts were like natural organisms in being subject to cycles of florescence and decay; hence the occasional need for sages or worthies to engage in therapeutic interventions, so as to restore balance.[59] Thus to master a text, one had to "put it in order," "master it," or even "heal" or even "cure" it (*zhi shu* 治書).

Such massive efforts directed toward remedying (also *zhi* 治) the flaws in hand-copied manuscripts would have led editors in the late Western Han imperial libraries to try to devise more reliable methods for evaluating competing variants and editions, with the result that those same editors would have themselves become more self-conscious authors, who showed ever greater selectivity in choosing the models for their own compositions. For instance, Yang Xiong's *Fayan* openly speaks of "borrowing" or "rejecting" the models and slogans associated with the Han and pre-Han philosophical masters. In tandem with this editing and cataloguing project came the invention or conventionalization of new textual forms, such as the addition of prefaces or postfaces (many in verse) as early Tables of Contents (e.g., the last chapter of Yang's *Fayan*). Even more importantly, such an unprecedented focus on the virtues and pleasures of close reading spurred the production of several of the first reference works in classical Chinese (see below). Attention to pre-Qin epigraphy grew in the wake of the library organization, since the emperor and his ministers found it useful to consult early narratives when weighing alternative policies or searching for plausible precedents for new initiatives. Imperial collecting would henceforth be

---

56 See FY 5/7-8.

57 See SJ 47.1936-37. Supposedly, Confucius in putting together his own recension of the *Odes* selected a mere 300 odes out of a total of either 3,000 or 6,000 odes known to him, and selected for his *Documents* classic a mere 100 or 120 chapters out of 3,240, in addition to compiling the *Annals* by excising, rearranging, and rephrasing archival materials from his home state of Lu.

58 See Kalinowski 2003; Nylan 2008.

59 I owe this observation to a wonderful conversation with Dirk Meyer (Oxford), in the spring of 2008. In writing of manuscript culture up to and including the Song period, Cherniack 1994: 12, put it bluntly: in her view, the early Chinese held a different concept of transmission, "with the Chinese scholars generally in favor of emending texts." As Christopher Nugent has shown, however, this is something of an overstatement. See Nugent 2007.

propelled by the notion that putting old writings in order (*zhishu*), the older the better, might aid government and even "restore antiquity" (*fugu* 復古).[60] Small wonder, then, that scholars like Yang Xiong who were lucky enough to be appointed to the imperial library staff felt that they had died and gone to heaven or to one of the Han paradises at Kunlun or Penglai.[61]

Scholars today tend to believe that a fully developed culture of the written word cannot exist absent three preconditions: the circulation of multiple copies of key works; the expansion of access to books via the growth of private libraries; and the development of public repositories for books. By those measures, a sophisticated culture of the written word did not emerge before the Song (960-1279), which witnessed phenomenal growth of private academies and libraries, as well as state-sponsored and private printings of the Classics, commentaries, and technical manuals.[62]

---

60 Cherniack 1994: 12. But Moses Finley 1995: 201, argues the deadening effect of reducing a liberal education to book culture; it is only after the freezing of the liberal arts, and their reduction to book culture, that learning increasingly was "expressed statistically in some figures of book ownership."

61 A story told of Ma Rong 馬融 (79-106), however, is that he irritated Dowager Empress Deng by writing a satirical poem, saying that "He had been stuck in the Eastern Lodge for ten years, without permission to transfer" (HHS 23.822; 60A.1954).

62 The only actual surviving Tang imprint is a Dunhuang copy of the *Jinggang jing* (Diamond Sutra), published in 868. McDermott 2006 would put this date much later than others, in mid-Ming, since he emphasizes (1) how few bookstores existed in Ming outside the major metropolitan centers; (2) how often books were acquired through gift exchange; and (3) how many titles were extremely hard to get, even sometimes of "basic" books.

In comparing the ways in which the imperial library functioned in comparison to modern libraries, Dudbridge 2000 is inclined to over-emphasize the similarities. Using any standard of evidence, public access was too limited to warrant the rosy account presented there. At present, there exist two main models of book circulation: (1) that proposed by Robert Darnton, which concentrates on the different human actors engaged in producing and distributing forms of knowledge; and (2) that proposed by Thomas R. Adamans and Nicolas Barker, which deals with individual books to analyze the circulation of these objects in institutional and individual collections. Neither model considers censorship or exorbitant prices.

LITERACY, AND YANG XIONG'S INTENDED READERS

"Why should words be a treasure to hold on to alone?" asked one early author.[63] Why indeed? What do we know about readers in Han? How did Yang view the select group of his readers, current and future? What practices and expectations were brought to acts of reading and reciting?[64] And what changes in reading habits transpired over the long centuries when manuscript culture predominated? These sorts of questions come flooding in as soon as we notice Yang's faith that later generations of discriminating readers would appreciate and transmit his writings. Yang presented himself in his writings as an anomaly: a classical master who intended to live most fully inside his manuscript rolls, rather than in the courts or schoolrooms of his day.[65] Some literary scholars imagine him to be the first self-conscious "author" intent upon maximizing his posthumous influence in Chinese history (more on this below). Of course, Yang was too intellectually ambitious to limit his ideal readers to the pool of potential or actual bureaucrats among his contemporaries; that ambition probably accounts for his steadfast refusal to allow his masterworks to circulate prematurely.[66] At the same time, he could reasonably expect only limited circulation for his writings among disciples and disciples of disciples, as was typical of manuscript culture.[67]

Several features of the early manuscript culture of Han compel our attention, the first being that "reading" in most cases meant "reciting." Given the paucity of suitable inexpensive writing materials in Yang Xiong's time, to learn the contents of a manuscript one often had little choice but to commit those contents to memory by reciting them again and again. Rough estimates put the pace of copying by seasoned professionals at no more than

---

[63] The Liu Xin/Yang Xiong correspondence, included in the *Han Wei congshu*, is usually appended to most editions of the *Fangyan*. See Knechtges 1977; Chung 1982: 482-95.

[64] On this, see Nylan 2001.

[65] Yves Hervouet 1964: 428 argued that Sima Xiangru was the first Chinese writer to regard literary production as a matter of primary importance in his life. However, this assertion is not particularly supported by the relevant texts.

[66] This is reiterated in Yang's poem "Expelling Poverty" and in his exchange of letters with Liu Hsin.

[67] As HS 87A.3515 (Yang's autobiography) says that Yang "thought that when a noble man got the right time, then he could do grand deeds; if not, then he would be a dragon coiling up like a snake."

one manuscript of average length per month of full-time employment.[68] Even so, the gist of legal, administrative, or religious notices, if not the precise wording, needed to be orally transmitted from literate to semi-literate and illiterate populations. We have no proof that literacy rates rose much in Yang's time or in the centuries immediately after him, despite the throne's boast that it patronized classical learning.[69] All the "evidence" routinely adduced for any such increase is shaky.[70] Readers/reciters generally sought from manuscripts the requisite knowledge to follow in their parents' professions, or consulted technical manuals that promised to improve their daily lives by providing the proper formulae for prayers, useable calendars of lucky and unlucky days, or sound advice on medical treatments, irrigation, or rhetoric.[71] Whereas many professionals – artisans, merchants, doctors,

---

[68] In 849, the Tang Censorate calculated that the professional copyists in the Imperial Library, whose numbers varied between twenty andtwenty-seven, according to the sources, could copy 417 scrolls per year. if working at full speed. See Drège 1991: 68-69. Liu Xiang's "Bie lu" 別錄 reportedly compared the process of collating texts to "enemies facing off against each other." See that work, cited in FSTY, *yiwen*; TPYL 618. Mary Beard 2009: 27, notes that the money to buy a top-quality copy of a manuscript of 500 lines would be enough to feed a family of four on basic rations for a year in Rome in the third century AD.

[69] Both Mark Edward Lewis 1999 and Robin Yates 2007, for example, presuppose comparatively high literacy rates, without paying due attention to the existence of oral commands and scriveners, distinguishing sufficiently between bare literacy and numeracy (such as might be found among low-ranking army conscripts) and high cultural literacy (such as would have been required by high-ranking officials at the Han court), or separating "reading and writing" from "composition," a much more demanding technical skill.

[70] The usual evidence adduced consists of (a) the proliferation of commemorative steles and letters; and (b) the numbers of "students" registered at the Imperial University. As has long been recognized, steles are a fashion imported from Central Asia, and the numbers of extant letters may be a function of preservation bias or the greater availability of lightweight writing material. The earliest extant personal letters (dated ca. 224 BC), are two letters on wooden boards from Yunmeng, Shuihudi, Tomb 4, which were exchanged between a soldier fighting in the Qin campaign against Chu in 224-23 and his brother Zhong, the tomb occupant. Transcriptions of those letters may be found in *Yunmeng Shuihudi Qin mu* (1981). Shaughnessy 1997: 181 translates one of the letters into English. Yates 2007 hypothesizes that a much larger group during Han may have commanded some rudimentary skills in numeracy and writing. As for the tallies for the number of *boshi* disciples at the Academy, these show a less consistent pattern that most (including Lewis) suggest. In any case, an increase in the number of disciples or Imperial Academy students probably reflects their bureaucratic patrons' growing power to absolve them from tax and labor services, and not necessarily advances in classical learning. See Nylan 2008 for details.

[71] As in most recorded societies, in Han some few geniuses advanced beyond their inherited station because of their extraordinary talents in reading, transcribing, and

soldiers, scribes, and functionaries – would have realized the advantages accruing from even a rudimentary grasp of a limited number of graphs,[72] the barriers to advanced cultural literacy were formidable. "High cultural literacy" meant producing as well as reading manuscripts that wove together elegant phrases and classical allusions (*zhu wen* 屬文) via complex prosodic and semantic rules,[73] thus magnifying the difficulties for those like Yang, who first had to translate their vernacular regional languages and non-standard script forms into the "refined" classical language of the court.

Judging from the available sources, reading did not become a virtue per se (not only a sign of diligence) until some time after Yang, nor were manuscripts fully commodified (reduced to a set price), even in the large metropolitan areas.[74] Indeed, writings by Yang Xiong and his famous peers consistently claim that the pleasurable associations of books derived chiefly from the manuscripts' associations with intensely gratifying relations binding master to pupil, father to child, patron to client, friend to friend, or ruler to

---

composition. For Yang's hereditary background, see the opening lines to his autobiography, recorded at the start of HS 87A. Yang may have attended Wen Weng's 文翁 Academy in Chengdu (see above), but this is speculation. In any case, J. Michael Farmer 2000 has cast some doubt on longstanding traditions regarding that "academy." Lü Simian 1982: 678-92 makes the case that many figures during Han experienced social mobility as a direct consequence of their learning to read and write, but Lü could only come up with a handful of names. For most, as Lü confesses, study in the capital or in the commanderies merely afforded men of good breeding the opportunity to cement good relations with office-holders in the administrative seats.

72 In early Western Han, and possibly in Yang Xiong's time as well, the first qualification for hiring scribes, diviners, and invocators was hereditary, as indeed it probably was in the upper reaches of officialdom. However, the phrase "scribes" in this case may mean "those in charge of astronomical records" who are also prayer-masters, as *Zuo*, Lord Zhao 20.6, makes clear but none have noted.

73 Scholars generally underestimate the difficulties associated with the transition from the vernacular regional languages to the "refined" classical language of the court, as they mistakenly assume first, that linguistic transformation is part of the natural order of human history, and second, that the discrete languages in early China were simply dialects, minor variants of the single model of a national language. Naquin 2008 has remarked upon this with respect to late imperial times. In citing such views, I part ways with scholars who minimize the gap between rudimentary literacy and numeracy and high cultural literacy (i.e., the ability to compose texts laden with allusions to other literary works), and who discount a phenomenon widely reported, the propensity to read out orders to the general populace, including conscripts. However, the most efficient coordination of the army's movements and operations depended upon some proportion of soldiers and officers having a modicum of reading skills plus numeracy, as did the efficient organization of manufacturing processes.

74 See, e.g., HHS 49.1629, 80B.2635.

subject. Almost every type of instruction or exposition was more reliant on oral instruction in late Western Han than it is today. Manuscripts often circulated within the context of gift exchanges. Via dictation and recitation students, disciples, officials and clients often put down in writing what they had just heard from their social or intellectual betters.[75] All this made early manuscripts a visible locus and medium of exchange in the promotion of social solidarity within relatively small communities. Meanwhile this strong association of manuscripts with social interchange made them into highly authoritative guides to deliberation and conduct in a culture avidly searching for exemplary models in life or in books.[76] Texts most transparently represented people when a single person or family was responsible for a particular composition or set of compositions that then circulated within small groups (Yang several times conflated text and person, whether creator or transmitter)[77] and this alone accounted for the propensity of Han scholastics to tie every act of composition to a particular person confronting particular circumstances. Broader and more casual access to textual culture threatened to strip away the pleasurable cachet attached to manuscripts as site and symbol of complex human relations.[78] (Until Sui and Tang times,

---

75 According to Yates 2007, this is also how the excavated Liye accounts describe the process of training and hiring of imperial officials, whether at the capital or in the commanderies and counties. Most of the Liye documents remain to be published, however.

76 See *Tongzhi*, 20.1821-22, "On Collating," claims, "In antiquity [by which he means Han], for those with high cultural literacy, whatever was produced by the hand of one person was thought to 'complete' the learning of that person's own family. In Sui and Tang, [compilation] started to use many hands; the Jin and Sui official histories are good examples...."

77 *FY* 2/20. *Analects* 8/17 does something similar when it compares the ardent pursuit of learning with the ardent pursuit of the person desired. Hence the common view of texts as desirable destinations. As texts were not widely available, often a person had to seek them out (as with Stone Classics in the capital, entry into the imperial library as a career goal, travels to specific masters for study, and so on).

78 One Tang writer, Li Deyu 李德裕 (787-850), complained in 845, "Everywhere you look you see men of breeding and cultivation, some already occupying important positions and some already at an advanced age, pounding away at composing texts, looking only for compensation." See Li Deyu rpt. 2000: 18.365. One wonders whether such comments were targeting Li's contemporary, Han Yu 韓愈 (768-824), who was very well paid for his compositions. If so, Han's stature would have paved the way for other scholar-officials to have adopted his methods. Han Yu supposedly got for one commissioned epitaph "one horse with saddle and stirrups, and a white jade belt," and for another, "500 bolts of silk," extraordinary sums that would have been three times one month of his official salary set at 150,000 cash/month.

surprisingly few jointly authored compositions were recognized as such.)[79]

Attitudes toward manuscripts copied by oneself or kin or kindred spirits could differ markedly from attitudes toward documents produced by scriveners and clerks.[80] Hand-copying texts could confer moral and intellectual benefits upon the copyist, but only when undertaken as a vital part of the learning process, designed to steep the copyist in the virtue of fidelity to the authority who conferred the gift of knowledge and experience, as well as fidelity in transcription and transmission.[81] These were the preconditions for inscribing the text's contents onto the copyist's heart and mind, for internalizing the manuscript's underlying message, and for instantiating the authorial intent. Readers were told that if they could "read and recite it [a manuscript] a hundred times, the sense of it would become apparent."[82] There was a profound faith in the transformative potential of hand-copying and memorizing model manuscripts, so long as the text and its author were thoroughly good. But, by the same token, if the manuscript so carefully hand-copied and memorized was inherently misguided, its errors might well color the learner's experience of the world and skew his judgments. Recall Yang Xiong's frequent warnings against reading any literature that was "mixed" (i.e., not strictly focused on the related tasks of governing the self and others).[83] As books carried such enormous transformative potential, it was incumbent upon the wise person to find a reliable standard by which to judge their contents. Yang wrote,

> 一哄之市，不勝異意焉；一卷之書，不勝異說焉。一•之市，必立之平；一卷之書，必立之師。

> Just as countless numbers of ideas exist in a single alleyway marketplace, so too innumerable arguments may co-exist in any one scroll of writing. Just as a balance must be set up for

---

79 See n. 76 above, citing Zheng Qiao's *Tongzhi*.

80 True, the skills of scriveners, clerks, and copyists – transcribing speech into writing or verbatim copying of documents – conferred no very great prestige during Han, even if the empire would have quickly collapsed without their aid.

81 However, "fidelity" in transmission may not have meant "verbatim transcription," which is a modern concept. Fidelity may well have allowed transcriptions in homonyms, when a piece of writing served mainly as an aide to memory.

82 *Sanguo zhi* 13.420.

83 FY 5/16, for example.

each little marketplace in a narrow alley, so too a teacher must be set up even for a single text only one scroll in length."[84]

Yang's insistence on the necessity of finding a good teacher made supremely good sense in his own era. First, before the regularization of formats, genres, and script types, and the development of scholarly apparatuses in Yang's lifetime and beyond, most readers could not reasonably expect to understand a text from the distant past without the aid of a teacher.[85] Second, perusal of a manuscript by a person on one's own still smacked of superficiality, if not indolence – a negative association strengthened through Yang's disparaging comments about the *fu* and alluded to in such seductive phrases as "floating of the glance" and "drifting of a look."[86] Once the moral reader, with the help of a teacher, had weighed the quality of the available texts and their contents, the reader was fully prepared to maximize his own potential through "immersion" (*qian* 潛) into the best sorts of manuscripts, i.e., dedicated credence in the true textual masters via properly copied and memorized manuscripts. According to Yang Xiong, the written traces of past masters trained the avid learner to emulate true greatness. After all, it was solely through the medium of old texts that "Confucius had inculcated in himself the qualities of the Duke of Zhou," in a manner as fully complete as Yan Hui emulating the qualities of Confucius, his master in life.[87] And once the reader/transcriber glimpsed the authorial intent behind the texts that invited reflection, he would himself become a virtual repository of such authoritative texts. This process Yang deemed "natural" but "not spontaneous"[88] – "natural" because it was natural for the best in people to want to imitate the best in others, yet "not spontaneous"

---

[84] FY 1/11.

[85] See *Wenxin diaolong*, 8.4/85/4 (Shih, p. 297) on the inability of post-Han writers to understand the works of Yang Xiong "in the absence of a teacher" and sufficiently "broad learning." Increasingly, text experts believe that a choice of a particular variant could be based as much on "conjecture" or "inspiration" (*divinatio*) as on earlier variants carefully preserved in earlier manuscripts. The age of a text "at best age gives only a rough indication of a manuscript's value." Cf. Cherniack 1994: 7, n. 7. For the continuation of multiple script types and orthographic variants long after unification in 221 BC, see Galambos 2006; Kern 2003 436; and Harrist 2008, passim.

[86] See Tao Qian, "On Reading the *Shanhai jing*," in Yuan Xingpei, 4.393 (Hightower 1970 Poem 54), no. 1 of 13 in the series, lines 13-14.

[87] For "immersion," see FY 5/1. Cf. FY 1/7, 1/18.

[88] FY 5/6. Cf. Veyne 1988, passim, writing of the Greek views on this.

because of the informed choices and hard work required for such immersion into the profundities.

Yang Xiong's ideal readers were those sufficiently learned and cultivated to engage in serious reading, transcribing, and composing of texts packed with classical allusions to works like the *Odes* and *Documents*. These readers would have memorized the vast majority of the manuscripts they encountered, so that antique phrases rolled off their tongues and their brushes. Such readers brought a keen thinking and a highly developed sense of style to their own writings. During Han, such learners were rare birds perched on high branches inescapably aware of their superior erudition.[89] But in Yang's view most who claimed to be learned were in the thrall of hoary traditions or crass ambitions and also inclined to mistake memorizing a heap of facts for attaining true wisdom. Hence Yang's sharp critique of the court-appointed Academicians who, misguided or self-seeking, misinterpreted the teachings of the Ancients.[90] Rulers, the ultimate patrons for professional writers and classical scholars, might themselves lack refinement.[91] Yang nonetheless was greatly cheered by the notion that like-minded people of sufficient taste might form a close-knit group defined by their love of classical learning.[92]

In Yang Xiong's view, two categories of texts attracted the best minds. Writings originating in the dicta of one or more authorities called for acceptance of the authority invested in the text. This class of writings

---

[89] See, however, He Xiu's 何修 (129-82) interesting, if impossibly idealized projection on the past of an account of social mobility via learning, from the winter lessons given by farming fathers to sons beginning in the tenth month and the selection of best students for the corps of court officials. See Chen Li 1936, 3.1259-61. Basic numeracy was taught together with basic literacy, but since it was hardly central to Yang's vision of the coupled pleasures of reading and classical learning, it is mentioned only in passing here.

[90] See below. Yang Xiong, as one of the *haogu* reformers, attacked the expertise of the imperial Academicians, official guardians of the Classics transmitted from antiquity, as well as the heavily accreted traditions, interpretations, and commentaries attached to the Classics and masterworks.

[91] Cf. Wu Fusheng 2007: 43, in talking of Sima Xiangru (not Yang Xiong).

[92] A later textual community is described in *Liangshu* 51.748. Conceivably, students could recite a Classic or a masterwork, without understanding its content, especially if the recitation mode (sometimes identified as the *ya* mode) entailed a special pronunciation. Therefore, recitation preceded being lectured on a text, and those lectures preceded full commitment to a text, in Drège's formulation, "apprenticing one's body to it." Yang would have had no sense of a "republic of letters" or an "empire of texts," however, following McDermott 2006: chap. 4. Further information about literacy in China during Yang's own era can be found at the www.changan26BC Website.

included contracts, edicts, legal documents, coins, seals, tallies, censuses, written orders, and so on – documents that neither wanted nor needed reflection, much less reinterpretation. By contrast, a second category of writings positively invited imaginative responses,[93] so that devoted readers, transcending time and space,[94] might bring to life the dearly beloved authors by ongoing engagements with and frequent resorts to the text. Only the second class of writings – those that required a series of ardent communications – struck Yang as "sexy" or "alluring." Manuscripts full of resonant patterns and inspired juxtapositions of images and graphs appealed to the imagination and mirrored the cosmos, thereby propelling humans to interact and conceive of cultural exchange beyond their own limited experiences. Yang considered this sort of rewarding engagement the most singular and valuable experiences of human existence. He therefore wrote, when he could please himself, texts to form rather than to inform; he spoke of "casting men."[95] That sort of manuscript, he believed, would be hand-copied by avid learners down through the ages.

As Yang Xiong himself remarked, writing can preserve long and intricate lines of argumentation across time and space, as oral discourse cannot. Writing in the most admired Han mode – weaving passages together in artful compositions – facilitated a merging of disparate ideas from disparate sources.[96] Witness Yang's own selectivity when harnessing the pre-Qin persuasions to his larger vision. Writing and composition could stimulate a higher level of reflection or abstraction than oral discourse, especially when repeated drafts precede the final fair copy.[97] And writing allowed authors and readers to try out various ways of sorting and categorizing knowledge, as is evident from the tales of Yang's shuffling and

---

[93] In other words, in the first case the Han reader would think that in reading the text he is rather hearing the voice of an authoritative person, with the piece of writing in hand merely meant to document, confirm, or preserve a speech or gesture. For this useful distinction, see Fischer 2003: 23, 28, speaking of Mediterranean cultures.

[94] FY 3/8, on humans and interaction: "Through human interactions human achievements may be realized" (*ren dao jiao, gong xun cheng* 人道交, 功勳成). Writing in the second category was seen to be far more than the mere "transcription" of speech (*pace* some linguists and sociologists today). Jack Goody is one expert of the latter sort whose enormous contributions cannot be doubted, and who still sees writing primarily as "reported speech."

[95] See, e.g., FY 1/8; 3/8.

[96] This is what is meant by *zhu wen* 屬文, literally "connecting" or "putting together" texts.

[97] This discussion is inspired by Meyer: 2008: 4-5.

reshuffling his set of file cards on flat wooden boards in his search for the most persuasive order. In the class of texts inviting reflection, Yang believed the Classics and neoclassics – whether composed by the Ancients or by latter-day sages like himself – afforded readers the closest possible analogues to sustained relations with the ancient sages and worthies,[98] the best possible medium for communicating with those "far away." But because verbatim transcription was an oxymoron in the pre-printing era, Yang saw that "engaging" texts meant encouraging the copying and re-copying that increased the chances that the original wording of any given text would be traduced, especially when so many of the learned in his day viewed manuscripts as mere aides to memory or pretexts for adaptation or playful acts of literary impersonation, or *prosopopeia.* With no apparent irony, then, Yang praised the "Redactors of the Canon of Yao, / Correctors of the *Odes* with Hymns."[99]

Because access to or ownership of each manuscript testified to a valued commitment – whether the manuscript came from a father, patron, ruler, or friend, or was acquired through a gift exchange or some other means – reading and writing strategies were based on the assumption that highly personal ties imbued all manuscripts. Those in power generally chose to restrict access to their most treasured manuscripts, lest these rare and valuable objects fall into hands that would use them to the discredit of the original owners. Even a prince of the Liu ruling house was denied access to the manuscripts in the imperial collection.[100] Xunzi, a writer whose works Yang knew well, once observed that silence is often the better part of valor,[101] since any piece or form of writing is liable to post-facto consultation, and writings placed in changed or changing contexts tend to acquire unintended meanings and associations. Yang remarked to an unnamed critic in one of his imaginary dialogues that a single ill-judged word could mean a fall from high office to bloody extinction for an entire clan.[102] At least twice

---

[98] FY 2/9.

[99] HS 87A.3552. The description of Yang's *Taixuan*, in HS 87B.3575, where "the three regions,... and 729 Judgments are divided into three *juan*" suggests that even this masterwork may have undergone reformatting.

[100] HS 80.3324.

[101] Xunzi 6.9; Knoblock, vol. 1, 225: "Speaking when it is appropriate to do is is practical wisdom; remaining silent when appropriate is also wisdom. Thus knowing when to remain silent is as important as knowing when to speak."

[102] HS 87B.3567. Han history is littered with the names of those proscribed, exiled, imprisoned, or even executed because of imprudent writings on delicate subjects under the

in Yang's career he was threatened with jail or worse because of what he had entrusted to writing. He had composed a letter of recommendation on behalf of a fellow countryman from Shu who later fell afoul of the law.[103] Worse, he had tutored a Liu clan member in the arts of "strange scripts," the rare or obsolete characters sometimes used in divinations about dynastic fortunes, in magical medicine, or in apocryphal writings.[104] As we have seen, after his aristocratic pupil was accused of high treason, Yang jumped out from the upper storey of the library where he worked, fearful that he would be implicated in the capital crime.[105]

Given the Han legal system, which charged the intimates of criminals with guilt by association, Yang's suicide attempt can hardly be dismissed as paranoia. But it is also true that Yang often groveled insufficiently before the powerful, risking charges of *lèse majesté* in many passages of his writings, as careful comparison of a *Fayan* passage with its parallel in the *Hanshu* shows.[106] And, in one *fu*, Yang Xiong had the temerity to implicitly compare his own emperor, Chengdi, to Jie and Zhou, the last tyrants of the Xia and Shang dynasties.[107]

One example from the *Fayan* shows Yang Xiong in his element, playing with words in artful ways that take off from the Classics yet drive his point home: a person's moral worth is easily assessed, he says, simply by seeing whether that person becomes the object of others' admiring gazes or a truly repulsive sight in their eyes. Odes 295 and 297, two temple hymns,

---

court's purview, such as Liu An, King of Huainan; Dong Zhongshu; and Jing Fang, to name but a few.

[103] See the Liu Xin/Yang Xiong letters, translated and assessed in Knechtges 1977.

[104] Cf. Emperor Xuan's order to Wang Bao and others 'to recite day and night strange writings and their own works" to help cure the heir apparent's illness (HS 34.2829).

[105] HS 87B.2584.

[106] FY 7/10 looks innocent enough at first glance, being a discussion of whether a person in service can "faithfully attend his ruler" by chess-playing. However, HS 64.2829 shows Emperor Xuan of Han justifying his love of the *fu* by a misemployed *Analects* allusion plus a comparison of chess and classical learning. No one would have missed Yang's attack on Xuandi.

[107] In the "Sweet Springs" *fu*, Yang talks of Chengdi's towers being "heir to the Jade Building and Jasper Palace," the palaces built by those two tyrants. See HS 87A.3528. Liu Xiang also criticized Chengdi harshly, according to HS 36.1956-57. Yang Xiong so seldom employed "indirect admonition" (*feng* 諷) that one wonders whether he was not thinking about another gloss for the same word, drawn from the *Zhouli*: "reading silently without the help of humming to the accompaniment of the *qin* or *se*." See commentary and main text of the *Zhouli*, "Chun guan" 春官 [e-Siku], 23/28a.

describe members of the governing elite "yearning" for Kings Wen and Wu of Zhou, paragons in their day and ever afterwards. With those odes in mind, Yang composed the following exchange, setting out the most basic qualities required of charismatic rulers:

> 或問：為政有幾？曰：思、斁。或問思、斁。曰：昔在周公，征于東方，四國是王；召伯述職，蔽芾甘棠，其思矣夫！齊桓欲徑陳，陳不果內，執轅濤塗，其斁矣夫！於戲！從政者審其思、斁而已矣。或問：何思？何斁？曰：老人老，孤人孤，病者養，死者葬，男子畝，婦人桑之謂思。若污人老，屈人孤，病者獨，死者逋，田畝荒，杼軸空之謂斁。

> Someone asked me whether there are any keys to good rule.
> Reply: "Yearning and repulsion."
> "What does *that* mean?"
> Reply: "It refers to that time long ago, when the Duke of Zhou launched a punitive attack in the east, and 'Him the Four States took as king'; also when the Lord of Shao faithfully carried out his duties, and he was said to be 'Lush and verdant, the sweet pear.' Those certainly had the effect of making others yearn for them, did they not? But when Duke Huan of Qi wanted his army to cross through Chen, and Chen refused, in point of fact, to let him enter, the duke detained Chen's envoy, Yuan Taotu. He certainly had the effect of making others feel repulsed, did he not? Ah! Those in power had better look to yearning and repulsion – that and nothing more!"
> Someone asked me what creates yearning or repulsion.
> Reply: "We speak of a ruler being the object of 'longing' if he treats the aged and the orphans as they should be treated, he tends the sick and buries the dead, puts the males to fieldwork and the women to silk production. But we label the person in power 'repulsive' if he mistreats the aged, humiliates orphans, neglects the sick, exposes the corpses of

the dead, or lets the fields become wasteland while the looms lie idle."[108]

By reference to classical models, Yang lays out in admirably succinct and clear terms his fundamental premises about the power of power to attract or repel, leaving no doubt about (a) the basic human capacity to evaluate people, things, and events correctly; (b) the inevitability that good judgments will be made by those whose classical learning puts them in a good position to judge; and (c) the consequences for human motivation that (a) and (b) must entail. To the written word Yang entrusts his final evaluations, since the Classics have so faithfully preserved the tenor of these examples drawn from history.

This chapter has sought to lay the groundwork for an argument that agrees in all the essentials with a recent formulation by Taniguchi Hiroshi 谷口洋 (1948-), the literary historian, though the argument seeks to go further than Taniguchi. Taniguchi has forcefully argued that Yang Xiong is the first fully self-conscious author in Chinese history.[109] As poets and thinkers

---

[108] FY 9/4. Yang's phrasing probably derives from the phrase *yi si* 繹思 twice in Mao 295 ("Lai") and *si wu yi* 思無斁 in Mao 297 ("Si"), an ode supposedly sung during the ceremony of the great enfeoffment in the temple. Ode 16 describes the Lord of Shao and the sweet-pear tree. As for the counter-example of good rule, in the year 656 BC, Duke Huan of Qi attacked Chu. On his way home, he wanted to take a route through Chen, but Yuan Taotu, the Chen counsellor, advised against letting him enter the state, whereupon the duke seized Yuan. See *Zuo* and *Gongyang* for Lord Xi, Year 4, whose stories show minor variations.

[109] Many have argued that this personae is first developed by Sima Qian (145?-86? BC), given his autobiographical "postface" in SJ 130, or, even further back in time, by Qu Yuan (fourth c. BC). But arguably, as we have seen, the development of Qu Yuan's persona in history owes a great deal to Sima Qian's lengthy biography of him, and the *Shiji* postface occupies but a small part of the two Simas' monumental project. Taniguchi Hiroshi 2010 would impress us with the thoroughness and perfection of Yang's persona as self-conscious author. I came across Taniguchi's recent essay (published Jan., 2010, but available in the library only in June) as I was putting the finishing touches on this manuscript. But because my view so closely corresponds to that of Taniguchi, I offer this summary of his far more extended argument here. I, like Taniguchi, think it crucial that Sima Qian's account says that he wrote the book "out of burning resentment" (發憤著書), in response to his own and his father's ill-treatment at the court of Wudi. Yang Xiong, by contrast, seldom refers directly to the Han court in the *Fayan*, except when he registers oblique criticisms of it through praise of those who were condemned by the various Han emperors. This is but one of the ways

during the Zhanguo period sought positions as clients of the powerful local lords in the Six Kingdoms, their compositions frequently alluded to what they perceived to be the all-important relationship of host and guest, ruler and client.[110] Once the empire's resources in men and materials became highly centralized under Emperors Jing and Wu (r. 157-87 BC), however, the single court in the Han capital of Chang'an superseded all others as the center of prestigious appointments and patronage. Nonetheless, poets such as Sima Xiangru, according to Taniguchi, continued to behave and to compose their *fu* as if they were still the "honored guests" of one or another local lord, proceeding along the old Zhanguo model. By contrast, Yang Xiong, a century later in Western Han, introduced several innovations in his writings. He (1) had his own prefaces to various writings imitate the most successful constructions of the "author" that he found in the *Shiji*, (2) arranged his works in chronological order, implying that he had grown wiser in the course of time's passing, and the ensuing alterations in his perceptions of things had, in turn, altered the intention, content, and style of his writing (a point he reiterated in the *Fayan*),[111] and (3) gave the impression that he was writing for a living, though he received a good salary from his rulers. Moreover, Yang rejected the primary formula used in the traditional display *fu*, which involved the pretense of a "guest's reprimands" delivered to the host and ruler for the latter's benefit. Instead Yang made himself, rather than the emperor, the central figure in his author's tale, playing virtual host to a gaggle of interlocutors in ways that allowed his mature writings to reveal his own experiences as author and classical master. (Even the *Fayan*, this author would add, seldom discusses the emperor or his proper role, aside from its final chapter of thirteen.)[112] Thus, Taniguchi concludes, did Yang manage to bring together in a seamless narrative, evidently *for the first time*, a compelling authorial voice, a corpus of memorable works, and a volley of statements detailing the author's hopes for the positive reception of his best writings, whether among contemporaries or posterity.

---

that Yang's writings nudge the Han emperors off center stage. Taniguchi notes that Liu Xin and Liu Xiang, Yang's contemporaries, may well have developed the same sort of authorial voice, but we have very few extant works by Liu Xin, and for Liu Xiang, only his official compilations.

110 One good source on the idealized patron-client (ruler-official) relationship is Pines 2002.

111 FY 2/1.

112 See Nylan (forthcoming-d).

Few authors in Chinese history have been as good as Yang in fashioning a distinctive persona which, despite a goodly dollop of eccentricity and gruffness, still exerts a powerful appeal upon discriminating readers who never knew him and might not share his particular viewpoints (though he can be very persuasive). Quite rightly, even those who disapproved of Yang's politics regarded his construction of the authorial voice as a model for all time – at least for more than a millennium after Yang's death.[113]

[113] Taniguchi cites Yang's "Dispelling Ridicule" (Jie chao) fu, included in *Wenxuan* 45.8b-20a. He notes also that Cui Yin 崔駰 early in Eastern Han regarded Yang Xiong as a perfect example of one who had "refined commitments" (*da zhi* 達志). During Southern Song, however, Zhu Xi and others of the True Way Learning persuasion tried to oust Yang Xiong from the Confucian temple (and so deny his role as exemplary classical master). For further information, see the Introductions to *The Canon of Supreme Mystery* (Nylan 1993) and to the forthcoming translation of the *Fayan* (2011); Wilson 1995: 55, 7781, 113, 158, 176.

III
Playing with Words

YANG'S PLAY WITH GRAPHS AND DIALOGUES

The seductive quality of words was hardly a new trope in Yang's time, even if it was being newly applied to the contents of old manuscripts. In texts from the classical era or in the Western Han *fu*, lists of enticing pleasures include fine rhetoric and elegant persuasions alongside sensuous music, beautiful women, fine palaces, swift horses, soft silks and warm wools, and the bounties of the banquet table. Artfulness (*qiao* 巧) was admired in every form, but the spoken arts were credited with moving hearts and minds as few other arts could do. Yang says of Qu Yuan, for example, that he "tried to outdo" the "pretty ladies in the harem" in "elegance and beauty," in "grace and charm," displaying his writing talent in the same way that they paraded their delightful artifices,[1] doubtless because Qu Yuan himself had couched his claims to political authority in terms of sensual beauty.[2] At least by the time of Sima Qian, a century before Yang, the case had been made that literary production could surpass biological reproduction when it came to delivering posthumous fame. Sima Qian's "Letter to Ren An" is the best known Han writing to plead that case, even if it is a post-Western Han literary impersonation or pastiche composed mainly of transmitted passages from the Senior Archivist's writings. The attribution of seductive qualities may have arisen because the character *xing* 興 denoted both literary inspiration and sexual arousal, with authors no less vulnerable than readers or listeners to a text's charms.[3] We should take Yang at his word when he

---

[1] HS 87A.3520; DRK 16.

[2] Qu Yuan (?), *Chuci* 1/1/25 couches his own political convictions and calumny by others in terms of sensual beauty and its detractors: "All you many [detractors] envy my 'moth' eyebrows/ Reporting of me that I use them to improve my lasciviousness" (眾女嫉余之蛾眉兮, 謠諑謂余以善淫).

[3] For inspiration and arousal, see Riegel 1997, which has shown that these issues appear as early as early Western Han commentaries on the Odes. The "Seven Stimuli" similarly alludes to the possibility of arousal in response to fine rhetoric, as well as a therapeutic result from that arousal. For "Qifa," see Mair 1988. When the protagonist

insists on his attachment to his craft and his vision, "Long have I taken it as my guiding precept that so long as I finish 'embroidering' my work, even death will be unimportant!"[4]

In this heady state of mind Yang Xiong sought in his *fu* and even more in his neoclassical works to formulate a new and highly distinctive aesthetic, a new way of looking at the realm of human perception and sensation in relation to conceptual thought.[5] In the pre-Han period, aesthetics was a discourse crediting the imperial person with an exquisite responsiveness rooted in extraordinary perceptiveness, supreme conviviality, and a profound appreciation for the physical orders; in this conceit, the emperor was forever "gilding the object whereupon he gazeth."[6] Yang adapted that aesthetic to his own vision of classical learning, allowing a comparable beauty and grace to distinctly non-imperial bodies with the requisite learning. So successfully did Yang co-opt the original discourse that by Eastern Han, emperors were wont to parade their own classical learning as a way of magnifying their own dignity and decorum. Yang, taking the medium to be part of the message, made sure that his most celebrated neoclassical writings demonstrated formal elegance and symmetry, balancing para-canonical moralizing prescriptions with novel plays on words in compelling ways. As each of the idioms employed by Yang has its special beauties and its rigors,[7] each of the processes through which these wordplays were achieved and imparted has its sensual satisfactions. Phrases replete with reduplicatives, verbal alliteration, and rhymes would have delighted the tongue and the ears. The eye would have been attracted by the dance of the black ink graphic patterns on the silk scroll or bamboo bundle, especially where there was visual alliteration. Even today the heart and mind thrill to the taut alignments and juxtapositions perceived in Yang's marvelously

---

prince hears that he will soon hear "essential words and marvelous doctrines of the world," his head clears, as if he had already heard the words," and he begins to perspire freely. This sense of exhilaration rouses his mind and body, aiding in his final "cure."

[4] Knechtges 1977: 318. Yang compares the importance of his project with those of Xiao He 蕭何 drafting the laws, and Zhang Tang 張湯 developing a calendar. See, e.g., HS 87A.3566; DRK 49.

[5] Here I think of Terry Eagleton, who writes of aesthetics as not limited to art, but to the whole region of human perception and sensation in contrast to the "more rarified domain of conceptual thought."

[6] For the characterization of the imperial person, see Huang 2010, chap. 2. For the quotation, see Shakespeare Sonnet 20, line 6, quoted in Vendler 1997: 27, substituting "he" for "it."

[7] Judith Farquhar 1994: 482, inspired this formulation.

inventive and carefully calculated writing, inducing the craving for classical learning that Yang celebrated.

Yang Xiong's preoccupation with capturing the spirit of past writings of true genius and translating it for his own era led him to faithfully replicate antique grammatical constructions, particle usage, and turns of phrase, mimicking the *Yijing* in the *Taixuan*, and the *Analects* in the *Fayan*. Being mindful that the best works need to balance ornament and substance, Yang paid equal heed to the propositional content of such works. By the time he arrived at the Han court in Chang'an, Yang had already begun harvesting the big ideas he deemed "worth borrowing" from the many works he had pored over. In Yang Xiong's mature work, the *Fayan*, these same powers of discrimination appear heightened, as when Yang applauds the ineffable wisdom of Zhuangzi's slogan "Lessen desires," even as he condemns Zhuangzi's subversion of ruler-subject relations.[8] As with authors, so too with cultural heroes: each the *Fayan* subjects to Yang's witty but probing analysis.[9] At times his style of inquiry into the past peers so deeply behind the signs and symbols that it nearly approaches the divinatory. (Shades of Yang's duties as an omen interpreter at court!) Yang Xiong's ideal reader would surely learn to read in others the main ways a person's commitments and predilections distinguished him from those who superficially resemble him, all such information being vital to the interpreter's fashioning of his own priorities.[10] Indeed, readers may never really come to know themselves, unless they can parse the signs they give out – thoughts, speeches, bearing, and deeds – in light of the signals that others, living or dead, pass on to them.[11] Yang's talk of "immersion" is no romantic or mystical call, but rather a dare to plunge into the unknown bourne where the Ancients swam, in the hope of gaining intuitions about the way they related their work to the world at large.

The long years Yang trained in archaic and modern styles of composition, and especially in the *fu* of the best Sichuan writers, would have given him an acute sense of cadences and aural patterns, and a predilection

---

[8] FY 4/26.

[9] For example, Yang indignantly demands to know the historical basis for the regent Huo Guang's high reputation, since Huo had failed to prevent his wife from interfering in affairs of state (FY 10/21).

[10] My work follows Paul Ricoeur in trying to shift the interpretive emphasis from the empathic investigation of hidden subjectivities toward the sense and reference of the work itself – in this, following Yang Xiong as well. See Ricoeur 1981: 58.

[11] Cf. Paul Ricoeur 1981: 65.

for repetitions and the copia of amplifications. The grand epideictic *fu* that became a Sichuan specialty was characterized by irregular alternation of rhymed and unrhymed passages that created lively cadences; by its exhaustive catalogues of rare animals, plants, flowers, and gems; and by its long alliterative, rhyming, and reduplicative passages.[12] With Yang Xiong, one epithet or image will never do if two or more are possible. Because this feature of Yang's writing carries over into the *Taixuan* and *Fayan*, something of these masterworks' style may be glimpsed in the following passage from the "Barricade Hunt" *fu*, which evokes the terror of the animals just now realizing the utter futility of resisting the coming slaughter:

> 亶觀夫剽禽之紲隃，犀兕之抵觸，
> 熊羆之挐攫，虎豹之凌遽，
> 徒角槍題注，蹙竦讋怖，魂亡魄....
>
> See the swift birds beat their wings in vain!
> Rhinos and buffaloes butt their heads without effect!
> Bears and sloths tug and pull at their ropes,
> Tigers and leopards tremble with fear,
> Only striking their horns and heads on the ground,
> They stand shaking and quivering.
> Their soul and animus is lost....[13]

As scholars have remarked, a sophisticated use of binomial *impressifs* marks Yang's writings throughout his *fu* and neoclassical works. These phrases impart an emotional flavor, although their precise meanings could not be pinned down even in Yang's day. In his magnificent *fu*, which set the standard for his and later eras, Yang Xiong had already worked to perfect the descriptions of sounds via onomatopoeia. "Strange characters" and odd rhymes are also a distinctive feature of his work, presumably thanks to local

---

[12] Mei Cheng [sometimes written "Sheng"] is probably one of the few writers of epideictic *fu* who did not come from Shu, but so many *fu* have been lost that we can only note the prevalence of Shu writers in the extant works. Knechtges points out that Mei Cheng was not from Shu, and he wrote the "Seven Stimuli" while at the court of Liang. As Sima Xiangru also travelled there, it is conceivable that the later writer was introduced to the epideictic style in Liang, rather than in his Sichuan home (private communication, August, 2010). Still, Chengdu was a city particularly famous as a polyglot entrepôt, where vivid sights and many tongues stimulated the senses.

[13] HS 87A.3542; DRK 64-65 (slightly mod.).

influence from Sichuan.[14] In his more mature work, the late "Justifications" and the *Fayan*, Yang neatly extracts intoxicating, almost incantatory expressions from their usual settings (descriptions of the natural world or of man-made grand spectacles) and affixes them to the legendary figures and historical eras that embodied ideal social roles. The obscure words appear to great effect in the generally plain-spoken *Fayan*, clustering as they do around rulers and dynasties in a way reminiscent of the sacrificial hymns.[15] At the same time Yang's riotous mixture of punning aural and visual word plays, propelled by his irrepressible delight in grouping ideas, images, and information by almost any conceivable method – be it by significs, entry headings, graphic symbols, or word lists – creates a delicious mélange of intricate conjunctions most pleasing to the eye, ear, and mind. "The various subgenres... may be compared to instruments of clay or gourds:/ All provide pleasure for the ear./ The zigzag and meander designs [of the graphs] are varied/ Both provide pleasure to the eyes."[16]

The *Fayan* provides more opportunity than the *fu* to display Yang's love of polysemy, and polysemy eminently suits the serious classical turn. For where words have more than one meaning, their appearance is apt to induce an initial state of confusion. This confusion proves useful if it makes readers aware that it is context and context alone that determines the values and valences that words assume in any piece of writing, binding author to reader in the construction and reconstruction of meaning. A typical example where a play on words takes on added significance is *Fayan* 11/11, whose assessment of Lü Buwei rests upon *zhi* 智 meaning both "clever" and "too clever by half." Still, the most striking feature of Yang Xiong's writing, in the late *fu* or the *Fayan*, is not the glittering volleys of erudition and wit, but rather the consistent interjection of the psychological dimension,[17] as witnessed in the "Barricade Hunt" passage above. The goal of that *fu* was to quicken the emperor's empathetic appreciation of the stark realities

---

[14] The Southern Song writer Dai Si 戴侗 notes that "strange characters" (*qizi*) are a feature in the work of both Sima Xiangru and Yang Xiong (司馬子長揚子雲皆好奇字. 故其辭賦太玄法言多奇字....). See his *Liu shu gu* 六書故 6.14b [E-Siku].

[15] Wu Fusheng 2007: 50, speaking of the Sweet Springs rhapsody.

[16] Preface to the *Wenxuan*, Knechtges trans., vol. 1, 87.

[17] Before 11 BC, Yang used figures with farcical names to deliver his moral messages, as Sima Xiangru had done before him. In the "Barricade Hunt *fu*," Yang for the first time constructs a dialogue between Someone (*huo* 或) and his unnamed critic (*lunzhe* 論者). Thereafter, Yang still delivers some criticisms through clearly fictional characters, for example Plume Grove and Ink-Grove, in the "Changyang *fu*.

experienced by the lesser creatures under his care while the ruler made his progress through the realm. Yang's *fu*, read reflectively, might lead the emperor to revisit and reframe his actions, and chapter 13 of the *Fayan* constructs an elaborate argument promising his emperor long fame and the ancestor's blessings, if he graciously condescends to supply the people's needs.[18] Though Yang eventually gave up expecting the desired response from his ruler, he never abandoned the idea that his empathetic writings might quicken the hearts and minds of future readers.

The *fu* genre in which Yang Xiong excelled was a performative genre that aimed to juggle formal rhetoric and entertainment with moral instruction. Often the most convenient way to achieve these disparate aims simultaneously was to populate the *fu* with multiple observers and commentators upon the splendid spectacles that pass before the reader's eyes. Dialogues heightened the dramatic potential of the most sober moral discussions, and the dialogue form had been employed for centuries before Yang, most notably in the *Zhuangzi* and *Xunzi* philosophical texts, in the *fu* of Sima Xiangru, and in Sima Qian's history of the known world.[19] In none of these earlier works, however, were the dialogues so sustained yet succinct, so wide-ranging yet so hard-hitting. None of the earlier works were so adamant that "making contact" (*jiao* 交) was the most fundamental business of human beings, nor so insistent about their role as communication qua conversation with the Ancients.[20] In none had the voice of the author's persona so dominated the highly theatrical exchanges.[21] Yang-the-speaker invariably enjoys the last word in the verbal pirouettes of the *Fayan*. Yet his innovative decision not to foreground his name and position or that of his interlocutors[22] made it hard to separate Yang-the-speaker or Yang-the-author

---

18 See Nylan (forthcoming-c).

19 Especially for Sima Xiangru, the "Da ke nan" sometimes treated as a verbatim account of an actual debate between Dongfang Shuo and a group of court academicians. For more information, see Gong Kechang 1997: 149-50; and Declerq 1998: 20-59. Kern 2003: 405, argues that the "Da ke nan" was "probably labeled as 'staged debates' or 'responses to questions' only in Six Dynasties times," i.e., long after Yang Xiong.

20 Of course, the *Fayan* makes it impossible for readers to forget that it is modeled on the *Analects*. Robert Ashmore 2010: 237, writing of Tao Qian, says, "showing mastery and claiming authority are not separate acts from the act of expressing oneself; rather all are simply different aspects of one [performative] act."

21 For example, in the *Xunzi* dialogue recorded in *juan* 15 ("Yi bing" 議兵), Xunzi's voice alternates with those of other prominent figures.

22 The *Mencius*, presumably compiled by disciples (before massive editing by the commentator Zhao Qi 趙岐 in late Eastern Han), who present him in conversation with

from the voices of the powerful masters of the past. Because for the most part the *Fayan* master and interlocutors remain faceless and nameless (though they are sometimes given stage directions), readers enjoy the freedom to try on various arguments without judging the argument by the reputation of its proponent, the better to learn how to live inside their own skins.[23] (Hence the imperative to script the dialogues as believably as possible.) Yang's dialogues would have us first witness and empathize with a wide range of attractive-seeming human foibles and logics, before exposing their inherent flaws. If successful persuasions, by definition, require words "both helpful and pleasing to life,"[24] the reader's careful deliberation on and final acceptance of the persuasion's propositional content must be coupled with a heightened consciousness of a pleasurable release from the consequences of bad choices. Hence the attempt in Yang Xiong's writing to lead readers inexorably back, by routes direct or circuitous, to the single question, What sort of pleasure-taking is more lasting and serene, because it would obviate "being of two minds" about one's absolute commitments?[25]

The earliest canonical texts in China, such as the *Odes*, envisioned the pleasures of textual production and reproduction arising chiefly "not from the page, but from the performance."[26] In classical learning, the chief dramatic site for displays of virtuosity pleasing to both the performer and his audience gradually shifted from the court to the page, but certainly not because of Yang Xiong's ineptitude as an orator.[27] Still, one impetus for the

---

local rulers from Qi and Teng and elsewhere. The *Xunzi*, by contrast, shows Xunzi in conversation with high-ranking officials.

[23] Yang himself was mindful of the chameleon aspect. See FY 5/5. The stage directions, I would argue, give the only indication that some inward psychic reevaluation will be needed, if one is to learn to delight in the Way and turn away from striving after conventional success. Mainly, the dialogues show an evolution of dramatic interaction rather than any inward development.

[24] Horace, *Arts Poetica* 139.

[25] FY 9/18 warns the ruler – and by extension, the exemplary person – not to be of "two minds." This fear of being torn by contrary impulses is discussed in many Zhanguo and Han texts.

[26] Beecroft unpublished ms., p. 368. (Obviously, I do not ignore here the fact that some odes articulate the pleasure, satisfaction, or necessity of composition.) Conventional literary historians often ascribe the origins of the use of the dialogue in the *fu* to Qu Yuan's poems, where the fisherman in a short dialogue, partly rhymed, argues with Qu's literary persona. However, this poem is surely not by Qu Yuan.

[27] As mentioned earlier, I suspect that Yang's "stutter," like that of Han Fei, may have derived from his late arrival, when he was in his forties, at the Han capital, from an area whose language sounded quite different.

shift, doubtless among many, was Yang's decision to insert spectacles and performances into the middle of his late and best compositions.[28] Yang as praise-and-blame historian does not hesitate to mete out swift judgments on historical exemplars good and bad, but Yang rightly senses that moral fervor alone is seldom persuasive. Thus the rapid-fire exchanges imbedded in the *Fayan* give Yang ample opportunity to set forth the most gullible and muddle-headed of human beliefs, which he can then demolish via didactic messages delivered in skilled rhetoric.[29] The sly *Fayan* dialogues, in adapting the irregular line length and alternations of rhymed and unrhymed passages that are typical of the *fu*, more closely mimic the playful banter of today's "backtalk" comedy routines than the solemn proclamations of a *Documents* or an *Odes* classic.[30] Large swaths of the *Fayan* are composed of snappy statements and the witty repartee, like the following lines taken from the opening chapter, which show Yang deep in conversation with the sages, not just contemporary interlocutors and future readers:

> 或問進。曰.水。或曰為其不舍晝夜與？曰有是哉。滿而後漸者，其水乎？
> Someone asked me, "But what about advancement?"
> Reply: "It's water."
> "Because it never stops, day or night?"
> Reply: "You've got it. After filling up, gradually and
> inexorably it spills over.[31] Such is the nature of water! ..."[32]
> (1/14)

---

[28] Many of the alliterative descriptions (visual as well as aural) in Yang's *Fayan* paint vivid pictures of the dynasties, while the dialogues "perform" virtue and moral ineptitude. Yang was said to stutter, but the same thing was said of Sima Xiangru, yet the differences between the poems of Sima Xiangru (Yang's ostensible model) and Yang's own writing (full of visual as well as aural alliteration) are obvious. Yang never wrote for Everyman or Woman, but for a highly select readership; anything else would have been unthinkable in manuscript culture. Cf. Pierre Hadot's remark on ancient philosophy in classical Greece, in Hadot 2009: 53.

[29] That Yang uses textual incongruities "as a means to convey the poet's didactic message" has been noted already by Wu Fusheng 2007: 53.

[30] This may strike some readers familiar with the *Fayan* as an outrageous claim, but that is because it is easy to overlook the many *Fayan* passages that do not take the form of dialogue, but which occupy long parts of text in some, but not all chapters. It is also easy to overlook the lengthy rhymed passages, for example, that concluding chapter 13.

[31] See *Xunzi* 103/28/26-29, for water as a metaphor for the Way and the virtues. Cf. *Analects* 9/17, in which Kongzi uses this phrasing to speak of the river's flow as

> 吾未見斧藻其德若斧藻其楶者也。
> I have never seen anyone whose love for carving out and embellishing his moral power matched the love he brought to having ornate patterns carved on the lintel struts of his home [i.e., for getting ahead in his career].[33] (1/15)

In *Fayan* 1/14, Yang's interlocutor asks himself about "advance," meaning "career advancement" through the ranks of the Han bureaucracy. Yang's retort uses "advance" in quite another sense: "improving in cultivation." For this improvement that should be the single goal pursued by every "noble man" worthy of the title and status, Yang employs a water metaphor well-known from writings ascribed to Kongzi, Mencius, and Xunzi, giving it a twist: whereas his predecessors in the classicist Ru tradition had referred in this metaphor either to a person's inexorable journey through life and his consequent inability to retain opportunities once they are gone, or to the ceaseless round of change in the cosmos, Yang directs attention to two sorts of activity that he insists are under each person's control, the acquisition of cultural attainments and more refined social relations. Again, In *Fayan* 1/15, Yang exploits a famous line, this time from the *Analects*, noting how few men and women crave virtue with the same intensity that they crave sex. Deftly, Yang implies that the people of his own day are even worse than those of Kongzi's time, being craven in their ambitions, intent upon making outward shows, and essentially devoid of the sort of passions that can be channeled into yet another kind of love, that for classical learning.

Like Shakespeare, Yang employs low comedy to soften the reader up before bringing on the high drama: the resolution of the practical dilemmas that confront those with power and learning. If comedy and tragedy in theater did indeed evolve from the dialogue form in Greece, the staginess of Yang Xiong's vivid performances in writing provided drama's functional

---

metaphor for life's journey, and *Mencius* 4B/18 (源泉混混，不舍晝夜，盈科而後進....). What is interesting is that Kongzi, Mencius, and Yang Xiong are using the same metaphor for different ends. For this whole paragraph, it is useful to compare *Yijing*, Hexagram 53 (Gradual Progress); and its counterpart, *Taixuann* Tetragram 14; each links advancement to gradual progress. Li Gui comments, "Water fills the pit and then proceeds to spill out; men study broadly and later serve." Certainly "advance" calls to mind "career advancement."

32 In other words, a person should not act until he or she has achieved a measure of cultivation.

33 Cf. *Analects* 9/18, where the contrast is between love of sex and love of power and wealth. The carved lintels signify high office and conventional success.

equivalent in China, all the more so, because Yang occasionally interrupts the dialogues to directly address the reader in the first-person, via short passages, usually rhymed, that encapsulate a slice of proverbial wisdom.[34]

Yang Xiong throughout the *Fayan* employs a full battery of rhetorical strategies besides the dramatic (where the speaker indirectly quotes an antagonist). Some exchanges emphasize time's passing; others display sharply conflicting moods or volatility (as with the "yearning or repulsion" passage cited above). Still others hinge on knowledge of the semantic range and etymologies associated with theological, legal, alchemical, medicinal, political, and aesthetic vocabulary, or turn philosophical, adapting analogies sacred to the literary tradition. To different effects, Yang employs different rhetorical structures, including successive and equal statements, hierarchical statements aiming to establish priorities, contrastive or even paradoxical statements, successively "louder" or "softer" claims, changes of rhetorical address from first to second or third-person, contrasts between rhymed and unrhymed passages, the use of puns, and the occasional use of misunderstandings.[35] As another academic has remarked of another master stylist, "The more conventional the topic, the greater the author's inclination to look to word-games" to prove his mettle and put him on his mettle.[36] The same can said for Yang Xiong, as the same ingenuity he displayed in writing *fu* often comes most spectacularly into play when he aims to convince readers of the simplest propositions. To take one instance, Yang argues that while each type of learning may have its own particular method and historical models, only classical learning qualifies a person for the title of "true greatness." Into two lines of text, Yang packs no fewer than seven dense allusions:

---

[34] These pronouncements/proverbs can be divided into two types: the positive pronouncements may well be well-known proverbs, in which case, we should add the implicit, "People say that..." It seems less likely that the negative pronouncements are anything but Yang's own inventions, and most seem to relate to contemporary debates at court, as I show in an essay (forthcoming-c) on the last chapter of the *Fayan*, where I discuss rhymed vs. unrhymed passages at some length. Cf. Vendler 1997: passim, on the problematizing aspect of the couplet in Shakespeare's sonnets. Andrew Colvin 2001: 2, 10, thinks that this irregular alternation between dialogue and first- and third-person pronouncements makes for seeming incoherence.

[35] Illustrations of these points, and more, can be gleaned from my forthcoming translation of the *Fayan* (University of Washington Press), also from the new translation of the *Fayan* into French by Béatrice L'Haridon (2010).

[36] Cf. Vendler 1977: 77.

> 孔子習周公者也，顏淵習孔子者也。羿、逢蒙分其弓，良舍其策，般投其斧而習諸，孰曰非也？
>
> Confucius inculcated in himself the qualities of the Duke of Zhou, and Yan Yuan, those of Confucius. If Archer Yi and Peng Meng had snapped their bows in two, if Wang Lang had thrown away his horse whip, or if Gongshu Ban had thrown away his ax – so as to practice the Way of a Duke of Zhou, a Kongzi, or a Yan Yuan – who would say that they were wrong?[37]

Yang Xiong also supplies textbook examples of changing feelings and altered understanding regarding a single topic. One brief example, about the relative folly of casting alchemical gold versus cultivating one's physical person, is typical:

> 或問：世言鑄金，金可鑄與？曰：吾聞覿君子者，問鑄人，不問鑄金。或曰：人可鑄與？曰：孔子鑄顏淵矣。或人踧爾曰：旨哉！問鑄金，得鑄人。
>
> Someone asked me, "In today's world, people are always talking about casting alchemical gold. Can gold really be produced in this way?"
> Reply: "From what I have heard, those who see a noble man ask about casting men, not about casting gold."
> He then asked me, "Can men really be cast and moulded like metal?"
> Reply: "Surely Confucius in a sense cast Yan Yuan."
> Startled, the interlocutor responded: "Well done! I ask about making gold and I get an answer about transmuting men."[38]

---

[37] FY 1/7. Yan Yuan is perhaps better known as Yan Hui 顏回. Hou Yi 后羿 and Peng Meng were the most famous archers of all time; Wang Lang was the best charioteer; and Gongshu Ban (sometimes written Lu Ban 班), a rough contemporary of Mozi, according to tradition, was the epitome of the master-craftsman, for he supposedly was able to build a "cloud ladder." See, e.g., HNZ 11.369-70. Meng Pen is the classic strongman. Note that the idea of "service" (*yi* 役) and "arts" (*yi* 藝 or *shu* 術) were closely related. See LSCQ 21/5.2 ("Ai lei" 愛類); Knoblock, pp. 560-561, 725; cf. HNZ 9. 313.

[38] FY 1/8.

Yang's two stated reasons for composing the *Fayan* are relevant here: first, that the various philosophical masters had each used "what they knew" to subvert the true Way, and second, that the world was "drowning in hearsay" (*ni yu suo wen* 溺於所聞) and received traditions,[39] with the result that even some of the best-intentioned men no longer knew what was false.[40] To dislodge ill-conceived ideas from this sort of person would require far more than merely pointing out the follies and short-sightedness of immoral conduct. What is particularly cunning about Yang's *Fayan*, then, is its careful interplay between the constructed dialogues – often heated and always engaged – and other sections of the text in archaic style featuring the latter-day Master's magisterial judgments with an air of moral inevitability.[41] Careful readers who would trace the unfolding logic outlined in these direct addresses, proverbs, and top-down pronouncements in the *Fayan* could easily reconstruct what Yang would have them see as first premises: mostly, the indispensability of classical learning, but by-the-by touching upon key features of Han court policy toward governance of the masses.

Yang Xiong begins with the notion that true learning consists simply of determining what is right in a given situation. Thus classical learning is mainly to be used in practical situations, in deed or in speech; teaching it to others is not its primary purpose, and far worse is using it merely to procure a career.[42] Careful comparison shows the superiority of the Classics over other writings, since only the Classics teach, in language that is as simple as is humanly possible, what is most important and what is useless to the conduct of life. The excellence of the Classics is likely to be especially appreciated during times of oppressive and tyrannical rule, insofar as they offer information, insights, and intuitions into better ages.[43]

---

39 For both "writings" and "speeches" by convention are "heard." For further information, see Nylan 2001; Geaney 2010.

40 HS 87B.3580.

41 These pronouncements occupy up to 58% of the text in some of the *Fayan* chapters, but as little as zero in others. Cf. Henry 1999. I am indebted to Hsu Fu-kuan 1975: vol. 2, 502, for his insistence that Yang Xiong borrows as much from the *Chunqiu* as from the *Analects*. These statistics are rough, but in chap. 1, out of twenty-four units of text, 58% contain these pronouncements, whereas in chap. 10, of thirty units, none takes the form of these pronouncements. In the other eleven chapters, roughly 31% of the text consists of these pronouncements.

42 FY 1/1.

43 See, e.g., FY 5/9.

A sustained focus on cultivation nearly insures its attainment.[44] As human nature is a mixture of good and bad, it is necessary to refine it of the dross, creating a second nature that is more "whole and intact," being fully humane.[45] And since the cultivation of human nature is the only aspect of one's human existence over which one may reasonably expect to exert substantial control,[46] achieving cultivation enhances life far more surely than vain attempts to calculate luck or timing.[47] A highly charismatic nobility of spirit requires a person to apply his whole heart and mind to the Way of the sages, for that Way constructively expands a person's imaginative experiences and encounters.[48] This nobility is the only protection a person can build against enslavement to his desires or to others' inappropriate demands.[49]

Even Yang Xiong surmised that not all the lessons that he hoped to inculcate were amenable to explication through conveniently staged dialogues. After all, his imagined mentor and peer, Kongzi, had apparently had to resort not only to the speeches transcribed in the *Analects*, but also to the *Annals*, a historical *narrative* supposedly designed to illustrate moral– or amoral – principles embodied in action and speech. By definition, the good teacher must, by justly meting out historical praise and blame, induce greater understanding in his pupils, as tradition claimed that Kongzi had done with the *Annals*. Given the frequency with which Yang pronounces on historical figures, court debates, and other events, especially in the last four chapters of the *Fayan*, Yang Xiong evidently saw himself as a professional historian who could compose a narrative about developments over time that would be in greater conformity with the values underlying the *Annals* than Sima Qian's 司馬遷 quirky *Shiji* 史記.[50] Noteworthy is Yang's propensity to commend historical exemplars who were condemned by the courts of their time, underscoring his barbed critique of the misuse of power.[51] His most loving

---

44 See, e.g., FY 5/12, 5/14, 5/17.

45 FY 4/3.

46 Following *Mencius*, Yang Xiong says that some who strive to perfect their characters may fail, but without striving, refining the self is impossible.

47 FY 6/13.

48 FY 7/2-3.

49 FY 7/4.

50 HS 87B.3580. Cf. FY 12/9. However, Yang admired Sima Qian; see FY 10/30. Chapter 4 of this monograph focuses on Yang's historical writing.

51 Those condemned by the Han court include Su Wu 蘇武 (who narrowly escaped being the victim of a political intrigue in 80 BC), Xiahou Sheng 夏侯勝 (accused of a capital

treatments he reserves for Kongzi and Yan Hui in distant times, as well as for his own Sichuan teachers and his son, a prodigy who died early. In so doing, Yang himself modeled the properly reverent behavior toward those who went before, and the proper benevolence towards the weak. In unambiguous language Yang laid out his views of the Han policies relating to land taxes, government monopolies, and frontier expansion.[52] Equally importantly, Yang condemned various philosophical masters (e.g., Mozi, Zhuangzi, Shen Buhai, Han Fei, and Liu An), men of derring-do (e.g., the assassin-retainer Jing Ke),[53] some rulers (the First Emperor of Qin, Shihuangdi 始皇帝, but also Han Wendi 文帝, Wudi 武帝, and Xuandi 宣帝), and the majority of court advisers, whom Yang casts, despite their claims to classical learning, as mere technicians parlaying factual information and immediate remedies.[54] The forthright way that Yang, the master of ambiguous phrasing, delivered major pronouncements is amazing, especially since most Han writers employed the most tortuous prose to lend their works plausible deniability at court.[55]

Why combine dialogues where Yang appears as master with anonymous assertions that beg to be accepted as proverbs or premises? Because Yang Xiong knew that readers might willingly accept the highly general statements asserted through direct addresses, and yet balk at applying the implications of those statements to the concrete situations and human dilemmas of daily life. The propositional content of the *Fayan* is not hard to grasp, yet Yang's injunctions are far from easy to carry out in daily life, requiring, as they do, an absolute commitment to a particular view of classical learning as it is embodied in social institutions and groupings.[56] Putting

---

crime but saved by a general amnesty from execution), the diviner Jing Fang 京房 (executed), Jia Juanzhi 賈捐之 (executed in public).

52 See FY chap. 13, esp. 13/21-22; 13/25-27, 29.

53 FY 11/4, 11/6.

54 Elsewhere I have argued that Yang and his contemporaries were instrumental in blackening the reputation of the First Emperor in ways unknown before them. See Nylan, "A Revisionist History of Han Ideas of Qin" (forthcoming-d). Of course, Yang implies that most Academicians are dunces, charlatans, or opportunists – a view he seems to have shared with Liu Xiang and Liu Xin.

55 See Hsu Fu-kuan 1975, vol. 2, 503. Hsu credits Yang with being the first real historian in China, as he swept away all the notions of cycles that Mencius, Zou Yan, and Sima Qian had employed, insisting on the importance of human agency (though not to the exclusion of other factors); cf. Taniguchi Hiroshi 2010.

56 As FY 3/9 succinctly puts it, "One who admires the great but does not emulate greatness will be anything but great!"

together the two types of rhetoric, the dialogues and the lofty pronouncements, promotes several of Yang's aims: (1) it puts the focus on Yang Xiong as supreme master, a position he only on rare occasions relinquishes in favor of Confucius, Yan Hui, or Yan Junping, Yang's own teacher in Sichuan, whose eminence naturally contributed to Yang's own stature; (2) it sets out in proper sequence the few premises for discussion that Yang, the master rhetorician, thinks it wise to accommodate; (3) it allows Yang to lead the reader at a pace that he, Yang, has determined until the reader sees that the interlocutor's position is faintly ridiculous, counterproductive, ill-informed or worse; (4) it meanwhile creates a sufficient distance between the fictional interlocutor and the reader, allowing the reader to believe that he in conversation would agree with the position championed by Yang, the master, rather than by the idiots posing the questions; and (5) it lets Yang parlay the most conventional images, drawn mostly from the Classics, while voicing the most unsettling assertions about the unreliability of conventional wisdom.

With respect to point (4), Yang's adulation of Yan Hui, which is quite unprecedented in earlier Han writings,[57] is rhetorically savvy, in that Yan functions as placeholder with whom well-intentioned learners can identify. Yan Hui shows that a sympathetic and reverent emulation of the truly great (Kongzi) produces a genuinely humane person.[58] By design, Yang's dialogues provide models for performative speech, while teaching us how to listen and observe and read, because understanding waits upon such activities. At the same time, Yang Xiong's late projects, just as much as his early epideictic *fu*, were invented to amuse others and to exhibit his own boundless capacity for creating works of spectacular artistry and versatility, capable of delighting readers by their proportion, musicality, and lexical profusion.[59]

Yang specifically devotes not a few entries in the *Fayan* to the problems of transmitting important writings over long periods of time: the explicit structures that he employed in the *Taixuan* and the *Fayan* are admirably suited to minimize unwitting errors, deliberate tampering, and inadvertent losses. That Yang would have labored mightily to reduce the likelihood of editorial changes initially surprises, since he lived in a manuscript culture in which the modern investment in the idea of a single

---

[57] See the remarks of Hsu Fu-kuan 1975: 504, corroborated in Matsukawa Kenji 1994: 27-47.

[58] For this emphasis, see Matsukawa 1994: 36-37.

[59] I would argue for musicality in Yang's *Fayan* and *Taixuan*, given the numerous rhymed passages, but not, obviously, in the *Fangyan*. Lexical profusion marks all of Yang's writings.

authoritative version of a text, even a Classic, was well-nigh unthinkable, given the vagaries of oral and written transmission. Evidently Yang's collating work in the imperial libraries, where he eventually joined Liu Xiang in Chengdi's mammoth editing project, had impressed upon him the great quantities of writing discarded, emended, or miscopied over time.[60] Hence Yang's decided preference for rhymes, punch lines, short sections, visual clues and emblems, strict attention to verbal forms and grammatical structures, and prefaces that served as signing statements, as all such measures could forestall, if not preclude certain forms of misunderstanding and interpolation.[61] Perhaps this feature of Yang Xiong's writing would astonish us most, were it not, upon reflection, the clearest illustration of how strongly Yang felt that he would live on in the words that he hoped would be transmitted to later generations.

YANG'S PLEASURE THEORY AS IT RELATES TO CLASSICAL LEARNING

For the thinkers of the classical world, desire, sensuality, and the daily struggle with competing desires is an essential part of what it means to be human. Aristotle's analysis of human behavior is predicated on the premise that "by nature all human beings desire to know,"[62] and halfway round the world, a few hundred years later, Yang Xiong's *Fayan* put forward a variant of the same proposition: that people take profound pleasure in knowing that they know something well, and they find that pleasure magnified when authorities or events corroborate their sense of things. Profound pleasure for Yang seems, then, to be a second-order pleasure: a self-conscious reflection on the joys of overcoming one's personal limitations via imaginative encounters with the antique great who are known mainly through books. This phase of thinking about the past in China promises that the distant past will remain intelligible, if careful resort is made to the only suitable tools at hand, the transmitted texts of the classical masters whose authority has stood the test of time.[63]

---

60 The project began in 26 BC, roughly five years before Yang Xiong travelled to the Han court from his native Shu (modern Sichuan), by Knechtges' reckoning.

61 See Yan Shigu's commentary to HS 87B.2580, n. 5.

62 Aristototle, *Metaphysics* 980a-b.

63 E.g., FY 7/6: "And yet that man [Kongzi] still seems to live."

More than once in his *Fayan*, Yang Xiong follows the "Zhongyong" and other texts in applauding the archer whose practice sessions find him gaining an increasing sense of his own prowess.[64] So far as I know, however, no precedent exists for the equation registered in Yang's *Fayan* between a living master and his writings, which collapses text into author, though authors like Sima Qian had claimed to discern a living master in the texts ascribed to them.[65]

> 或曰：惡睹乎聖而折諸？曰在則人，亡則書，其統一也。
>
> Someone asks, "But how is one to spot a sage, so as to evaluate them?"
> Reply: "If he be alive, one takes the person as model, but if he be dead, one consults his writings. The principle is one and the same."[66]

In fact, Yang Xiong's equation of text and author runs directly counter to nearly all earlier traditions found in the Classics and the pre-Qin masterworks. No one before Yang accorded writing this sort of living power. Canonical statements recorded before Yang's time tended to stress the great *inadequacy* of language, whether speech or writing, to fully capture reality; most cast writing as one step further removed than speech from the ideas and intentions that led an author to communicate. Hence the "Great Commentary" passage ascribed to Kongzi that "writing does not fully convey speech, nor speech fully convey the ideas [of the sages]."[67] This sense of the gap between speaking and doing similarly informs the *Zhuangzi* episode in which Wheelwright Bian laments his inability to transmit his craft to his own

---

64 E.g., FY 3/1; 6/15. The received text of the "Zhongyong" essay also likens the process of learning and cultivation to the archer's practice sessions. The same metaphor found in the "Zhongyong" figures largely in Aristotle's *Nichomachean Ethics*, 1049a24-26 – and for the same reason: to show that it is a pleasure to knowingly hit the target (recognize something that is true).

65 SJ 47:1947: "When I read the books of Kongzi, I imagine what type of man he was" (余讀孔氏書，想見其為人). The distinction I see to make here is between Yang and many earlier Confucian masters (Xunzi being a prime example), who privileged access to masters far above access to their books.

66 FY 2/21.

67 However, a late tradition probably known to Yang Xiong had Kongzi saying, "The wording conveys [the authorial intent] –that and nothing more." See *Zuozhuan*, Lord Xiang 25. Even this emphasizes the inability of wording to express all that is in existence.

son through speech or writing; the *Laozi* slogan that "the Way that can be spoken is not the true Way"; and the *Han Feizi* anecdote that avers, "knowing and knowledge cannot be stored in writing."[68] All the complaints about writing testify to an acute awareness of the inevitable slippage between the lively pleasures gained from knowing and then embodying a technique, an art, or a way, and the lifelessness inherent in the notation of those experiential pleasures in didactic texts for novices.[69]

Yang Xiong's pairing of reading and pleasure represents a notable departure from these earlier accounts. Yang readily concedes pleasure's immediate impact in the presence of an object of desire (e.g., wine, women, rhetoric, or touch) or in the powerful sense of relief experienced as a release from deprivation (the "filling up" of a void).[70] He also sees pleasure as an activity (doing whatever conduces to pleasure) or an event (the pleasurable sensation itself). Yet Yang is far more preoccupied with the pleasurable recognition that comes to the person whose enlarged capacities allow him to derive and value a true narrative about the world and his place therein. And enlargement of one's capacities, Yang believes, comes only after years invested in disinterested reading in classical texts. Yang Xiong cares not a jot whether this pleasure is recognized after the event or before it, in *memory* or in *expectation*. But he deems pleasure in recognition of the truth to be the supreme pleasure for three main reasons: first, it results from the learner's conscious exercise of that set of capacities which is most characteristic of human beings, as opposed to lesser creatures; secondly, the sense of expanded capacities becomes so ingrained in truly great people that others can never disturb or diminish it; and thirdly, recognition of what is beautiful and fine (*mei* 美) also entails recognition of the "substantially true and real" (*chongshi* 充實),[71] diminishing the number and intensity of conflicts between

---

[68] For the *Laozi*, see chap. 1, the opening line. *Han Fei* 21/44/18-21, the entry with Xu Feng 徐馮. Even as late as Hong Mai, one can see a bit of this attitude toward writing. See Inglis 2006: 19, where Hong writes, "As for the writing of books, this comes from the basest of motives, yet I cannot release myself from this folly" (*Sangzhi ding*, 34th installment, preface). Elsewhere, Hong Mai says that he does not claim to write the sort of book that "Yang Ziyun would have read" or "the sages would have said." See p. 51, citing *Ding zhi*; and Campany 1996: 138, linking Yang's words with the *zhiguai* tradition.

[69] This acute awareness was known to Socrates as well.

[70] Cf. Konstan 2006: 4, who notes that in classical Greece an emotion is frequently deemed a "reaction to an impinging event or circumstance," and so somehow dependent upon the outside stimulus to which it responds.

[71] *Mencius* 7B/25: 充實之謂美.

the desiring person and the world. As Yang writes, "For the person who recognizes the Way, knowing things in advance [of the time when to use that knowledge] functions like the faculty of sight, with whose aid even the faintest, most minute, or most indistinct thing becomes absolutely clear."[72]

Yang further insisted that one can derive no real sense of accomplishment absent an external measure by which to gauge progress while learning. Many thinkers before Yang Xiong had sought to devise a convincing calculus weighing short-term versus long-term gratifications to be had from the experiences of self-fashioning, of sharing and friendship, of hearing music, of seeing clearly, and so on, with an emphasis on pleasurable objects or pleasurable sensations. By contrast, Yang argued that the most reliable source of pleasure lies in the sense of satisfaction that comes when *one knows that one knows* the best method to weigh the relative merits of different courses of action. It goes without saying that wiser life choices can be made by reference to external measures, but more importantly to Yang, the chosen course of action is imbued with greater meaning when it knowingly participates in larger patterns of significance. Desires for the serious satisfactions of the reflective life then lead dedicated learners to seek out the masters and models that inculcate improved habits through a variety of methods, including a profound love of play that escaped condemnation as gross careerism.[73] Proper tutelage, brought to bear upon real experience, can bring real expertise and its attendant satisfactions to the former novices.

The dialogue format could preclude lifelessness in a text. Besides, contact with the Ancients through books was just as likely to prove satisfying as tutelage with living masters, given that (a) the most famous living teachers in Han allowed their so-called disciples minimal personal contact, in utter departure from the Confucian teacher-student model; and (b) great books like the *Analects* could impart some sense of truly great men like Kongzi.[74]

---

[72] FY 9/1.

[73] Jia Yi was one of many Han masters (Yang included) to say that developing a refined and selective taste depends upon prior training. He ascribes to Kongzi the saying that "Practice makes it seem perfectly natural." See Jia's biography in the HS. *Fengsu tongyi* 11.22/162/2-3, defines the Ru by this love of playing with old traditions (written and not), and contrasts this propensity to play with the words of the sages and worthies with the career ambitions of the "vulgar classicist."

[74] Dong Zhongshu 董仲叔 (c. 179-c. 104 BC), for example, in the mid-second century was said to have "taught" his students by chanting texts to his chief pupils, who then transmitted those texts to the relative beginners. Minimal contact was made, in other words, with many who were registered as his "students." That the same was true centuries later is suggested by the famous story of Ma Rong 馬融 (79-166), who supposedly never met with

Even limited acquaintance with truly great men could inspire the inexperienced and inept to undertake the arduous course of study that makes greatness possible. Yang Xiong, writing this way, offered a vision of propositional pleasure-taking that seems at once more detached (in its steady focus on books as well as on larger-than-life personalities) and more demanding (in requiring the radical expansion of memory and experience via reading in classical-era texts). Yang's stated goal was to persuade readers to relish the art of measuring the inherent value of people, things, and events; to engage in acts of apprehending and narrating the true features of the social world, and to find in such comprehension a source of profound pleasure. In Yang's telling, a distinctly lesser pleasure could be had from the purely instrumental view that a truer account of the world and one's place in it would most likely prevent future disappointments based on miscalculations.

Yang's vision of the primary and secondary pleasures can be extracted from all his masterworks, but especially from the *Fayan*, his most prismatic piece of writing. That Yang Xiong delivers his theory there through a series of dialogues is hardly coincidental, for he intends to put readers in dialogue with the most lucid and farsighted teachers and teachings of all time. The teachers – Confucius and Master Yang himself chief among them – are to be approached as "doors" that can never be substantially improved upon to readers' insights about themselves and the world,[75] though the insights may be expressed in new and different ways without diminishing their significance or impact. In the *Fayan*, Yang's decision to employ dialogues with unnamed interlocutors results in a continual interplay that fairly compels readers to hunt for the unambiguous, univocal messages planted throughout the text, on the assumption that masters worthy of the title had managed to formulate a vision of life at once cohesive and comprehensive (*quan* 全). Apparently, Yang looked to his followers to work out the implications of his moral teachings for themselves ("I grew weary of explanations..."').[76] As a pedagogical method, forging connections between seemingly disparate things and people was far more likely to hone his followers' powers of deliberation than simply parroting back a list of rules. Meanwhile, Yang Xiong strove to raise exegesis and philology to the level of

---

"his pupil" Zheng Xuan 鄭玄 (127-200) in the years Zheng studied at the capital. See SJ 121.3127; HHS 35.1207; cf. *Guanzi, pian* 59, "The Duties of Students."

[75] FY 5/21. This explains first, why Yang Xiong does not envision progress, but instead looks back for good models to a time in the distant past; and second, why he is nervous about innovation.

[76] *Analects* 7/8. Cf. Jiyuan Yu 2007: 13.

a single new "technology," driving in a single direction what might otherwise be a series of disconnected operations subsumed under the rubric of "the learning process."

The main outline of Yang's argument in the *Fayan* is fairly easy to grasp, even if the most subtle points are harder to capture. For the early chapters of that masterwork build a strong case that the conventional attitudes toward learning in general, and classical learning in particular, are mistaken, and that these mistakes prove very costly throughout life. Yang's reasoning goes something like this:

(1) Convention holds that learning in general, and classical learning in particular, are mere tools toward specific goals in life (e.g., career advancement, long life, the acquisition of factual knowledge, etc.), but it is unlikely that the sages would have directed their lifelong efforts to such paltry ends. Moreover, the conventional goals are either unattainable for humans (as with immortality)[77] or not solely dependent upon the efforts of the person who desires them (as with career advancement).

(2) Further inquiry into the proper ends of learning shows that the sages' inventions are meant to facilitate human interaction within the social and cosmic orders, since this is the one subject about which all sages speak.[78] Humans share with many other creatures the need for food and sex, but unique to humans is a strong desire for active membership in a flourishing community that endures through time. This sort of community, however, can only be sustained through the beauty and rigor instantiated in the aesthetic orders of ritual, music, and classical learning[79] that "add ornament

---

[77] FY 12/20-22.

[78] By definition, the sages understood the inherent nature and capacities of human beings, and so any devices they created should be eminently suited for human beings' use. Cf. e.g., FY 3/15: "Someone asks, 'What is this that we call 'being human'?'"

Reply: 'To seize upon four things as important and eschew four things lacking in consequence: that, then, is what is fit to be called human'."

[79] What is truly extraordinary about classical learning – whether it is encountered in books, in rites or music, in institutions or in living masters – is the degree to which it is economical yet compellingly lucid, effective yet gentle, since it has no admixture of lesser qualities in it. See, e.g., FY 11/21. FY 2/4 notes that "moderation and propriety" as two features of classical models; FY 2/7 insists that substance be balanced with ornamentation.

to the basic substance."[80] One analogy likens human beings to jade: while the basic substance of both is inherently valuable, the true luster of both is brought out only through painstaking grinding and polishing.[81] Far from being at odds with people's basic nature, cultivation brings out the captivating beauty inherent in that nature, imparting to people all of beauty's associations: animation, tension, poise, balance, resolution, coherence, integrity, and virtuosity. Mindful of this, the sages urged people to "refine and refine [themselves] again,"[82] so that they might more effectively engage others in social settings.[83]

(3) The institutions devised by the sages – chief among them the Five Relations (ruler-subject, husband-wife, parent-child, sibling-sibling, and friend-friend) – therefore refine the Five Social Virtues (humaneness, commitment to duty, ritual decorum, wisdom, and trustworthiness),[84] and even improve the Five Capacities for interaction (sight, hearing, speech, bearing, and thinking) that the "inborn nature possesses."[85] "Learning" simply means learning how to maintain these institutions and to exercise these virtues. Without learning, people are hard put to maximize their potentials, for only "through learning do the capacities come to function correctly."[86] For human nature requires the artful application of the sage's institutions and models, if the best in it is to shine forth. There is no other way for humans to become fully human. Since, "great discernment"

---

80 FY 4/5 says heaven, unlike men, does not "carve and cut" forms. FY 9/7 characterizes the sages as those who "added ornament to substance," and then says it is through these aesthetic orders that one may still glimpse the sages.

81 This metaphor Yang repeatedly returns to, in FY 1/4; 2/6; 6/19; 7/7; 8/17, 12/7, etc.

82 For "refine and refine again," see FY 7/6. FY 7/7 says, "Someone asked me: 'Good jade should not be carved, nor should fine words be embellished.' What does this mean?" Reply: "If jade was never really meant to be carved, then the precious *yufan* 璵番 ornament would never have been made into a ritual object. And if words were never really meant to be embellished, then neither the Canons nor Counsels [of the *Documents*] would ever have become part of the classic." I speak of being "fleshed out," since ritual embodies or "fleshes out" (*ti* 體) this capacity for aesthetic goodness. Han glosses frequently play on the visual pun between *li* and *ti*.

83 FY 1/9; FY 1/17.

84 See FY 3/12.

85 FY 1/9. FY 9/19 insists that the sages do not detach themselves or flee from the world.

86 FY 1/9.

presupposes "acquiring considerable experience,"[87] merely to accumulate facts or theories can in no way conduce to the correct functioning of the human faculties. Such accumulation tends rather to create the confusion and lack of focus that undermine true pleasure.[88] Repeated failures to use a capacity or to use it correctly then risk the loss of that capacity altogether.[89]

(4) Only mature people – not beasts or birds – can learn to distinguish apparently similar things.[90] The great difficulty for humans is to discriminate between mere mimesis and the true aesthetic orders. The former relies upon superficial patterning but the latter derives profound pleasure from recognizing the value of the old orders ("rites and music") and applying them to new situations. Even though the institutions of learning take into account people's inclinations, continued support for these aesthetic orders presupposes a sustained commitment to propriety and decorum, and an equal determination to live in accord with that hierarchy of values those reflect.[91] A failure to see the need for a hierarchy of values (which sets priorities in action) is a denial of the most significant aspect of the human potential for pleasure.[92]

(5) Learning in general and classical learning in particular greatly expand the person's awareness of human potentials. Classical learning invariably entails imaginative immersion in examples from the past, and so it multiplies the number and range of experiences to which a single person in a lifetime may lay claim.[93] By hearing all and seeing all,[94] good learners first contemplate

---

87 FY 7/3: "FY 13/7 discusses the potential for the apparent classicist to be a faker.

88 Thus FY 5/10 casts the Five Classics as "retaining walls for the masses of explications." FY 5/16 deplores writings that are "mixed" in their approaches to ethical problems.

89 FY 3/14. By comparison, a prolonged period of not using the eyes risks blindness.

90 FY 2/12-13; 5/26.

91 For the first point, see FY 5/22; 7/2. For the second, see FY 1/13; 3/3.

92 FY 8/28. FY 1/10, 3/15, 6/3, etc. Cf. Yang's condemnation of the social engineers working for Qin, as in FY 7/22, 10/6-11, 11/11. Still more despicable (because less human) are those who insist that humans are not social beings whose powers are capable of radical expansion.

93 FY 7/1 suggests that classical learning provides fleeting glimpses of times and places that are otherwise too remote to be apprehended (and so all the more to be treasured), which makes classical learning a great pleasure. Interestingly enough, a recent essay by Benedict Carey 2009, reports on scientific experiments that suggest that what we see in our

and then confirm the human possibility of creating new aesthetic orders, drawing upon personal experiences, the teachings of the past masters who have created successful orders, and newer writings that agree with the Classics in form, style, and quality.[95] (Yang believes that his own masterworks fall into this rubric of edifying and empowering Classics.) Thus excellent writings – classical and neoclassical – encourage a pronounced taste for the aesthetic orders exemplified in great people and preserved in great books.[96] Yang is quick to counter objections that applying the models and institutions of antiquity to the present day is unduly confining, like "applying glue to the fret before tuning the zither." By his reckoning, the sages demonstrated great flexibility in the ways they adjusted past models and institutions to meet the exigencies of their times.[97] Others can do the same today.

(6) To see the wisdom of applying to current problems the flexible orders associated with the sages is also implicitly to acknowledge that the sages' talk of human nature and their creation of institutions were premised alike on a true idea of human capacities and humans' place in the social and cosmic orders. As Yang puts it, "Someone who thoroughly understands heaven, earth, and humans we call an [ideal] classicist (*Ru* 儒); someone who merely comprehends the cosmos but not humans, we term a [mere] technician or craftsperson (*ji* 技)."[98] Yang Xiong allows that good technicians and craftsmen can make very useful things, but the classicist's efforts produce an artful way of being in the world which cannot be wrested from the learner.[99] For

minds' eye affects our neural pathways as substantially as what we have ourselves experienced. Cf. FY 12/12, which talks of the sages' transformations recorded in writing.

94 FY 6/2; cf. 8/29.

95 For the past masters, see, e.g., FY 1/10; 9/26; and 9/8: "In every case in the past, the models of the sages had a direct bearing upon the flourishing or decline of the realm." History attests past achievements, and we can expect equal achievements to be possible in the present and future (FY 4/12). For the authority of new writings adopting good models, see FY 1/19. Yang here refers to his own writings or to the obscure writings handed down from the past that he is expert in.

96 FY 2/9, and one's appreciation of the utility of the Five Classics.

97 FY 9/8 claims that Kongzi once managed to "make things pure" – return them to the best spirit of bygone days.. Yang cites examples showing that the sages institute satisfying aesthetic orders, rather than stultifying straitjackets.

98 FY 12/17.

99 I take this to be Yang's point in FY 1/2, which states, "True learning does not covet a particular end [external to the self]." Aristotle made precisely the same point.

classical masters, success is self-mastery,[100] and the Way and its embodiment in exemplary people have no inherent limitations, their activities consisting simply of "expanding the capacities and potentials of oneself and others."[101]

(7) By Yang's definition, whatever allows humans to operate supremely well in distinctively human ways constitutes an inexhaustible source of pleasure; hence the pleasures of the process of classical learning must be stupendously gratifying. Throughout life, learners in the Way experience the pleasures to be had from conscious improvements to their characters and capacities. Advanced learners in the Way grow increasingly sensible of their great good fortune,[102] acknowledging that their chosen path has allowed them to become "the very finest examples of their own species."[103] Hence the significance of the epigram coined by Yang, "The sages take pleasure in acting as sages."[104]

Yang goes so far as to allege that the sages as a rule experience great pleasure even when their labors seem to bear no fruit within their own lifetimes.[105] Ordinary people may be apt to confuse "taking the fullest measure of pleasure" with conventional success and the promise of being "free of care," but this equation is demonstrably false, in Yang's view.[106] Since only the sages cleave to their most distinctive qualities as humans, only they are the apogee of humanity.[107] In addition, those wise enough to devote themselves to developing their own potential pay homage to the best in others, with the result that all but the most benighted people come to care for them in return.[108] Thus does an intense regard for one's own humanity evoke civility in others.[109] "Steadfast in adversity," free of societal snares, and attuned to the larger cosmic patterns, the sages are fully aware that they have

---

100 FY 3/14; cf. 6/18. FY 3/21 says, "The sages like to become their own teachers and models."

101 FY 4/1-2.[But the quote doesn't actually appear in either of these passages.]

102 FY 3/22; 6/18; 8/12; 11/26. Cf. SJ 24.1212: "The *junzi* is happy to get the Way, while the *xiaoren* is happy to get his heart's desire."

103 FY 13/27.

104 FY 6/5: 聖人樂聖.

105 See, e.g., FY 5/27; FY 8/8.

106 FY 1/16; 3/14; 5/21, etc. Nor does it suffice to be a "master of pleasantries." See FY 11/21, speaking of Dongfang Shuo.

107 FY 5/4: "It is only the sages who continually grasp hold of it so as to preserve it! The sages preserve their godlike aspects and seek perfection."

108 FY 12/18.

109 Johan Huizinga 1943: 66, remarks, "This display of civility to others lies in intense regard for one's own honour."

created in their own persons, if not in their own societies, something of ineffable beauty. They have created this beauty by consciously "adding to or subtracting from" the orders they have inherited in response to the times.[110]

(8) Of course, some sorry creatures will always find ways to abuse their humanity and denigrate the sages' institutions.[111] Of those who are weak, some may recognize true greatness but not seek to emulate it, while others may try to emulate it, but fail.[112] The vast majority of people fail, however, because they put off the learning process for a later time, because it seems to them unrewarding. Such men either do not see that their time is short, or they are distracted from classical learning by lesser pursuits.[113] Still, Yang Xiong is not so foolish as to guarantee that the learning process will be a pleasure at each and every moment. Often the ardent desire to learn is spurred by an equally strong sense of shame in those who are relatively ignorant or uncivilized, a paradox illustrated in the *Fayan*:

> 曰：顏苦孔之卓之至也。或人瞿然曰：茲苦也，祇其所以為樂也與？
>
> "Yan Hui was deeply troubled by the perfection of Confucius."
> The interlocutor is startled.[114]
> "That particular form of trouble – was that not the very means by which Yan made himself truly happy?"[115]

The sage who would attract lesser human beings must work with their own love of sensual pleasure, inspiring others to emulate his splendid charismatic

---

[110] FY 6/19. The phrase "steadfast in adversity" comes from *Analects* 15/2.

[111] In FY chaps. 10-13, Yang Xiong discusses historical figures, by way of providing a model for just praise and blame.

[112] FY 3/10: "One who admires the great but does not emulate greatness will be anything but great."

[113] FY 3/20. That life is short and all other claims on one's attention inherently less valuable is a constant theme in the FY. See, e.g., FY 6/13-14.

[114] Tentative translation. Perhaps the interlocutor is startled by his own insight? Normally, *ju* 瞿 does not refer to one who is "delighted," rather than fearful, but see Han Jing, p. 24, n. 8. *Ju* can mean "timid," and perhaps the interlocutor hazards this observation.

[115] FY 1/23. Cf. *Shuoyuan* 16.208/139/5: "The noble man studies broadly, fearing that he will not have a chance to put it into practice; once he puts it into practices, he fears he will not be able to promote it; once he can promote it, he fears his inability to give way."

person or persuading them of the manifest attractions of reading and classical learning. Since the sage is a master connoisseur of life's pleasures, this he can do.

Yang's set of eight linked propositions about pleasure evokes the opening line of the *Analects*: "To learn and at due times to repeat or put into practice what one has learnt – is that not a delight after all?", as well as the *Analects* line that described Confucius as "the sort of person who ... forgets his cares in his pleasures."[116] Whereas the Confucian *Analects* tends to collapse the gap between knowing and acting, insisting that if you really know something to be true, you will invariably act upon that knowledge,[117] Yang Xiong's *Fayan* introduces a much more complex picture of human agency and desire, conceding that humans may acknowledge the truth of some proposition, yet feel insufficiently motivated to pursue that truth wholeheartedly. Yang's remedy for this malady is to emphasize the compelling beauty of the sages. As one astute historian put it, "If the matter did not pertain to the sages, it was not one that Yang Xiong deemed worthy of rapt contemplation" (其事非聖, 楊雄所不觀).[118]

This admission is the proper background against which to place Yang's ruminations about the role of classicists at the Western Han court. In theory, members of this group had dedicated their lives to the pursuit and transmission of classical learning, yet they regularly failed to practice what they preached. Still less did they embody the spirit that infuses all the teachings ascribed to the sages. One *Fayan* passage acknowledges the conventional successes the career classicists have nonetheless racked up as a group, securing posts at court on the basis of their rhetorical skills, their erudition, and their mastery of past precedents; Yang Xiong suggests that the careerists among the Ru have "learnt *something* from the sages,"[119] even if they have inexplicably failed to learn the crucial thing from the antique masters. Yet Yang's attention is drawn more to the great confusion engendered in the well-intentioned learners by the apparent similarities between true and false lovers of classical learning. The *Fayan* therefore discusses the use of patterned rhetoric, in speech or writing, considering the end to which the

---

[116] *Analects* 1/1, 7/9.
[117] The *Analects* implies this in many passages.
[118] Liu Zhiji, in *Shitong* 5.106-7.
[119] FY 6/7.

patterns may be put, in weighing the relative value and impact of those patterns upon the viewer/reader:

> 或曰：有人焉，曰雲姓孔而字仲尼，入其門，升其堂，伏其幾，襲其裳，則可謂仲尼乎？曰：其文是也，其質非也。敢問質。曰：羊質而虎皮，見草而說，見豺而戰，忘其皮之虎矣。聖人虎別，其文炳也。君子豹別，其文蔚也。辯人貍別，其文萃也。貍變則豹，豹變則虎。
>
> Someone asked me: "Suppose there were a man who took the surname of Kong and the sobriquet of Zhongni [like Confucius]. Were he to enter Kongzi's door, ascend his hall, lean on his armrest, and wear his robes, could he be rightly called Confucius?"
> Reply: "The surface pattern would be right, but the substance would be wrong."
> "I dare to ask, what about the substance?"
> Reply: "A sheep in wolf's clothing is delighted when it sees some grass, but terrified by the sight of a jackal because it will have forgotten all about the skin that it wears."
> "The sage is as distinct as the tiger, with patterns bold and brilliant! The noble man is as distinct as a leopard, with patterns fine and elegant. The rhetorician is like the fox, its patterns dense enough to provide cover." Yet a single change can transform the fox into a leopard, and with a single change the leopard can become a tiger!"[120]

The rhetorician is concerned only to protect himself with ornate speech. But since he already has trained himself in that discipline, by redirecting his energies and enlarging his aims and views, the rhetorician can emerge as a

---

[120] FY 2/12-13. The first passage speaks of a wild dog (hence my jackal), instead of a wolf, but I wanted to retain the association of sheep and wolf in English; in addition, both tiger and leopard are associated with advanced cultivation in the lines below, and the leopard "changing its spots" suits improvements in cultivation. Note also that the *li* 貍 is actually a raccoon-dog, but "fox" seems a good substitute in context.

true classical master.[121] Yet another *Fayan* passage squarely addresses the question of classical learning's utility:

> 或曰：聖人無益於庸也。曰：世人之益者，倉廩也，取之如單。仲尼，神明也。小以成小，大以成大。雖山川丘陵、草木鳥魯，裕如也。如不用也，神明亦末如之何矣。
>
> Someone said to me that the sages are of no benefit to the ordinary person.
> Reply: "The men of this age consider the granary to be of great use, but the more you take from it, the more it is depleted. Confucius had godlike insight. Small men can use him to perfect themselves in small things, and the great in the great. Even mountains and rivers, hills and mounds, grasses and trees, birds and beasts, flourish under his influence. But if his Way is *not* employed, then of what possible use is even his godlike insight?"[122]

Although Yang did not hesitate to identify the pretences of some professional classicists, he saw that the court classicists, even as poor imitations of the sages, performed a useful function, insofar as they put before other people's eyes and ears models of behavior that wiser men can then appreciate and adopt. Even poor imitations sometimes serve to remind others of the excellence of the original. The inestimable value of classical learning lies in the perfection with which it works upon human nature and the world at large.[123] As with a bottomless well, men can draw from the Master's teachings a sufficiency to slake their thirst, whether their thirst be great or small.

Yang Xiong never doubted that it was the classicists alone who were up to the task of perfecting human beings:

---

[121] See FY 11/18, where Yang denies that Gongsun Hong and Dong Zhongshu were true classicists.

[122] Punctuating after *mo* 末. Alternatively, "But if his Way was not like this, then even his godlike insight would be of no avail!," reading *mo* 末 as *wuke naihe* 無可奈何. Because the passage seems more about employing the Way than its fundamental character, my rendering is different.

[123] FY 5/1 insists that it's the will to emulate the sages that makes one like the sages.

天之道，不在仲尼乎？仲尼駕說者也，不在茲儒乎？如將復駕其說，則莫若使諸儒金口而木舌。

The Way of Heaven– was it not invested in Confucius? But the harness traces of Confucius's carriage were set down at his death. Is the Way not [now] invested in these classicists? Were one to try to take up again the conveyance that was laid down, then the best way of doing this would be to cause all the classicists to make their voices ring out loud and clear, like wooden tongues giving voice to bells of bronze.[124]

In Yang's pleasure narrative, even superficially impressive people have the potential to act as compelling emblems of the orders, institutions, and modes of operation favored by the sages; in so acting, they function as "doors" to insight.[125]

Since trained classicists, in Yang's view, function either as second-rate mimics or as compelling correlates to the ancient sages, depending on the degree to which they instantiate the sages' aesthetic orders and breathe new life into them, much of Yang's *Fayan* is taken up with the question of what constitutes a true model or teacher, as suggested by his title *Exemplary Figures.*[126] In Yang's view the same criteria define a true model, whether a teacher or an instructive institution: (a) the degree to which its account of the world matches reality, especially the social realities;[127] (b) the degree to which it formulates and inculcates an aesthetic of inexhaustible beauty and rigor;[128] and (c) the degree to which its aesthetic vision contributes to human flourishing via increased numbers of constructive exchanges between responsive humans.[129] Yang's definition of the good model does not pretend

---

124 FY 1/3. To Yang's comment, compare those of Ban Gu (HS 21A.978), which claims that those who are wearing Ru clothes are reciting words that are "not right"; and of *Lunheng* 13/36/15-17: "The person with wisdom and ability could better serve the court with his tongue of three inches and a writing brush of one foot," meaning he should talk less and write more of the Classics.

125 See FY 4/9-10; 4/13-15.

126 FY 1/11.

127 FY 12/20-22.

128 E.g., FY 4/17, 5/9, 8/10.

129 E.g, FY 7/2. FY 3/15 uses the phrase *ke guan* 可觀 ("worth contemplating") when answering the question, "What is this that we call 'being human'?" [可觀 is not in my

to be anything but circular, since it begins and ends with the excellence of the sage kings: "The noble man does not take to be a model anything that fails to conform to model of the former [sage-]kings."[130]

The most peculiar aspect of the *Fayan* is the role that Yang Xiong assigns to composition. Composition for Yang is far more than an aesthetic endeavor in which to display excellence. The relative value of a piece of writing depends at least as much upon the writer's refining his definition of and attachment to greatness as upon his literary talents.[131] Following one longstanding tradition, Yang viewed the very act of assigning names to reality as incorporating aspects of reality in coherent systems of cultural, moral, and aesthetic significance. Hence his excoriation of the type of *fu* he had composed as a young man, which took mimesis as its highest goal, without striving for coherence. Insofar as Yang's early epideictic *fu* failed to supply a true and complete picture of the way the world actually works, his immature writings gave off mixed messages about the way things are.[132] However stylistically appealing the *fu*, mimesis lacks substance and refinement.[133] Why waste time on writing *fu*, when the same taste for stylized display could generate a yearning for good order and for the transformative power of ritual and music, merging pleasure with self-improvement?[134]

In Yang Xiong's theory, the classical writings worthy of the name "canon" share certain features that elevate them above all other forms of text: (1) they balance substance (propositional content) and embellishment (rhetorical phrasing),[135] avoiding the over-use of decorative elements that masks the true model as surely as the over-use of cosmetics obscures a

text of 3/15, though it does appear in Li Gui's commentary]Cf. FY 2/9; 7/15, with the latter speaking of the Zhanguo period as "not worth contemplating."

130 FY 2/8. FY 3/6-8 says that human interaction and human contact is fundamental to human's well-being. Cf. FY 11/21. FY 3/10 goes further, defining the "way of humans" as "making contact."

131 FY 4/25.

132 See, e.g., FY 2/1; 1/10. Hence Yang's dismissal of parts of many pre-Qin masterworks, but his tendency to salvage something from them.

133 FY 2/6, citing the example of Qu Yuan's poems.

134 Contra Kern 2003: 431, which only addresses a part of Yang's writings (his rejection of the epideictic *fu*). This chapter emphatically argues that neither Yang Xiong nor Liu Xin rejected the faith that the pre-Qin texts reveal about the fusion of pleasure and morality, as might be guessed, in the case of Yang, given his admiration for Mencius.

135 FY 2/7; 12/10.

woman's natural beauty;[136] (2) thus they exemplify moderation, with the result that their value endures repetition;[137] (3) they enjoin the modes of cultivation seen in the finest Central States traditions, in contrast to the inferior orders prevailing elsewhere;[138] and (4) they "everywhere communicate virtue,"[139] as attested by socially constructive acts they inspire and guide.[140] In other words, for Yang the best sort of composition differs from lesser sorts of writing in its aims, its literary excellence, and its unparalleled potential to convey how to act as a fully mature human being in a world of flawed human beings.[141] Texts become truly iconic when they draw no undue attention to themselves, but instead inspire allegiance to a community of moral purpose more encompassing than that of any single person. Iconic texts supply images that correspond with experiences and resonate with those experiences in ways that prompt further reflection about the human condition. Hence, their power and authority surpasses those of emperors and kings,[142] revealing the propensity toward the divine in the human spirit.

With the foregoing in mind, Yang Xiong's longest *Fayan* pronouncement about the potentials of speech versus writing renders up its meaning:

> 言不能達其心，書不能達其言，難矣哉。惟聖人得言之解，得書之體。白日以照之，江河以滌之，灝灝乎其莫之禦也。面相之，辭相適，捈中心之所欲，通諸人之嚍々者，莫如言。彌綸天下之事，記久明遠，著古昔之㫚㫚，傳千裏之忞忞者，莫如書。故言，心聲也。書，心

[136] FY 2/5. Cf. FY 5/17: "Writing that does not embody the classical principles is not proper writing, and speech that does not embody them is not true speech. Speeches and writings that do not embody the classical principles are absolutely superfluous."

[137] FY 2/14: "To like books yet fail to see the centrality of Zhongni's [Confucius's] writings is to be nothing more than a bookstall. To enjoy rhetoric yet fail to see the centrality of Zhongni's sayings is to make nothing more than tiny tinkling sounds."

[138] FY 3/20; 4/11.

[139] FY 6/23.

[140] FY 8/18.

[141] FY 7/5: "Someone asks whether the Five Classics contain any disputations. [Reply]: 'Only the Five Classics are really discerning language! ...Were we to discard these texts, all disputations would become paltry affairs'."

[142] One of the interesting aspects of Yang's writing is his willingness to de-mystify even his heroes, including Mencius, whose theory of "sages arising every 500 years" he shows to be false. His chapter "Xian zhi" 先知 has nothing to do with premonitions and foreknowledge, but rather extols the sorts of training that leads to predictable results.

> 畫也。聲畫形，君子小人見矣！聲畫者，君子小人之所以動情乎！聖人之辭，渾渾若川。順則便，逆則否者，其惟川乎？
>
> They say, "Speech cannot fully express what is in the heart, nor can writings fully express speech." What a difficulty! Only sages apprehend the true meaning of words or achieve the substantial embodiment [of things] in writing. [Of Kongzi it was therefore said:] "The white sun shown down on him; the Yangzi and Yellow River cleansed him. So powerfully does [his example] flow onward that none have been a match for him!"
>
> Nothing is as good as speech for exchanging fitting remarks during face-to face meetings, expressing the heart's desire or communicating people's pent-up emotions. And nothing compares with writing for fully delineating the affairs of the whole realm; for recording events of the distant past or for making one see clearly what is geographically remote; for bringing out what has been obscured by the mists of time or for transmitting over a thousand miles any murkiness in affairs. Therefore, speech is the sounds of the heart, and writing, its images. As soon as sounds and images assume form, then the noble and petty appear in high relief. Certainly, sounds and images are the means the noble and petty alike use to motivate themselves and others.
>
> The sages' rhetoric flows on and on like a river. When one follows that current, things go easily and well. But when one goes against the current, that makes for hard going.[143]

Speech and writing are likened here to music and painting, two aesthetic traditions promising to capture internal ideas and emotions and render them visible through external conventions. Elsewhere in the *Fayan* Yang insists that text is far superior to painting, because a verbal portrait of an exemplary figure never fades, yet it conveys the innermost thoughts and feelings of its

---

143 FY 5/13-14.

subject, being more than mere mimesis.[144] This passage emphasizes the scope and power of speech and writing to express and describe the full complexity of humans. Significantly, however, writing generally excels speech, given its greater potential to transcend the limitations of time and space, and to describe things more fully at greater length.

Mencius, one of Yang Xiong's heroes, purportedly told a disciple that a sensitive reader could expect to glean from poetry or prose not only the main thrust of the text but its underlying authorial intent, so long as one did not get tangled up in the verbiage. Seeing authors "as humans" was the first step on the rewarding path that Mencius called "looking for friends in history."[145] Meaning accrued from restoring the original context to the piece, and careful restoration rewarded the restorer with an "insight into words" that in turn encouraged "cultivating a flood-like *qi*" via a "firm grasp of the essentials."[146] The final result: the resolute integrity that came with "being whole in power." Yang Xiong in his own writings, especially the *Fayan*, insists that writing adequately expresses "the heart" – the emotions, drives, and thoughts – of the sages, who alone can appreciate and compose the sorts of writing that facilitate the human desire to know. Here Yang has subtly shifted the focus from reading to writing.[147] Reasoning that it was only Kongzi's writings that allowed his "rhetoric to flow on and on," so that the Master appeared to succeeding generations in all his brilliant clarity, like a force of nature, Yang saw the crucial importance of such writings, even if he doubted that many shared his vision:

> 吾寡見人之假者也。邇文之視，邇言之聽，假則偭焉。
>
> "Rarely have I seen people prefer what is remote. Recent writings, those they look at. Recent sayings, those they hearken to. The remote, they turn their backs on."[148]

---

144 See FY 12/11 for mineral colors that fade. See FY 12/13 for good writing that "gets clear through to [i.e., communicates with and instantiates] the inherent patterns [of things in the world]."

145 *Mencius* 5A/4, 5B/8.

146 *Mencius* 2A/2, with Gongsun Chou.

147 One helpful introduction to such passages in Yang's work is Gu Ming Dong 2005: 35-43, though my translation departs from Gu's. We agree that Yang's main focus is on the writing and reading of texts (p. 37).

148 FY 7/1.

The *Fayan* repeatedly insists that "heaven's constants" – the only standard for humans intent upon gaining a true sense of reality – can only be found in the "brushes and tongues" of the sage-kings of antiquity."[149] Then what prevents the capable from grasping the crucial idea that the essential truths about the human condition must be sought in the writings of the sages? Yang offers several plausible answers, some of which we have seen before: (1) the instrumental use to which classical learning has been put makes people see the Classics as a means to a prestigious end, rather than as open-ended invitations to expand one's capacities and views; [150] (2) the idea that imperfections in the Five Classics' transmissions makes them poor sources for history and for morality;[151] (3) the common complaint that the Classics are too difficult to understand and memorize;[152] (4) the silly notion that human beings change in their fundamentals from age to age; and (5) the more bizarre idea that the Classics embody a set of ideals that is too rigid to cope with social changes.[153] Yang Xiong readily concedes distortions and lacunae in the transmission of the Classics and of the pre-Qin system of rites and music.[154] Many of the classicists feared that their own inability to read – and make sense of – the pre-Qin writings was a severe impediment to devising any new order on the classical model. Hence the fervor that Yang brought to his study of pre-Qin script forms found in pre-Qin texts.

In deciding who and what to emulate, Yang Xiong naturally confines himself to the concerns of members of the governing elite, since only they have the leisure for prolonged reading in the Classics. Notably, however, Yang's theorizing about composition, classical learning, and pleasure allots surprisingly little space to the ruler's role – a notable omission that sets Yang apart from his predecessors, all of whom saw the ruler as central to any civilizing effort (*jiaohua* 教化). This must have been intentional, since Yang has an unnamed interlocutor bring the omission to his – and our – attention in the *Fayan*. Yang believes that some rulers have been great, but most have

---

149 FY 4/12; cf. FY 1/22.

150 FY 12/12.

151 FY 5/6-8.

152 E.g., FY 5/10; 8/11. This objection Yang counters by emphasizing the wide-ranging character of the Classics, which is not easily constrained or captured, and yet the Classics do adequately mirror the times in which they were written (FY 5/9).

153 FY 7/16: "Someone asks, "Why was the territory of Lu whittled away even when it employed classicists?"

154 FY 5/21.

been mere blockheads.[155] In Yang's writing, the "dragon who soars" or "scales the heights" is most typically not the ruler but men like himself who have enjoyed the heady experience of seeing their own abilities expand to the point where they can roam freely through the texts transmitted from remote antiquity.[156]

As Yang Xiong saw it, whoever desires to "scale the heights" cannot do better than to study and emulate the thoughts, purposes, and characters of those deemed great by the great. He would have agreed absolutely with the linkage between good reading and good composition proposed by one who shared his love of ancient forms:

> 夫鎔冶經典之範, 翔集子史之術, 洞曉情變,曲昭文體,然後能莩甲新意雕畫奇辭...
>
> If one casts his work in the mold of the Classics, soars and then lands in the techniques of the ... masters and historians, clearly understands the changing of emotions, and intricately exhibits the proper style, he will be able to generate fresh ideas and carve out unusual expressions.[157]

In consequence, compiling a person's achievements, lending them life through verbal adornment, and submitting them to others to contemplate and study was not a task to be undertaken lightly.[158] With utmost seriousness and a sense of urgency about the possibility of restoring moral order, Yang Xiong devoted his talents and erudition in his later years to history and epigraphy, in the hopes that his efforts might help men of his own circle to learn from the Ancients. At the same time, however, he insisted that a sense

---

155 Yang's denunciations of the First Emperor of Qin and Han Wudi are outspoken. As we have seen, he also did not hesitate to criticize Xuandi or Chengdi.

156 That texts create discursive spaces akin to geographical spaces is made abundantly clear not only in Yang's works, which compare the Classics to the great mountains and rivers in the Central States lands, but also in Tao Yuanming's work, which observes, in Poem 33, line 3, of "Written at Tukou, at Night, Seventh Month Poem": "The Classics remain my old source of pleasure," which means Tao has never ceased reading them. Cf. Poem 68, line 17 of "In Sacrifice for Myself" (*Zi ji wen* 自祭文): "I delighted myself with books"; also Poem 54, concluding couplet of "On Reading the *Shanhai jing*" 讀山海經: "In the space of a moment, I've reached the ends of the world./ If this is not pleasure, then what is?" See Yuan Xingpei, 3.193, 7.555, 4.393, respectively.

157 *Wenxin diaolong* 6.6a-6; Knechtges *Wenxuan* trans., Introduction, vol. 1, 15.

158 See Isocrates, *Evagoras*, 75-77.

of playfulness be brought to the study and selection of the *mot juste* – the delight that would sustain serious study, as he saw it – in this, defying earlier Confucian masters, such as Xunzi.[159] Because of his phenomenal propensity to find that *mot juste* that says a great deal with economy of style Ban Gu dubbed Yang Xiong one of the three best writers of the "subcelestial realm."[160]

---

159 Xunzi, *juan* 21 ("Jie bi" 解蔽), specifically condemns "toying with unusual language (*wan qi ci* 玩奇辭), so as to vex and confuse others" -- advice Yang ignored. Distrust of strange language or verbal tricks is evident in many Han texts, including SJ 102.2752; HS 50.2307, with the latter criticizing "verbal disputation that has nothing to do with reality."

160 HS 28B.1645.

IV
At Play with the Ancients

For millennia students of Chinese history have been taught to vastly underplay the enormity of the changes that has occurred over long centuries, in the belief (partly valid) that the principal subject of antique history – the playing out of human needs, desires, predilections in society and politics – has changed remarkably little over the ages. Hence Mencius' famous pronouncement, "Those who truly understand people know how to assess the different ages" (*zhi ren lun shi* 知人論世).[1] Certainly, by Zhanguo times, the benefits of dressing up new rhetoric in old finery had become apparent to all aspirants to prominence at the court, since cultivation then, as in all premodern civilizations, was synonymous with knowledge of the past.

Arguably, however, Yang Xiong and his peers in late Western Han, even as they relished more recent narratives like the *Zuozhuan* and *Shiji*, were the first generation to truly "love antiquity" (*haogu*) in the specific sense of wanting to *restore* a distant past they believed to be hugely better than their own time and organized along markedly different principles.[2] The prominent thinkers of early to mid-Western Han uniformly celebrated the newly unified empire and presumed its benefits so long as it was guided by the right sort of men. But, in the view of Yang Xiong, his followers and some of his famous peers, the necessary restoration of ancient institutions and practices was best accomplished through reading ancient texts, so when Yang spoke of one remote figure, the Duke of Zhou, he portrayed him less often in his usual guise as regent than as author and influential model for the successful life lived through books, a portrayal quite at odds with that offered by more conventional advisors at the Han court.[3] Given the slow pace of copying and

---

1 *Mencius* 10/8. The expanded phrase is: 論古之人, 頌其詩, 讀其書. 不知其人, 可乎? 是以論其世也. 是尚友也.

2 Poo Mu-chou 2010 registers some astute observations on the multiple pasts invoked at the Han court.

3 See, e.g., FY 4/24. Prior to Yang Xiong's time, multiple pasts (some quite recent) qualified for consideration as worthy models, and earlier texts had referred to those pasts, and the leading figures identified with them, almost indiscriminately, apparently thinking no

memorizing in a manuscript culture largely dependent upon oral instruction, the final authority of even the most renowned model and his writings could be trusted only insofar as circles of admirers committed themselves to preserving and transmitting their favorite texts. At the same time, every act of copying in early China was seen as an invitation to reinterpret the text. Thus the sincere admiration of successive generations did not always prevent emendations to the Classics and masterworks during transmission, as Yang readily acknowledged.[4]

In company with Liu Xiang and Liu Xin,[5] Yang was deeply troubled by the carelessness with which his classicist peers had handled past traditions, in the way they promoted exemplary figures and evaluated early texts. Thus Yang and the Lius, father and son, became the leading advocates of a counter-cultural "return" to classical learning that really represented – as such "revivals" often do – a reinvention of the revered past accomplished through a careful selection of useable features. (That does not mean that Yang and the Lius invariably saw eye-to-eye.)[6] Given the fame of Confucius as a "praise and blame" historian, Yang Xiong's self-conscious claims to being a good historian speaking truth to power are an expression of his ardent love for the antique sages, just as his innovative proposal to use pre-Qin inscriptions to correct the texts of the Classics (see below) was part of a larger concerted campaign to restore integrity to the court-sponsored traditions associated with Confucius. Apparently, the *haogu* campaign was effective, most probably because a cash-strapped throne was forced to consider new ways to shore up its legitimacy, and linkage to the past, largely constructed in the imagination, was far cheaper than public or palace spectacles or wars. In any case, frequent allusions to pre-Qin sources in authority-based arguments became commonplace in Yang's time, where before they had been comparatively rare, even perfunctory.[7] Meanwhile,

---

one past era particularly merited scholarly attention. Yang focused on the Duke of Zhou as model for Kongzi. See FY 1/7; the verse summary for chap. 2; 7/8; 7/16, etc.

[4] See, e.g., FY 2/11, 5/7, 5/8.

[5] Xiao Wangzhi 蕭望之 and Kuang Heng 匡衡 are two earlier figures praised for their elegant writing style, who evidently paved the way for *haogu*, as had Jiao Yanshou 焦延壽 and Jing Fang 京房, the master-prognosticators. See Liu Rulin 1935: vol. 2, 55.

[6] Liu Xin and Liu Xiang disagreed over the relative superiority of two traditions to the *Chunqiu*, with Liu Xiang preferring the *Guliang* and Xin, the *Zuo*. Yang Xiong seems to have disparaged Liu Xin for starting the fashion for the curious, when he presented his edited version of the *Shanhai jing*. See Liu Rulin 1935: vol. 2, 109; cf. FY 12/9, on Sima Qian. Another conflict is recorded in the "Letters" translated in Knechtges 1977.

[7] See *Wenxin diaolong* 8.1/81/5 (Shih, p. 63), on "allusion and reference."

Yang took considerable pains to challenge the supremacy of the literary genre that he excelled in, though it had dominated the literary scene at court for at least a century, since the time of Han Wudi (r. 141-87 BC).[8] In his estimation, not even the best *fu* could ever hold a candle to the Classics, masterworks, and neoclassical works, in beauty or in the practical effects they encouraged.[9]

Yang Xiong did not hesitate to excoriate members of the Han court for abandoning the model of the sages and preferring the methods and institutions associated with those fabled tyrants Jie and Zhou of old and the First Emperor of Qin. Indeed, some of the very passages in Yang's writings most likely to strike today's readers as insufferably insipid and eminently forgettable would have been recognized by Yang's contemporaries as harsh criticisms of the reigning emperor, his immediate predecessors, and their inner circles of advisors, all of whom were charged with falling far short of the sublime model of the Ancients. For instance, an innocent-sounding query in the *Fayan* about the advisability of courtiers amusing an emperor by playing chess with him was, in fact, an allusion that few of Yang's peers would have missed to Xuandi's (r. 74-48 BC) inattention to the matters of state and his consequent willingness to twist a phrase ascribed to Kongzi to defend his love of games of chance.[10] Episodes in Yang's life and passages in his writings reflect his fervent desire to "play with the Ancients" in more demanding ways more faithful to the Master. First, Yang labored long and hard as a historian, in chronicles (no longer extant, but presumably incorporated into Ban Gu's *Hanshu*), as well as in the *Fayan*, all of which assert the profound play of history in the present, with four *Fayan* chapters consisting mainly of pointed historical judgments on major historical figures.[11] Second, Yang spent nearly three decades collecting many examples

---

8 Whereas Liu Xin had simply said of the *fu* that "To recite without singing is what we mean by *fu*. He who climbs on high and can compose a *fu* may become a court councilor," Yang issued a serious challenge to the moral legitimacy of the *fu* in several of his works, as is well known. See HS 30.1755-56. Liu Xin, however, also criticizes some *fu* writers as "submerging the intention of satire and analysis."

9 FY 6/22;

10 Compare FY 7/10 and HS 64.2829. Xuandi tried hard to justify his love of *fu* by constructing a forced analogy between *fu* and dice or chess, on the one hand, and the Classics, on the other. But Yang's subtle reworking of Xuandi's retort conveys his profound disgust at the imperial jest, making it clear that first, Xuandi had the temerity to mock Confucius by citing him out of context, and second, banal games and contests simply waste time and preclude more rewarding types of cultural play, such as emulation of the Ancients.

11 *Tongzhi, juan* 5 下中, lists Yang Xiong as one of the compilers of the Basic Annals draft chapters for the reigns Jingdi to Pingdi (156 BC-AD 5). See Yang Haizheng 2003: esp.

of pre-Qin script and obsolete regional expressions, in the hope that their methodical application to textual studies would breathe new life into the manuscripts of the Classics and make them more reliable guides to the past. Third, Yang was thought of as "a historian's historian" by historians of later ages, including Liu Zhiji.[12]

For those in power, the chief subject of epistemological inquiry in pre-Han and Han times was not "knowing facts" but "knowing men": knowing how to gather and weigh evidence about the character and proclivities of candidates for office. Accordingly, aspirants to greatness sought in history a useable past and a secure professional status. Deliberation on exemplary historical and contemporary figures gave historians the material from which to construct impressive arguments about controversial topics before the court that were "worthy of careful consideration."[13] Pointing to contrasts between the time of the sages and the present day afforded authors opportunities to take stances and provide rationales for them.[14] The assumption of the role of impartial judge over historical figures and events could elevate an author in the eyes of his contemporaries, given the widespread assumption that only the most astute of men, the sages, understood how to evaluate men and their activities properly.[15] That the root word for "investigate" was cognate with the word for "aged" (*kao* 考 = *lao* 老) was hardly lost on men like Yang.[16]

21-31; *Lunheng, pian* 60 ("Xu song"), which says that Yang "recorded" (*lu* 錄) the reigns from Xuandi (r. 74-49) to Pingdi.

[12] See Ren Naiqiang's comments regarding Liu Zhiji's assessment of Yang, for example, recorded in *Huayang guozhi* 10A.543 (n. 3).

[13] For the phrase "worthy of careful consideration" in connection with Yang, see *Shitong*, 5.106-7.

[14] DeClercq 1998: 41-55, offers a brilliant analysis of Yang's "Dispelling Ridicule *fu*" (Jie chao) (HS 87A.3566-73), emphasizing Yang's use of past to criticize the present.

[15] This is the argument put forward in the *Documents* chap. entitled "Gao Yao mo," which is the most frequently cited *Documents* chapter in Han times, as reported in Nylan 2001: 149.

[16] This linkage between lao and kao, which appears in the Shuowen jiezi [e-Siku] 8A/23a, a full century after Yang, as well as in such early collectanea as TPYL, 383/1a, is accepted by scholars thereafter, in commentaries to many texts, including the Shiji, the Liji, and the Jinshu, as a search in the Siku quanshu electronic database shows. Later texts seem to regard these as loan characters, as in, e.g., Shiji 63/1b; and Wei Xu 韋續 (Tang) Mou sou, 墨藪 1/1a [both e-Siku]. William Baxter (University of Michigan) notes (personal communication, Sept. 2010) that the authoritative Ji Xusheng (2002) says the two characters were written identically in oracle bones and early bronzes; also that neither character is related to xiao 孝. That the ancestors were called "kao" (as in kaofu 考父) in texts that

PHILOLOGICAL MATTERS

Much of what follows is premised on a hard-won insight (possibly off) that virtually requires an expansion to the standard definitions given two basic terms in Han classicism, *xiaoxue* 小學, and *qiwen* 奇文. The term *xiaoxue* is usually translated as "elementary education" (i.e., training for beginning students), and it indubitably carries that meaning in most contexts in Han literature.[17] However, any serious discussion of the catalogue divisions in the *Hanshu* 30 "Treatise on Literature" entails careful consideration of the possible implications of its assignment of a host of *xiaoxue* texts to the division entitled "the Six Arts" (i.e., the Five Classics plus a lost *Music* classic) (not to mention the discrepant accounts offered in the "Treatise" and *Shuowen*).[18] A summary appended to the *xiaoxue* subsection in the "Six Arts" division makes those implications fully explicit, for it describes the several versions of the *Cang Jie* (including that compiled by Yang Xiong), the *Erya*, the *Shi Zhou pian* 史籀篇, and other wordlists containing small- and large-character seal script[19] and "many old characters"[20] as the major philological works fundamental to the responsible decipherment of the Five Classics and the necessary excision of extraneous accreted readings attached to the Classics by careless scholars of previous generations. It moreover shows that the important work of compiling these *xiaoxue* Classics is best left to acknowledged adult masters (not children) steeped in erudition and, as often as not, laboring under the express orders of the court.[21] That means that *xiaoxue*, depending upon circumstances, means not only "elementary education," but also "Philological Classic."

Turning to a second phrase, *qizi*, readings in Han classicism again spur a rethinking of this term. The binome *qizi* 奇字, well known from both

---

predate Yang's era is indisputable, but we cannot prove that this association predates Yang's time, since no early excavated texts make the same link, so far as I know.

[17] For example, HS 30.1721 specifically says that students "at eight *sui* are to enter primary school [or, the elementary educational phase]," and be taught "the fundamentals of how to form characters." For more on "elementary education" and "philological studies," see Lei Hanqing 2000, esp. 1-2.

[18] Hsing I-t'ien 2004 reminds us that the *Hanshu* and *Shuowen* accounts do not agree.

[19] See, e.g., HS 30.1716-1717, 1720. Hsing I-t'ien 2002: 446, agrees that the *Cang Jie* originally must have been written in seal script. Wang Guowei 2004: 43-44, reminds us that both seal and clerical scripts were current (*jinwen* 今文) in Han times.

[20] HS 30.1720.

[21] HS 30.1721.

Hanshu 30 and a few later texts,[22] is often defined as one of the six calligraphic styles practiced by children destined or aspiring to high office. The *Hanshu* "Treatise on Literature" equates *qizi* with one of the "eight forms" of writing (*bati* 八體), which would seem to support that definition. However, the standard commentary to the "Treatise" unambiguously defines *qizi* as "archaic script characters that differ from those found in the writings taken from the wall of Confucius' house" (古文謂孔子壁中書...奇字即古文而異者也).[23] This evidence, considered in light of recent scholarly studies plus several additional facts,[24] strongly suggests that this script style represented far more than a mere school boy's calligraphic exercise. The relevant facts are: first, that Yang Xiong was known for teaching "strange characters" to adults, including the adult son of the classical master Liu Xin (歆子棻);[25] second, that knowledge of this script was viewed somehow as "dangerous," since it gave access (or appeared to the credulous public to give access) to heavenly commands and revelations;[26] third, that part of the reputation of Yang's own classical masters came from their knowledge of such scripts and regional expressions;[27] fourth, that relatively early sources

---

22 HS 30.1721.

23 HS 30.1722, n. 7. For the story (part of it fictionalized) about the writings taken from the wall of Kongzi's house, see Nylan 1994, 1995.

24 On recent studies of calligraphic script styles in relation to archaeological finds, cf. Hsing I-t'ien 2010, which reviews other work on Han lexicons. Hsing (p. 437) agrees that only those with advanced learning could read *qizi*.

25 *Qian Hanji*, 30.15b. According to the CHANT database, there are only four other uses of this term, two of them being HS 30.1721 and Yang's own autobiography. The binomial phrase does not appear in the main text of the *Shuowen*, though commentaries to that text identify five characters in that text as *qizi,* i.e., a special type of archaic script. The binome appears once in the postface to the *Shuowen*, which is ascribed jointly to Xu Shen 許慎, the primary author of the *Shuowen*, and to Xu Xuan 徐鉉 of Song, who wrote "additions" to the postface. That postface appears to cite HS 30.1721. For further information regarding the postface, see Thern 1966; Greatrex 1994 (passim).

26 The "tallies" that were seen as revelations from on high about dynastic changes employed "strange script." See *Qian Hanji*, 30.5b. Apparently, the calligraphic forms functioned during the transition from Western to Eastern Han (and long afterwards) in a manner akin to the so-called "cloud writing" of Daoism, which supposedly can be read only by Transcendents. For examples of "cloud writing," see Little et al. 2000. Andrew Colvin 2001: 42-45 discusses "Tokens for the Mandate" (*fuming* 符命) within the late Western Han court context.

27 *Huayang guozhi*, 10A.533.

claim one special aspect of Yang Xiong's writing to be its inclusion of *qizi*;[28] fifth, that interest in strange characters was on the rise, thanks to the works of the two contemporaries Du Lin 杜林 (d. 33 BC) and Yang Xiong;[29] and sixth, that the author of the "Treatise on Literature" deemed the ability to recognize and then decipher these individual antique characters the key to understanding the subtle meaning of the Five Classics.[30] Furthermore, at the end of the first century BC, fine calligraphy was still not yet taken to be the transparently "readable" sign of the gentlemen, so office-holders routinely ordered scribes to draft and brush their documents for them.[31] Therefore, it seems clear enough that the study of *qizi* cannot be reduced to a schoolboy's exercise in rudimentary literacy, but instead it must refer to a form of adult training in one of the most demanding prerequisites for substantive erudition in the pre-Qin Classics.

A word of caution: a total of six short passages in extant pre-Tang texts mention *qizi*, invariably in connection with Five Classics learning, with five of those six essentially repeating the elliptical phrasing of *Hanshu* 30. In light of the skimpy evidence, one is forced to admit to informed speculation when trying to piece parts of the historical puzzle together, so as to avoid the utter bafflement induced by the reflexive adoption of the conventional renderings for *xiaoxue* and *qizi,* a bafflement experienced by all earlier scholars when confronted with, to take but one example, the postface to the *Shuowen.* A close reading of all the early sources lends itself to the conclusion that knowledge of both *xiaoxue* and *qizi* or "strange characters" – mentioned already in connection with Yang's distinctive style of writing – corresponds to the very highest level of learning and cultivation, in the view of Han thinkers and historians identified with the *haogu* movement, and it forms the basis for their preferred methodological approaches, as argued below.

---

28 One Southern Song authority on script styles, Dai Si 戴侗, author of the *Liu shu gu* 六書故, characterized several of Yang's writings in this way. See *Liu shu gu* 6.14b [E-Siku]: 司馬子長[=Sima Xiangru] 揚子雲 [Yang Xiong] 皆好奇字. 故其辭賦太玄法言多奇字而不適於用. 予所不取也.

29 See Bottéro 2003 for details.

30 HS 30.1721.

31 Nylan 2001 (passim).

YANG THE HISTORIAN

In line with the strong historicizing impulses of his era, Yang Xiong sought to define himself as a "praise and blame" historian on the model of Confucius. For example, Yang's *Hanshu* biography, based on his autobiography, gives this account of the circumstances leading to the compilation of the *Fayan*:

> 故人時有問雄者，常用法應之，譔以為十三卷，象論語，號曰法言。
>
> Whenever people came to pose questions of Yang, he would invariably use a method [of reading history] to answer them, and thus he came to compose the thirteen *juan* of the book made in the image of the *Analects* that is entitled *Exemplary Figures*.[32]

While no one today places Yang Xiong in a long line of eminent "praise and blame" historians, that great Tang historian Liu Zhiji 劉知繼 compared Yang's writings on history, which for Liu included the *Taixuan* and the *Fayan*, to his own project.[33] Much closer to Yang's era, Wang Chong testified to the existence of a chronicle compiled by Yang for the reigns of the Han emperors from Xuandi to Pingdi (r. 1 BC-AD 5). The chronicle was to serve the court as a continuation of Sima Qian's monumental work[34] and the Ban family in Eastern Han presumably consulted copies of these chronicles (now lost) when compiling their history, the *Hanshu*.[35] Echoes of Yang's *Fayan*

---

32 HS 87B.3580. Knechtges' translation, cited as DRK, puts this in the first-person, rather than the third, on the assumption that Yang's autobiography is still being cited here.

33 See *Shitong*, 10.264-66; where Liu compares his own work to that of Yang in four respects. Cf. 12.306, where Liu Xin and Yang Xiong are singled out for condemnation for their "praise of false Xin" [i.e., Wang Mang], which deluded many who came later. See also Ren Naiqiang's comments to *Huayang guozhi* 10.543, n. 3.

34 *Lunheng* 60/263/4. Wang, of course, revered the man he called "Master Yang" more than Kongzi or Mencius.

35 HHS 40A.1324. The Li Xian 李賢 (Tang) commentary says Yang was one of the writers.

evaluations also pervade many chapter appraisals in the *Hanshu*,[36] and in describing the state of historical studies in their own day, the Bans likened Sima Qian and Yang Xiong to "the Yellow and Han Rivers" – i.e., the two great sources from which there flowed all streams.[37]

The continued coupling of the names of Sima Qian and Yang Xiong in the post-Han period almost certainly owes a great deal to Yang's decision to champion Sima Qian's work as a "true record" at a time when it was barely in circulation, even at the Han court.[38] For the concision of Yang's historical evaluations in the *Fayan* and elsewhere presents a stark contrast to the lengthy judgments recorded in Sima Qian's *Shiji*. Yang felt Sima Qian's full-length treatments of exemplary figures, good and bad, far too sympathetic to the morally dubious characters among them. This probably spurred Yang to compose for a host of historical figures the pithiest of final judgments only one or two Chinese characters in length – judgments that in many cases reversed those offered in the *Shiji*.[39] Many of Yang's historical evaluations anticipate Ban Gu's "Tables of Men, Ancient and Recent," or the "Pure Talk" (*qingtan* 清談) epigrams so admired by the leading figures populating the fifth-century *Shishuo xinyu* 世說新語, but, far more importantly, these brief but unambiguous pronouncements show Yang's unwavering support for dovish policies, periodic land-redistribution schemes, and low taxation rates on peasant households.

Yang Xiong's mature writing, focused though it was on deliberate narratives of actual events, lest his followers be misled by "empty words" detached from human realities,[40] was married to his delight in beauty and stylistic rigor. Yang's motivations in writing history, as in writing everything else, seem to have been complex, particularly in light of the loss of so many of his historical pronouncements and allusions. Yang's construction of the Qin First Emperor as double for Han Wudi drastically revised earlier

---

36 Examples include FY 11/19 and HS 76.3239; HS 72.3057, citing FY 8/25, 6/19; HS 74.3144 and FY 10/27. I am indebted to L'Haridon 2006: vol. 1, 209-30, for these references.

37 *Lunheng* 83/361/20.

38 FY 10/30. See Yang Haizheng 2003: 21-31.

39 Nonetheless, Yang expressed disdain for Sima Qian's "penchant for the strange" (*ai qi* 愛奇). See HS 80.3324. And while FY 10/30, for example, associates Sima Qian's work with the *Zhouguan* (i.e., *Zhouli*) and the *Zuozhuan*, Yang was generally distressed by Sima Qian's cavalier attitude toward the Classics.

40 SJ 130.3297, citing Dong Zhongshu (in a passage that appears in *Chunqiu fanlu*, "Yu xu" (6.780B).

assessments of these two larger-than-life rulers, setting the tone for later treatments of the centralizing program of the Qin and early Western Han rulers.[41] With equal force, Yang laid out the unmistakable outline of a program of institutional reforms that closely followed the Mencian prescriptions for benevolent government.[42] To bolster such reforms, Yang's "imitations of the Ancients" were designed to help those with the requisite cultural sophistication and access to power or wealth to reinvent themselves and their society.[43] Yang's writings in conscious emulation of the Ancients, along with his philological work, should not be equated with impulses toward nostalgia, let alone antiquarianism;[44] his contributions to classical learning lent color and substance to the post-Han discussions of the Classics and para-canonical works. Nonetheless, not long after Yang, settled convention virtually required a person to measure himself and others against the magnificent example of the Ancients, especially when judging the quality of a set of writings. After all, such comparisons between past and present allowed the wise person both to "see himself" and "make himself seen" (*zijian* 自見).[45]

Background to the *Haogu* Movement

Before late Western Han the courts of the powerful had been unabashedly enamored of the new. In the dominant discourse, new institutions and policy proposals had to be created for the new realities of the

---

[41] For the late Western Han construction of the First Emperor, see Nylan (forthcoming-d). Critics of Wudi, such as Ji An, complained that Wudi had written a solemn "hymn" not in honor of the ancestors or to promote moral suasion, but in celebration of pride of possession, after Wudi acquired a fine horse. Also, Li Yannian 李延年, Music Master under Wudi, introduced seventy singers and dancing girls into the State Sacrifice ceremony. All these offended Yang's sense of propriety.

[42] See, e.g., FY 9/25, for taxation measures.

[43] This is the argument made by Zhiyi Yang in her unpublished dissertation prospectus (2009) at Princeton University.

[44] Nostalgia (*huaigu*) is mentioned first in connection with failed aspirations, in YTL 5.1/29/9: 懷古道而不能行 (said of both Kongzi and Mozi).

[45] See, e.g., HS 62:2733 (吾何以自見於後世哉). Thanks to Owen 1992: 59, we see this motif in later authors, including Cao Pi. Cf. 聖人執一, 以為天下牧. 不自是故彰, 不自見故明, 不自伐故功... 夫唯不爭, 故莫能與之爭.

newly centralized empire laying claim to vastly more territory than any of the old pre-Qin states. Frequent wars, population transfers, treason trials, as well as the imposition of unified weights and measures and a single script for bureaucratic purposes[46] – all these threatened massive disorientation. This the Han court initially proposed to ameliorate by reorienting society, under its supposedly beneficent lead, to the public good (*gong* 公).[47] By late Western Han, however, many in the court were in sympathy with Yang's contention that aspects of highly centralized rule had actually undercut the Han throne's ties to its subjects, thereby alienating local populations and calling the very legitimacy of the dynasty into question.[48] The wars of expansion and the steady proliferation of imperial cults had proven ruinously expensive, and extra taxes and labor services had burdened the poorest in the land. If the Liu clan was to continue in power, it had to staunch the flow of imperial spending, even in the all-important state affairs of "war and sacrifice."[49] Frugality was firmly (if erroneously) associated in the *haogu* reformers' minds, if not in the standard rhetorical handbooks, with a return to earlier and supposedly simpler times.[50] As the extravagant forms of public display, inherited from earlier aristocratic eras, were draining the resources of the relatively cash-strapped throne in late Western Han, why not compensate for the privy purse's lack of cash by the creation of additional cultural capital? The construction of the emperor as scholar and evaluator of old texts, even the dynasty's collecting and sponsoring of Five Classics learning – these were relatively inexpensive ways to assert the court's preeminence. Hence the

---

46 Here, of course, I allude to the likelihood that the "modern" clerical script forms were employed mainly for bureaucratic purposes, as there is increasing evidence for the continuation of non-standard scripts in the Qin, Han, and post-Han periods. See Galambos 2006.

47 In writing this, I have thought of Berry 2006. Note that Yang is profoundly uninterested in the rhetoric of *gong* vs. *si* 私. Wolfgang Bauer 1976: 89, speaks of the "sense of intimacy due to the smallness of a single state" giving place "overnight to the feeling that one was living in a gigantic dominion governed by a distant capital... which continued to expand."

48 For Gan Zhongke, probably the best source remains Arbuckle 1995. For Yi Feng's memorial (48 BC) to move the capital, see the Loewe 2000 entry on Yi.

49 See *Zuo*, Lord Cheng 13, for the identification of "war and sacrifice" as the two main matters of state.

50 Yang's memorial on the Xiongnu is entirely pertinent here (see above); as are his remarks on the futility of the northern and southern campaigns (FY 13/29-30).

concerted efforts to portray good emperors as scholar-arbiters of the allied fields of Classics and history.[51]

None at court would have dared to register blanket opposition to centralized rule. Many, moreover, would have found such a notion unthinkable, as suggested by the degree to which the *haogu* reformers identified early Western Zhou rule as unified rule under strong kings who forged lasting ties with their underlings throughout the realm. Certainly, Yang Xiong publicly applauded the throne's grand ambitions to nearly universal sway.[52] Like the other *haogu* reformers, he simply asked what would make for long-lasting achievements and continued dynastic legitimacy, portraying retrenchment as a better option than continuing as before. However conservative the *haogu* movement's calls for a return to earlier models of good government and reduction in administrative expenses appeared to be, it was more radical in the boldness of its arguments for technical refinements in reading and writing, and for new ways of looking at the past.[53]

Yang Xiong entered court at a time when knowledge of the Classics had long been seen as one qualification for office-holding, even if birth and connections played greater roles in selections for prestigious posts.[54] All manner of polemical pieces, official pronouncements, and policy proposals alluded, if sometimes perfunctorily, to the Classics. Still, classical learning before Yang's era had been too often employed in the prosecution of treason

---

[51] We see these efforts on display in HS 88.3589-92; HHS 79A.3545-46.

[52] FY 13/25, for example, says, "Han rule – how truly cherished' it may be said to be! From south of Huangzhi and west of Daxia, in Dongti, and Beinü: all come [to the Han court] bringing rare items as tribute." Cf. HS 87A.3523, where Yang, in the "Sweet Springs *fu*" (and with predictable hyperbole), compares the Han house with the Three Lords and the Five Sovereigns, or HS 87A.3533-34, which compares the emperor to high Heaven.

[53] To give one example: many, including Yang, supported Wang Mang's call for the "restoration" of a well-field system that would effectively abolish private landholding, the most important form of wealth in Han, in return for greater income equality among Han's subjects and more secure tax revenues for the court. Michael Loewe 1974, therefore talks of the "modernists" (i.e., those who refused to look back) and "reformers" (those who would correct a degenerate present with the models of an idealized past).

[54] By a legend recorded in *Mozi* 83/47/33, the Duke of Zhou read every morning 100 *pian* of documents. Similar claims are made of the First Emperor of Qin, though there no suggestion is made that he read anything else but administrative documents. Note also that the phrase "a hundred" often means just "a great many."

trials or in portent interpretation.[55] A few portent specialists were even manipulating hallowed interpretive traditions to predict the imminent collapse of the dynasty.[56] Yang Xiong despised as mere "clerks" and hacks the *wenli* 文吏 in their judicial posts, and he advised followers to look to the society, not to the stars, for guidance in their deliberations.[57] Fortunately for Yang, the word *xue* 學 ("study" or "learning") still retained a whiff of its old flavor of "emulation," in addition to "learning to govern" or "learning a special technique" (e.g., swordplay, dice, or divining).[58] The concept *xue* extended to emulation of a master or model,[59] not just "studying" texts, even the texts of the Classics and masterworks.

But Yang's sort of generalized complaints about the supposed failures of the classicists at court might never have gained traction, leading to the development of a coherent *haogu* program, had it not been for the chance discoveries of pre-Qin bronzes – usually thrown up by natural disasters that made them seem doubly portentous and urgent. The seal script inscriptions on these bronzes could no longer be deciphered, let alone parsed. One spare account in the dynastic history of a find made near the capital a few decades before Yang's arrival at court reveals the predicament that each new find of undecipherable inscription must have posed to the court classicists charged with knowing the past, especially its rites and music:

> 是時美陽得鼎，獻之。下有司議，多以為宜薦見宗廟，如元鼎時故事。

---

[55] As late as 18 BC, Zhai Fangjin 翟方進, a classicist, won renown (or notoriety?) for his prosecution of thousands in Changling, an imperial mausoleum town, after which he was promoted to Capital Intendant. See Liu Rulin, *Han Jin xueshu biannian*, II, 74.

[56] For Gan Zhongke, see Arbuckle 1995.

[57] See, e.g., FY 8/13-14.

[58] In Han times, fashionable people still read books and wielded swords; there was none of the later disparagement of the martial, exacerbated by the An Lushan Rebellion of 845. Yang Xiong's student, Huan Tan, wanted initially to study with him and another master, an expert in swordplay. See *Yilin* 3/10a. Huan Tan was hardly the only one to combine an interest in reciting texts and swordplay, as this is reported of Jing Ke and Sima Xiangru as well (SJ 86.325; SJ 57.2529). Liu An, King of Huainan, took an interest in reciting texts and playing the *qin*; by contrast, he was uninterested in hunting and other more conventional pursuits of the nobility.

[59] *Zuozhuan*, Lord Xiang 31.12. Note that the same word is used for the private school house (*jingshe* 精舍) and "meditation chamber," just as the same word (*di zi* 弟子 serves equally well for "disciple" or "student," or for "client" and "retainer." For example, see HHS 67.2215, speaking of Tan Fu 檀敷 (fl. ca. AD 150) in Shandong.

> At this time [ca. 51 BC], at Meiyang [part of Fufeng county, in the capital district], they found a tripod, which was duly presented to the throne. The emperor ordered his officials to discuss it at court. The majority thought it ought to be presented to the ruling line's ancestral temple, since this had been done with a similar artifact during Wudi's reign.

Zhang Chang 張敞, then Governor of the Metropolitan District and one of the few early experts in the *Cang Jie pian*, a word list composed (at least partly) in pre-Qin script,[60] "was fond of reading archaic script characters," and so he tried to read the inscription. He believed it had to do with the founding of the Zhou dynasty, an event worthy of such commemoration, which supposedly took place near the Han capital of Chang'an. He then took the inscription to read:

> 王命尸臣官此栒邑，賜爾旂鸞黼黻琱戈。尸臣拜手稽首曰「敢對揚天子丕顯休命。」

> The King orders the official in charge to make his office at Xun City [near Bin, the ancient Zhou capital]. The king confers the official banners depicting the *luan* bird; ceremonial robes with ax designs on them; and spears with engraved designs. The official in charge, in accepting the king's decree, said, "I make bold to carry out the grand decrees of the Son of Heaven."

Zhang apologized to the throne for his inadequate understanding of archaic script, but it seemed to him that this tripod in all likelihood commemorated the Zhou rulers' decision to reward a high-ranking official, and that the official's sons and grandsons had had the tripod cast to honor their ancestor's merit, in which case the tripod originally would have been stored in that family's ancestral temple.[61]

---

[60] HS 30.1721 reports that the *Cang Jie* had "many old characters" (with "old" almost certainly meaning "pre-Qin"). It also reports Yang Xiong's activities in expanding the classic.

[61] HS 25B.1251.

Finds like these continued in Yang's own era, including a remarkable cache of sixteen old musical chime-stones (*qing* 磬) during Chengdi's reign, widely hailed as highly auspicious.[62] Since the pre-Qin bronze inscriptions were typically regarded as omens delivered by Heaven to the throne, and Yang Xiong was regarded as an authority on omen interpretation,[63] Yang in company with the other members of the court must have been alive to the new possibilities of reading the distant past via pre-Qin inscriptions.[64] Yang could hardly *not* formulate a response to such discoveries, especially when he was among the scholars selected by the Han throne to revise thc imperial holdings for the new imperial library, and moreover commissioned to summarize the results of a state-sponsored conferences sparked by the pre-Qin writings.[65] In addition, Yang was known to have received expert training from several Shu masters in the reading of "strange scripts."[66] The result: Yang, along with several of his most learned peers, a group that included his mentor Liu Xiang and his part-time rival Liu Xin, set out to devise the "most reliable, upright, and good method" to decipher classical texts so as to emulate the Ancients; they intended to put to good use their knowledge of

---

62 *Quan Hou Zhou wen,* 6/4b ("Yi biao" 遺表); *Quan Hou Wei wen*, 21/10a-b (上表乞定樂舞名). Nor should one forget the 102 *pian* version of the *Documents* produced by one Zhang Ba 張霸, in response to Chengdi's call for genuinely old versions of the Classics; this version was pronounced a forgery by Chengdi's librarians. See HS 3607.

63 Readers will recall that earlier Yang was identified as an expert in omens.

64 FY 2/11 praises the *Cang Jie pian*, for example. Other early traditions make Yang a devotee of the *Erya* (see below), as in *Huayang guozhi* 10A.533.

65 See Greatrex 1994, which notes that a *Cang Jie xun zuan* 訓纂 written by Yang Xiong, was the product of a court conference convened in AD 5 by Wang Mang in the Weiyang Hall (Weiyang ting); this conference was attended by over a hundred scholars, according to Xu Shen's preface to the *Shuowen.* Yang Xiong reportedly removed the repetitions from the *Cang Jie pian* and added a further thirty-four sections, so the *Xunzuan pian* amounted to eighty-nine sections, containing 5,340 characters. (The work is no longer extant.) That this work was designed to consider pronunciation and semantic issues occasioned by the transition from pre-imperial scripts to clerical script seems clear from Bottero 2003. It seems that when the *Shuowen* talks of the *Cang Jie*, it is this revised version of which it speaks, rather than the original. A Han find of a *Cang Jie* shows it to have used 7-character phrases instead of 4-character phrases. See Zhang Cunliang and Wu Hong 2009; Zhang Shichao 2009.

66 FY 6/19 and 11/23, discuss these masters. For Yang Xiong and Du Lin as major figures in the reading of *gu* 古 ("ancient") script, see HS 30.1721. The same passage names Yang as a specialist in the *Shi Zhou pian* 史籀篇 (cf. FY 2/11), a word list that, like the Han *Cang jie*, reportedly contained "many old script" characters, presumably of seal script.

the pre-Qin writings,[67] as well as their privileged access to old texts and archaic scripts.[68] (Their general preoccupation was with old scripts. Only Liu Xin was singularly enamored of *some* parts of what is now anachronistically dubbed the Old Text corpus.)[69]

The *haogu* movement offered itself as a viable alternative and an implicit rebuff to the reigning culture of learning at the court.[70] In company with other formidably learned *haogu* reformers, Yang queried the common wisdom that piling up pseudo- and para-classical texts would reveal the essential meaning of the Five Classics. He, in company with Liu Xin, alleged that in blessed antiquity the Classics were routinely mastered without the aid of massive annotations.[71] After all, Kongzi himself had preserved the *texts* and *meaning* of the Classics, but he did not do much explaining of the texts.[72] With seeming innocence, Yang Xiong joked that were the greatest exemplars of antiquity like Kongzi to return to life at the Han court, they would either flunk their "Class A" exams or join the miserable ranks of "candidates awaiting appointment," if they were lucky enough not to be dismissed outright.[73]

Echoing the complaints of Liu Xin, Yang insisted that the Academicians, acting like "clerks and scribes," wanted at all costs "to protect

---

67 FY 1/22.

68 FY 4/12.

69 This important distinction continues to elude some early China historians. See, e.g., Sukhu 2005.

70 The standard narrative makes Wudi's reign the start of the classical learning movement. It is possible that Yang Xiong was invited to court as much because he was student of Yan Junping (i.e., Zhuang Zun) as because of his remarkable abilities in writing *fu*. Neither possibility excludes the other. See HS 72.3056, which seems to attribute an interest in Yan's teachings during Chengdi's reign at the court; moreover, a member of the Wang family (early patrons of Yang Xiong) was an early patron of a person associated with Yan.

71 For Liu Xin, see HS 30.1723. For the *Fayan*, a time period of three years is also mentioned. While the *haogu* advocates had been gaining strength since 48 BC, one of the strongest opening salvos came in 28 BC, when Wang Feng sharply lambasted the King of Dongping for his request of the emperor to see the works by the various masters and by Sima Qian. Wang argued that not all the masterworks were the works of sages; some discussed topics best ignored (e.g., the spirits, strategic locations of the realm); and many enjoined the sort of thinking employed by the Zhanguo strategists-for-hire. By contrast, the Classics were all the works of the sages, and they covered every conceivable topic. See Liu Rulin 1935: vol. 2, 54-55.

72 Thern, ii.

73 HS 87B.3570. For the Grade "A" exams, see HS 88.3596; those candidates were tested by the *taichang* 太常, the minister for rituals.

the flawed and deficient readings" in order to support their interpretations. He therefore reserved his sharpest attacks for the unthinking court officials who considered the Academicians "the most broadly learned scholars of the age."[74] From the Qin dynasty onwards, the Academicians had merely "maintained their own families' theories," he said, neglecting their other duties "to set out the ritual platters and vessels" for the rites of the Confucian Way.[75] In Yang Xiong's day, as readers will recall, the Academicians tended to be appointed according to their allegiance to particular *shuo*, rather than to particular *jing*, and in the eyes of the *haogu* reformers, the correlation between career advancement and expertise in a *shuo* diluted the impact of the "core" texts on cultivation.[76] Accordingly Yang joined Liu Xin in calling for a strict mental separation between texts and their associated traditions, in part to prevent the gradual submersion of the *jing* 經 (the core texts) in the ever-accumulating piles of *shuo* 說 (explanations).

The *haogu* reformers proposed several constructive solutions for this regrettable situation. Liu Xin asked the court to insist that its Academicians avail themselves of a handful of writings transmitted in earlier script forms, even if newer recensions of the same texts employed modern script.[77] The

---

[74] HS 36.1970-71. According to Liu Xin (HS 30.1969), only Jia Yi 賈誼 (200-168) was worthy of the name of "classicist" (Ru). The lowest rung was occupied by the *wenli* 文吏 (the scribes and functionaries who kept the penal system functioning). This accusation occasioned such enmity at court that Liu Xin feared he would be charged with a capital crime, unless he took measures to leave the court for a time. See HS 36.1972; Knechtges 1977: 312. For Academicians "in the "family business" of transmitting texts as a private money-making venture (*jia fa* 家法), see Li Qing 2003:235ff.

[75] See "Boshi jian," in Li Zhen'ai 2001:305-8. The first line translated here (*jia yan shi shou* 家言是守) could conceivably mean "preserved the [inferior] talk of the technical experts," but that seems unlikely. See below.

[76] Of course, each *shuo* had its own textual history, but, generally speaking, far less was known about the individual histories of the *shuo* than about components of the Five Classics corpus.

[77] For Liu Xin's famous "Letter Addressed to the Academicians," see HS 36. 1967-71. Much of Liu Xin's letter presents a narrative that is undoubtedly wrong. For example, he argues that until the time of Huidi (r. 195-88 BC), aside from *Changes* divinations, there "were no other texts" (p. 1968); he also cites the very dubious story of finding "archaic script" texts in the wall of the former house of Kongzi. The context for that letter is Liu's perception (shared by Yang Xiong) of widespread attacks on classical learning either as "useless" or a form of technical knowledge of limited utility. But a great many Han scholars did not agree with Liu Xin, as can be seen from the Preface to the *Shuowen* (Thern 1966: 15): "Many people, however, reject [this story about texts like the *Zuo*]. They consider them curiosity-hunters, who have intentionally and cunningly altered normal forms, and cut

response from the throne and the Academicians was predictably hostile. Liu Xiang spent the last years of his life implementing quite another strategy, that of activist editing, though we cannot know what hermeneutical principles he invoked when deciding to excise passages and occasionally entire texts from the record.[78] Yang Xiong proposed an alternative strategy: that his followers commit to a set of reading practices capable of fostering a common set of values or orientations.[79] The key thing was to spend more time in reading the Classics, until one became cognizant of the special pleasures that they offered. Yang boasted that there was hardly a book that he had not read,[80] and extraordinarily wide-ranging reading was a requirement for those who would cleanse the pre-Qin writings of the numerous flaws, interpolations, and lacunae the texts had acquired as they "were copied over and over again and passed down through the generations."[81] Accordingly, Yang Xiong's ideal lover of antiquity would be well-versed in the many "arts" (*yi* 藝), meaning the Classics, and conversant with the *Erya*, a lexicon organized by synonyms and written, at least partly, in archaic script.[82] Still, broad learning had to go hand-in-hand with a rigorous selectivity in choosing among the

---

windows in the walls [of Kongzi's house] to fake unintelligible books." Françoise Bottéro 2003 shows that Sima Xiangru's *Fanjiang pian* was the first text to give only the "archaic script" (*guwen*) characters, while suppressing alternate forms.

78 Centuries after Yang, at the end of Eastern Han, Zheng Xuan (127-200) would attempt to "correct" the Five Classics corpus: by contrasting and comparing the language of the disparate parts of the whole corpus, and by "taking the best readings of various schools and rejecting the rest." Zheng forced the Classics (especially the three ritual classics) into a unitary framework, in hopes of forging a unified moral system. See Wagner 2000: 42.

79 As Yang explains it, in HS 87B.3565, under the troubles when the "Ding and Fu clans and Dong Xian controlled affairs of state," he kept busy drafting the *Taixuan* "as a means to keep to myself and remain tranquil" despite misrule. That Yang also had a "sabbatical" under Chengdi, when he was allowed to forsake his usual duties at court, also speaks volumes. After Yang's death, the Eastern Han throne found it convenient to predicate some of its claims to legitimacy on such textual "restorations," though books of any sort, whether manuscript or printed, were as likely to reinforce regional identities as to subvert them. One wonders, then, if the push to accept "archaic texts" was not a way of leapfrogging over regionally-based scholastic lineages of interpretation, in the belief that the distant past was less disunified and more coherent than the multiple recent traditions better known to scholars of the day.

80 HS 87A.3514: "I read quickly; there is nothing I have not seen."

81 A saying from *Yanshi jiaxun,* 30.305.

82 See, e.g., FY 2/9, 5/11, 5/17, 5/21, 5/27. For the citation, see Sun Xingyan, *Han guan liu yi*, item 4.3 citing *Han guan jiu* yi, item 3.3, where this is said of the ideal Academician. Since the *Erya* was a Han text, during Han it must have included characters in the pre-Qin script forms, if this statement is reliable.

various early traditions in writing. By composing neoclassical and lexicographical works, one would prove the wisdom of one's choices in reading. Yang saw himself more as a reader than a listener, and it is a course of reading that he consistently urges upon his readers.[83] That Yang's own later readers fully grasped the main thrust of his proposals is clear from Lu Zhaolin's 盧照鄰 (638?-84?) lyrical evocation, "Silent and lonely is the place where Yang Xiong lived/ Over the years, nothing left but a bedful of books."[84] Largely thanks to Yang, the reciting of texts, once a form of public performance at ceremonial banquets, funerals, and sacrifices, gradually came to be regarded as a form of welcome refreshment for the spirit.[85]

Since the ultimate persuasiveness of any strategy depends in part upon the appeal of its rallying cries, Yang Xiong must have been a brilliant tactician, for it was he (if Fukui Shigemasa is correct) whose writings coined the term "Five Classics,"[86] the rubric that neatly substituted for the notion of competing interpretive traditions backed by rival factions the idea of a cohesive corpus that would promote unified empire. Yang pressed the point that Five Classics learning lent a writer that "perfection of eloquence" that was quadruply powerful, being a convergence of all the best that could be achieved in the rhetorical, imaginative, political, and moral realms.[87] Yang compared the Five Classics to high mountain ranges that inspired awe, to high towers permitting wider vistas, to the profundity of seas, to the sun and moon in their dazzling incandescence, and, perhaps most movingly, to warm and sensuous furs that keep off the chill of winter. For Yang, the "really

[83] Kern 2003: 428.

[84] From Lu's "Chang'an: Ancient Theme" (Chang'an guyi 長安古意), 2.73.

[85] As the CHANT e-database shows, the Rites canons mainly discuss *dushu* 讀書 ("reciting texts," and only later reading them silently) in the context of ceremonial banquets, funerals, and sacrifices. By Eastern Han, however, perusing texts (*lan shu* 覽書) was seen as a form of relaxation distinct from conducting the business of government. See *Quan Hou Hanwen* 50/8b (Li You 李尤, "Dushu zhenming" 讀書枕銘).

[86] Fukui Shigemasa 2005. However, perhaps Yang popularized rather than invented the term *wujing*, as the "Five Classics" corpus is mentioned in a letter attributed to Liu Xin. See the "Letters" in Knechtges 1977. Doubts have been raised about the authenticity of that letter (and Yang's return letter), but both Serruys and Knechtges believe the two letters are genuine. The predecessors of the *haogu* reformers, including Kuang Heng, were still talking in 46 and 36 BC of the Six Arts (*liu yi* 六藝), not the Five Classics. See Liu Rulin 1935: vol. 2, 25, 44.

[87] For example, the Kongzi of the *Analects* insisted that the student or learner, upon completion of his learning, should apply himself to the task of securing an official post. See *Analects* 9/13. Cf. Fischer 2003: 45.

eloquent disputations" of the Five Classics were a virtual feast for the ears and eyes, even as they served the supremely pragmatic function of acquainting the attentive reader with all the significant prospects of the human and cosmic realms ("Were we to discard these texts, all disputation in rhetoric would become paltry affairs.").[88] Meanwhile Yang argued cogently, if quietly – never pressing the point beyond what was seemly – that his own philosophical masterworks merited consideration as a variation on the Five Classics corpus.[89] After all, he had presented a supremely cultivated form of homage to the Ancients that offered all the enticements of an intriguing game, in hopes that his rhetoric's exegetical functions might finally dislodge the error-ridden oral traditions promoted by the Academicians.[90]

To elevate the Five Classics, Yang's *Fayan* presumes to assess the real strengths and weaknesses of various works deemed "classics" by Yang's peers, including some of his disciples. These books included the *Laozi*, the *Zhuangzi*, the *Lüshi chunqiu*, *Huainanzi*, the *Shiji*, the *Cycles of the Yellow Emperor* 黃帝終始, and the poetic works attributed to Qu Yuan, as well as such military classics as the *Sunzi bingfa* and two works (now lost) entitled the *Swordmen's Treatise* 劍客論 and *Models for the Colonel* 司馬兵法. Some texts accorded the title of "classic" Yang rejected on the grounds that they focused on topics too unimportant or that their style was prolix or insufficiently grave.[91] Other works he discarded on the grounds of the author's personal failings (the book being a stand-in for the author in Yang's view), as with the poems ascribed to the suicide Qu Yuan. Still other candidates for the status of "classic" Yang disdained because they promoted anti-social or self-destructive behavior.

---

88 FY 7/5. The most common Han gloss for *li* 禮("rites") is *ti* 體 ("embodiment"). The character *zhi* 志 (here, "the heart's affects") covers everything felt in the heart. By "affects" I mean "the affections," "commitments," and "aspirations." The "Yaodian" cites the phrase 詩言志, as does the *Odes*, in order to describe the effective power of music. See *Shangshu tongjian* 020681.

89 FY 2/10; cf. HS 87B.3566-67. HS 87B.3570, 3572, has Yang comparing himself to the most illustrious ministers of the past. *Wenxin diaolong* 10.2/98/9 (Shih, p. 357), says of Yang that he "may be deemed the most profound [of writers], both in the language he employs and in the themes he treats. His ability to couch his brilliant thought in firm language is due to his sagacious and profound ideas, to his relentless search for wondrous and beautiful expressions; and to his untiring effort to think things through." He is, in other words, a sage.

90 Cf. Lee 2007, which argues that the imitation genres in the Six Dynasties had commentarial and exegetical functions.

91 Numerous passages in the FY excoriate these masters; see, e.g., FY 3/20, 4/6, 4/25, etc.

But most of the books which Yang refused to accord canonical status lacked, in his opinion, either the Five Classics' insistent focus on social refinement and self-fashioning or a comparably reliable and accurate account of things as they really are. As Yang concluded his list of works to be downgraded (though he was then speaking more narrowly of the *fu*), "I saw that the various masters all used their knowledge to gallop off in different directions.... Some engaged in strange convolutions, with hairsplitting arguments and paradoxical language that sowed confusion in the affairs of this world."[92] Thus to "restore" the pre-eminence of the Five Classics corpus – in fact, to elevate the Five Classics for the first time above other rival classics and masterworks – became one of the avowed goals of the *haogu* movement leaders.[93]

Liu Xin, in a letter to Yang Xiong, spoke of yet another strategy that in retrospect seems central not only to the larger *haogu* movement, but to Yang's individual projects as well. Supposedly, Liu Xin's father before his demise had proposed to "correct" the Classics using the *Erya*.[94] On apprising

---

[92] HS 87B.3580; DRK 56 (slightly mod.).

[93] See Nylan 2008, which emphasizes the usual (and continuing) importance during Han of the other classics, as compared to the Five Classics.

[94] For the letter, see Eva Chung 1982: 482-95. If the exchange of letters by Liu Xin and Yang Xiong is genuine (see above), this is the earliest reference to the *Erya*, which was right then gaining immense stature, as the possible work of the Duke of Zhou. Another early attribution of the *Erya* to the Duke is by the fifth-century commentator Zhang Yi, in *Huang Qing jingjie*, 667A/1a-2a. (For the dating of the *Erya* compilation, see n. 96 below.)

Yang's attempt to use the lexicon to "correct the Classics" may have provided the model for Yan Zhitui's (531-95) later call to use the Five Classics texts and interpretations based on a more recent wordlist, Xu Shen's 許慎 Eastern Han *Shuowen* (comp. ca. 100), in*Yanshi jiaxun*, 17.305 ("Shu zheng" 書證). In Yan's view, the SW was touted as even older and more authoritative, because (a) all its characters were written in seal script (small seal); and (b) it gave etymologies for the characters (some of which we now deem to be wrong). As Yan writes, "Classical scholars of the past even changed the texts to fit their own interpretations – to say nothing of how difficult it was to avoid errors when the Classics were copied over and over again and passed down through the generations. I have never thought that the *Shuowen* was always right... But by and large I admire it as a book that corrects many mistakes, has reasonable organization, and ample examples; also, in its analyses, which frequently trace the meaning to its origin and exhaust the sources... If we do not follow the views in the *Shuowen*, we will then be in the dark with respect to graphs and will not know what a given dot or line signifies" (Teng, ii). The same presumptions underlay Wang Anshi's 王安石 (1021-86) commentaries to the Classics, to which he added his "Explanation of Characters" (Zishuo 字說), yet another etymological attempt to interpret the classics. Wang, often portrayed as a wild-eyed radical, intended to rigorously reinforce

Chengdi of his eagerness to undertake such a project, he found the emperor disinclined to spearhead a project that could potentially upend longstanding interpretive traditions.[95] If a later tradition can be trusted, Yang Xiong agreed with both Lius about the seminal importance of the *Erya*, believing that its ancient origin made it the right text "to correct the Six Arts [i.e., the Classics]." The *Xijing zaji* tells of a learned official who asked Yang Xiong about the dating of the *Erya* and its intended use. Yang allegedly replied,

> 子雲曰 孔子門徒游夏之儔所記, 以解釋六藝者也。...爾雅之出遠矣。
>
> This was recorded by the likes of Kong's followers Ziyou and Zixia, *in order to explain the Six Arts*....[As they say,] "The origins of the *Erya* are remote indeed!"[96]

---

the traditional exegesis style; transforming politics and ethics into a "unified moralistic system." See Mittag 1993: 215.

[95] Liu Xiang had been patron and supervisor to Yang Xiong, but the relationship between Liu Xin and Yang was considerably more fraught. *Huayang guozhi*, 10A.533, names Liu Xiang and Xin (father and son) and Huan Tan, "and others" as admirers of Yang's, but Liu Xin and Yang hardly saw eye to eye on a number of issues. For example, Wang Chong, *Lunheng* 13/37/25 reports that Liu Xin objected to those who would "reduce desires" (a slogan Yang borrowed from a Zhanguo master, according to FY 4/16. See also the sarcastic tone of the letters supposedly exchanged between Liu Xin and Yang Xiong, and translated in Knechtges 1977.

[96] *Xijing zaji* 3.96. Note that the final sentence does not appear in the current *Da Dai Liji,* contra the attribution to that book in *Xijing zaji.* Both Ziyou and Zixia were especially known for their learning (*wen xue* 文學, here taken as "study of graphs"), according to *Analects* 11/2b, and Sima Qian says of the *Chunqiu* that it is so perfect that Ziyou and Zixia could not have emended in it even a single phrase (SJ 47.1944: 游、夏之徒不能措一辭). In Han times, there circulated several stories about the origins of the *Erya*: that a three-*pian* (expanded) version of it had been produced by Kongzi, or by Zixia, or by Shusun Tong. Lu Deming 陸德明 (556-627), and the later Qing commentators on the *Jingdian shi* wen also presumed the *Erya* text to be a product of Wudi's time, if not earlier. Jiang Xia'an 1931: 163-64, also cited the *Da Dai Liji* passages quoted below, but that para-canonical work dates from late Western Han as well. Note: Some mistakenly attribute this reliance on the *Erya* by the better educated to Wudi's time, on the basis of SJ 24.1117, but there the term "erya" refers not to the book by that title, but to the style of lyrics ("approaching elegance") of the nineteen sacrificial hymns composed at that time.

To this author's mind, Zhou Zumo 1984 proved, beyond a reasonable doubt, that the text postdates Wudi's era, even if some modern scholars, most notably the linguist Xu Chaohua 徐朝華 in his Introduction to *Erya jin zhu*, resist Zhou's skeptical position and posit an earlier date of composition or compilation, citing the many variant traditions

Admittedly, the book in which this passage appears is a work of literary impersonation that dates to the early sixth century AD, centuries after Yang's era, yet it manages to capture the excitement engendered by lexicons, especially the *Erya*, which appeared at the Han court no earlier than Wudi's time, or even decades later.[97] The ritual classic, *Da Dai Liji*, a late Western Han compilation, describes the same lexicon with equal excitement:

> 爾雅以觀于古足以辨言矣。傳言以象. 反舌 [?= 古]. 皆至可謂簡矣。
>
> The *Erya* is the way to see what is ancient, such that it is surely sufficient to use to discern the proper phrasing. Its transmitted phrases employ images [whose graphic forms preserve older characters], which if then returned to the tongue (?), can all be deemed [marvelously] 'simple'![98]

Lexicons were the mainstay of "elementary learning" and philological training (both *xiaoxue* in Chinese), with the former the premier teaching tool for

---

regarding the date of compilation for the *Erya*, which include, for example, the extant version of the *Hanguan jiuyi* 3.3.1839/17, which alleges that during Wudi's reign, the highest ranks among tested applicants were given to those conversant with archaic writings and the *Erya*, who could then compose texts by weaving phrases (*shu wen* 屬文) together. For the trope of Yang answering difficult questions brought to him by scholars and officials, see HS 87B.3580.

[97] In addition, the modern experts Wu Xiaorun and Wu Tongbin 1982: 82-84, emphasize three points whose relevance will soon be apparent: (1) the striking similarities between the texts of the *Erya* and the *Fangyan*; (2) the fact that the *Fangyan* preserves "not a few" ancient expressions; and (3) that the present text of the *Fangyan* is definitely not the original version of the text.

[98] *Da Dai Liji* 11.1/65/2. This claim is introduced by the passage: "The Master said: 'To be discerning but not petty is the goal. Petty wording breaks the meaning; and petty meaning breaks the Way. Petty and minor ways are neither comprehensive nor wide-ranging enough. Comprehensive and wide-ranging ways must be exquisitely spare. This is why one follows the string [with the finger] in order to see the music; that is sufficient to discern the wind'" (子曰: 辨而不小.夫小辨破言, 小言破義, 小義破道. 道小不通,通道必簡. 是故循弦以觀於樂,足以辨風矣.). My translation must be tentative, because the phrase *fan she* 反舌 (here "returned to the tongue") usually appears as the name of a foreign polity or group. One wonders whether *fan she* could be a mistake for *fan gu* (反古), "return to antiquity," but the text seems to be corrupt.

those who would turn fine phrases. Until about Yang's time, however, no one seems to have upheld the tradition that Confucius employed one particular lexicon, the *Erya* written in pre-Qin script, "to explain the Six Arts" (i.e., the Five Classics plus the lost *Classic of Music*), though this belief became settled convention by Eastern Han.[99] Lexicons helped to define the classical corpus insofar as they drew upon a limited range of sources. The *haogu* reformers' main interest in lexicons rested on the belief that lexicons, painstakingly compiled and carefully digested, could elucidate age-old textual problems and restore integrity to the hermeneutical processes. Some lexicons were mere word lists with examples of contemporary usage, but the *haogu* reformers' attention was drawn to a single type of lexicon originally composed in archaic script, which grouped words by their underlying categorical connections, so as to reveal the deep structure of human society and the entire universe. Under Xuandi, in 51 BC, the court had summoned experts who supposedly knew the correct pronunciations for the "ancient characters" included in the *Cang Jie* 倉頡 primer,[100] causing a sensation in academic circles. And in AD 5, under the boy emperor Pingdi and his regent Wang Mang, over a hundred experts were summoned to the main imperial residence, the Weiyang Palace in the capital, to explicate the graphs in the same *Cang Jie*, which by this time, thanks to Yang's additions, numbered roughly 5,340 graphs.[101]

Meanwhile, Wang Mang and his circle of *haogu* supporters saw to it that teachers of the *Erya* received a special summons to take up office in the capital and interpret omens via the *Erya*.[102] Pingdi – or, more probably, Wang Mang – then assigned Yang the task of drawing up the final report on the teachers' findings, for Yang's studies had yielded at least three

---

[99] See *Lunheng* 52/256/6, which says that the *Erya* is the basis for explications of classical learning (爾雅之書, 五經之訓故), and a source badly neglected by ordinary classicists (Ru).

[100] See HS 30.1721 for further details; this presumably follows upon the Shiqu conference, as it was used to "correct the characters." This gives a variation on the story usually told of Yang Xiong's compilation methods for "strange" and "old" characters.

[101] HS 99A.4069 describes Wang Mang and the group promoting classical learning as issuing a special invitation (*gong che* 公車) to experts in the *Erya*, the *Shi Zhou pian*, and other Classics and para-canonical works to speak about their specialties; many subsequently traveled to the capital. A later entry, HS 99B.4161, speaks of courtiers interpreting omens in Wang Mang's favor according to the *Erya*. Cf. Wang Xianqian 99.9a-11a; Dubs, III, 239. It is certainly significant that HS 30.1718-19 puts the *Erya* in the same category as the Shiqu pavilion conference text.

[102] See n. 96 above.

lexicographical works, the compilation we now know under the title of *Fangyan* 方言 (usually translated as *Dialect Words*, but just as plausibly *Correct Words*);[103] a glossary; and a one-*pian* summary and expansion of the *Cang Jie*. The last two works are now lost, almost certainly because later scholars, including Xu Shen, built their own word lists and philological studies on Yang's efforts – and so obviated the need for anyone to preserve Yang's earlier and less complete versions.[104] Notably, Yang Xiong devoted some twenty-seven years to compiling lists of "obsolete expressions" and "regional languages"[105] – a figure that dwarfs the time spent on the two philosophical

---

[103] This comment recalls the HS 30.1718-19 gloss for *Erya* (to which the *Fangyan* is compared in *Huayang guozhi* 10A.533: "Approaching Correctness" (*jin zheng* 近正 [the Five Classics]), not "approaching elegance," as when the phrase describes Wudi's literary styles (see n. 88); *zheng* 正 is a standard gloss and even substitute for *ya* 雅 throughout the Han and post-Han Middle Period.

[104] Yang compiled, with "strange characters" (*qi zi* 奇字), the *Cang Jie xun zuan* 倉頡訓纂, whose significance is described in Greatrex 1994. Xie Qikun 謝啟昆, "Xiao xue kao" 小學考, in *Ershi wushi bubian*, vol. 2, 1578 (p. 54), writes of a one-*pian* analysis by Yang of the *Cang Jie* (a tradition or commentary) "Yang Xiong wrote out his [its?] ideas" (*shu qi yi* 書其意). Some time during Han the *Cang Jie*, originally composed of rhymed lines, four characters per line, was expanded to seven characters per line, and this expansion may relate to Yang's version, but we cannot say for sure. For further information, see Zhang Cunliang and Wu Hong 2010; also Zhang Shichao 2009; Kong Deming 2010: esp. 37, on Yang Xiong and Shu as a special linguistic area.

Later, no fewer than twenty-one scholars, including Ouyang Xiu, wrote a *yinyi* 音義 ("sound and meaning") guide to Yang's works, probably focusing on the *Fayan*. See Yan Lingfeng 1993: vol. 5, 323. Hand in hand with the compiling of lexicons of obsolete expressions went the ethnographic impulse, asking about the folk traditions that may have preserved earlier forms of learning. See HS 36.1970 for Liu Xin's discussion of this under Chengdi. For Du Ye's 杜鄴 (d. ca. 2 BC) work in lexicography and Wang Mang's interest in it, see Liu Rulin 1935: vol. 2, 128, 133.

[105] See the correspondence between Liu Hsin and Yang Xiong, trans. in Knechtges 1977; cf. Greatrex, "An Early Western Han Synonymicon." As Kenneth DeWoskin 1982: 57, n. 6, writes, "To the reader unfamiliar with the tradition of etymologizing in China, it may seem strange to look for historical clues by dissecting words. Reading history into the components of characters is a methodology in the native traditions of scholarship that goes back at least two thousand years.... Whether by modern standards their opinions can be sustained or not, their [the Han scholars'] writings on the etymology of a character ... [provides a way] of entering into their epistemological world." Ying Shao's preface to the *Fengsu tongyi* specifically mentions a work presumed to be the original *Fangyan* as preserving words from "different eras" (*yi dai* 異代). The preface to the *Fangyan* by Li Mengzhuan 李孟傳 (1140-1223) is particularly interesting, for it ties the composition of the *Fangyan* to all of Yang's other works, for philology and pre-Qin archaic script style: " and so the *Fangyan*

neoclassical works for which he is known today. This should give us some rough sense of the relative importance to Yang of "truths" garnered from etymology.

Since modern lexicographers generally put little faith in tracing words back to their origins, it behooves us to consider what Yang and his peers thought they were accomplishing by investing so much time and effort in that sort of project. Under the influence of what might be called an "etymological fallacy," the history of words – far from representing a neutral record of changes in meanings over time – took on the appearance of a full-blown narrative correlating different values with diachronic differences.[106] The *haogu* reformers hoped their research would recover at least traces of the pristine state of language, before misuse, dilutions, distortions, and inadvertent errors had corrupted it. This vision of prelapsarian truth closing the gap between sign and signifier exerted a powerful hold on the collective imaginations of the best scholars in Yang Xiong's day. In the view of the *haogu* reformers, both script and writing had the potential to become more than straightforward and efficient means of communication. Like the graphic symbols found in older texts, expressions from the peripheral places that were presumably more immune to the changing fashions than the polyglot metropolitan areas could serve as repositories of older meanings, which might then guide would-be reformers in restoring an Ur-language in its purest and most powerful form. (Paul Kroll has made the astute observation that Yang intended his philological works to function like an *Erya* 爾雅 in reverse: rather than listing the elevated expressions used in literary Chinese – virtually a foreign language to many Han subjects, Yang listed obsolete expressions and regional patois, both of which, he may have assumed, preserved still earlier forms of language anterior to the *Erya* itself.)[107] Yang and his peers would finally be "rectifying names" in the manner advised by Confucius – and on an unprecedented scale.[108] Yang's

---

generally makes understood strange characters 奇字, and the *Taixuan* generally deploys these in unusual language (奇語, possibly hapax). Still, when he, Yang, used these, each for its part was appropriate. When Yang Xiong composed his *fu*, they were replete with ancient graphs, but when it came to the *Fayan* and the "Denigrating Qin and Praising Xin," the number he used were rather few." See Hua Xuecheng 2006: 4.

[106] Cf. Davidson 1997: 30-31, describing comparable Greek impulses.

[107] Paul Kroll (private communication, August, 2010).

[108] Liu Xin says that he has learnt that Yang has gathered "obsolete words from former dynasties and unusual expressions from strange lands." See Knechtges 1977, on the "Letters."

philological works were part and parcel, then, of a larger ethnographic impulse in Han asking whether local folk traditions preserved earlier forms of learning.[109] For unless the criteria by which to correct the Classics were found outside the texts of the Classics themselves, contradictory readings would inevitably multiply over time and diverge ever more sharply from the sage's ideas and intentions. At that point, the gross inaccuracy of the Five Classics readings would render them fit for little else save citation by trial judges (*yi xian yu wen li zhi yi* 以陷於文吏之議).[110] From that unhappy fate, Yang and his fellow reformers were determined to rescue the Five Classics, so as to achieve a meeting of the minds with the antique sages whose spirit informed them.

That Yang Xiong, like his fellow *haogu* reformers, had a major impact on the course of Chinese history is undeniable. Historians need only take note of the fact that the first emperors of Eastern Han, Guangwu (r. 25-57) and Mingdi (r. 57-75) were the first emperors to portray themselves in highly choreographed settings as patrons of classicism and donors of texts, as well as in other guises.[111] Enthusiastic adherents of Yang Xiong's vision included most of the major thinkers of the Eastern Han. Xun Yue 荀悅 (148-209) spoke for many when he said of the Five Classics that one should "recite them, sing them, strum them, and dance them!"[112]

CODA

Analects 2/10 argues for a character analysis that closely examines a man's motivations, and, more specifically, what imparts to him a pleasurable sense of ease and security.[113] For Yang Xiong, the supreme pleasures were undoubtedly the allied pleasures of reading and classical learning. Yang's own style of writing suggests that much of the pleasure he derived from reading good writing lay in discovering the lexical and thematic links that

---

109 See HS 36.1970 for Liu Xin's discussion of this at Chengdi's court.

110 HS 36.1971.

111 See, e.g., HHS 79A.2545-46.

112 See Liu Rulin 1935: vol. 1, 58.

113 *Analects* 2/10 says, "Look closely into his aims and observe what motivates him, look to what brings him contentment and security" (觀其所由, 察其所安) The close ties between "pleasure" and "security" – reiterated throughout the early literature – are the subject of Nylan 2004, 2007, and forthcoming-a.

animated it, also the degree to which authors pushed experimentation within formal structures.[114] Yang's intention to "use sex and beauty (*se* 色) to illustrate ritual [and morality]," in the manner of the early Odes' commentaries, was itself a playful attempt to illuminate the past.[115] It was Yang Xiong's fond hope to cultivate in others a taste for, even an addiction to the Way (*dan dao* 耽道). Yang's ideal followers would then happily perform their lives in the prescribed dance of conventions, precedents, and social desiderata that he and his fellow reformers laid out.[116]

Because Yang delighted in such play, he dedicated his later years to "warming up the old"[117] in entirely novel ways: composing neoclassical masterworks on the model of the *Analects* and the *Yijing*, while putting together what seems to have been the earliest etymological dictionary, the precursor to Xu Shen's famous *Shuowen jiezi*. Yang's mature neoclassical writings openly solicit reader responses as preludes to self-awareness and self-fashioning. It was that quality of openness in his own person and in his writings that may have eventually made Yang's works the centerpiece of the curriculum at the most important private academy of the late Eastern Han,[118] Jingzhou, as well as the chief inspiration for Shu Xi's 束皙 (d. ca. 300) "*Fu* on Reading"[119] and the model for the Six Dynasties poets Tao Qian and Xie Lingyun.[120] Four great biblioclasms occurred between Yang Xiong's era and

---

114 Cf. Mack Horton, unpublished ms. on the *Manyoshu*, p. 32.

115 For "sex and beauty" within the context of moral discourse in Han classical learning, see Riegel 1977. For the contrary metaphor of "cutting windows in the walls [of Kongzi's house] to fake unintelligible books," see Thern 1966: 15.

116 Cf. Horton, *Manyoshu*, unpublished ms. p. 24.

117 This famous phrase, as readers will recall, comes from *Analects* 2/11.

118 One wonders what course of study was followed in Yizhou (Chengdu), at the Academy of Wen Weng, which was supposedly still in existence in AD 172. Chang Qu, author of the *Huayang guozhi*, of course, may also have favored the works of its native son, alongside those of Yan Junping and others.

119 For an addiction to the Way acquired through reading, see Shu Xi, "Dushu *fu*," cited in *Yiwen leiju*_55.991. This piece is translated in Jack Chen 2009. It mentions Kongzi, as well as Yan Hui and Ni Kuan, among other "sages and worthies" (Chen, p. 62).

120 For Tao, for example, "Impoverished Gentleman," Poem 1, says: "The *Odes* and *Documents* are piled about my couch." In "Composed on a Certain Occasion," Tao's last line is, "I have many teachers in antiquity" (though here there is irony, clearly). Tao's set of poems opens with variations on the "unit poverty/farming" and moves on to the unit "reading/Classical learning."[give citation for original text in an edition of Tao's works] Cf. *Jinshu* 51.1409, said of Huangfu Mi 皇輔謐. (215-282); cf. 82.2152, said of Xie Chen 謝沈 (early 4th-c.); 9.2352, said of Fan Long 范隆 (early 4th-c.). For Xie Lingyun, see Frodsham

the Wei-Jin period when Tao and Xie were living and writing,[121] yet in those intervening centuries Yang's fame had only grown, so much so that Yang's insistence on the pleasures of reading and classical learning came to define the person of genuine worth in the post-Han period, and reading, a virtue. For example, Sun Jing 孫敬 in Eastern Han proclaimed his own "inner taste for learning"[122] in lines that recall Yang, and Li Yanzhi 李琰之 of the Wei declared reading a pleasure incomparably greater than a fine reputation or more tangible benefits.[123] Similarly, Ge Hong (284-364) and Huangfu Mi 皇甫謐 (215-82) depicted the sage as someone marked by his love of reading, and men of cultivation, as preoccupied with books and textual learning.[124] Yang's powerful writings, in other words, had succeeded in ascribing to reading the Classics and neoclassics the ineffable power to transport readers into the pleasurable company of the Ancients. Acquaintance with Yang's writings would equip the reader for that journey backward in time. Visions of serried delights and the real possibility of setting aside mundane cares attended the thought of conversing with the sages of old. "Rapt in the way," the heart would be free of the confines of time and space.[125] Thus did ideas about the edifying influences of texts and morally exemplary persons become interwoven into a pervasive feature of early medieval thought.[126]

1967; and *Xie Lingyun zhuzi suoyin*, e.g., 3.1/43/8, 12; 4.11.1/64/10-11; Harrison Huang 2010; also Jack Chen 2009: 69-70, translating Xie's "Reading within my Studio."

121 The supposed "Burning of the Books" under Qin (213 BC?) was followed by the destruction of the palace libraries under Wang Mang in AD 23, in 193, when Dong Zhuo razed the capital; and in 311 at the fall of the Western Jin. Another biblioclasm would date to the reign of Emperor Wu of the Liang dynasty in 554. One might also mention the razing of the Qin capital of Xianyang by Liu Bang, but that would be impolitic, by the early conventions of historical writing in China.

122 For Sun Jing, see *Yiwen leiju* 55.991, citing a certain *Hou Hanshu*; cf. *Beitang shuchao* 101.1a.

123 *Weishu* 82.1798 has Li asking, "Why wear myself out to acquire a reputation or benefit?"

124 For Ge Hong, see *Baopuzi, waipian* 3.2a (Sailey, 31-32). For Huangfu Mi, see *Jinshu* 51.1415.

125 The phrase "rapt in/addicted to the Way" (*dandu* 耽道) is the opening two-character phrase in Shu Xi's 束晳 "*Fu* on Reading." Knechtges, "A Western Jin Poem on Pasta" (forthcoming), n. 1, presents a brief survey of the various dates proposed for Shu's life (generally ca. 265?-305?).

126 Ashmore 2010: 6-8.

Yang Xiong could be thin-skinned when recalling perceived slights by his moral inferiors,[127] but one of his self-styled disciples, Zhang Heng 張衡 (78-139) got closer to Yang's more mature spirit in a *fu* entitled "Returning to the Fields" (Gui tian fu 歸田賦) that describes the pleasures of "bidding farewell to worldly affairs" and "rising above the dust and dirt."

> 極般遊之至樂，雖日夕而忘劬。
> 感老氏之遺誡，將迴駕乎蓬廬。
> 彈五弦之妙指，詠周孔之圖書。...
> 苟縱心于物外，安知榮辱之所如。

> I am so enthralled by the perfect pleasure
> to be had in rambling and roaming,
> Even as the sun sets, I am oblivious to fatigue.[128]
> Moved by the warning left by Laozi,
> I turn my carriage back to my thatched hut.
> And strum the sublime airs of the five-stringed zither,
> Reciting the writings of Zhou and Kong....
> If I let my mind roam free beyond the material world,
> Why need I worry about honor and disgrace?[129]

Yang Xiong would have been gratified by the allusion to the Duke of Zhou and Kongzi, as well as the *fu*'s linkage of old writings and exemplary lives to the good life.[130] A mere hundred years or so after Yang's death, Ban Gu

---

[127] It sometimes rankled Yang that the Han court cast him as hired entertainer rather than a master of morality and erudition. See FY 2/1-2. Yang was not far off the mark in this complaint, for as a mid-ranking official, he was assigned to the Music Bureau, charged with supervising and registering one thousand-odd actors, jugglers, acrobats, and musicians. See Huan Tan, cited in *Quan Hou Han wen* 13/5a-b. Cf. HS 87B.5136: "People despise what is near and admire what is far. People saw for themselves that Yang Ziyun's salary, position, and appearance was not such as to move the people, so they scorned his writings." Or HS 87B.3579: "Lao Dan has left a saying, 'I am honored that those who understand me are so few.' Is this not the proper principle?"

[128] Implying "even as I grow old..."

[129] *Wenxuan* 5.29b-30b, citing Zhang Heng, "Gui tian fu"; trans., Knechtges, vol. 3, 140-43 (slightly mod.). Cf. *Baopuzi*, "Autobiography," which defines the model gentleman as one who has perused all the books of antiquity (4/61a; Ware, p. 8): 行為士表, 方冊所載.

[130] Of men like this, Confucius supposedly remarked, "Such men ...wander beyond the realm... They borrow the forms..., unaware of where they start or finish. Idly they roam

would similarly equate "playing with the texts of the Classics" with the admirable Way of antiquity.[131] So, too, would Yang have relished the traces of his memory that lingered centuries after his death, making him a cultural hero, though there was "nothing left, but a bedful of books."

---

beyond dust and dirt, wandering free and easy in the service of no-action." See the portrayal in *Zhuangzi,* chap. 6, of Kongzi in conversation with Zigong.

131 See HS 30.1723, which claims that the Ancients who knew the Classics in the proper way would *wan jing wen* 玩經文 ("play with the text [or phrases?] of the Classics").

Works Cited

PRIMARY SOURCES

Analects: *Lunyu* 論語. See the standard paragraphing, as in the Harvard-Yenching Sinological Institute series.

Aristotle, *Metaphysics,* cited according to standard numbering used for sections.

_____ *Nichomachean Ethics*, cited according to standard numbering used for sections.

Baopu zi 抱朴子. Ge Hong 葛洪: See Sun Xingyan 孫星晏. *Xin zheng Baopu zi* 新校正抱朴子 ed. of 1885. n.p. Zhu shi Huai lu jia shu, indexed in *Baopu zi neipian tongjian* 通檢; *waipian tongjian* 通檢. Paris: Bali daxue Han xue yanjiu suo. 1965; rpt. 1969. See also *Alchemy, Medicine, Religion in the China of A.D. 320: The Nei p'ien of Ko Hung (Pao-p'u tzu)*, trans. James R. Ware. Cambridge, Mass.: M.I.T. Press, 1966. For the *waipian*, see Jay Sailey, *The Master who Embraces Simplicity: a Study of the Philosopher Ko Hung, A.D. 283-343*. San Francisco: Chinese Materials Center, 1978.

CHANT: ICS Concordance Series, ed. D.C. Lau. Hong Kong: Commercial Press, 1992- present.

Chuci 楚辭. Qu Yuan 屈原 et al. See *Chuci zhuzi suoyin* 楚辭逐字索引. Hong Kong: Commercial Press, 2000.

Chuguo xianxian zhuan 楚國先賢傳, in *Beitang shuchao* 北堂書鈔 (comp. 630, Yu Shinan 虞世南). Beijing: Zhonghua shuju rpt., 1982.

Da Dai Liji 大戴禮記: See *Da Dai Liji zhu zi suo yin* 大戴禮記逐字索引. Hong Kong: Commercial Press, 1992.

Dai Si 戴侗. Southern Song. *Liu shu gu* 六書故 [e-Siku].

Documents: See *Shangshu.*

Dongjing meng Hua lu 東京夢華錄. Beijing: Zhonghua shuju, 1962.

DRK: See David R. Knechtges. 1982.

Early Chinese Texts: See Loewe, Michael. 1993.

Ershi wushi bubian 二十五史補編. Ershi wushi bubian committee. Beijing: Zhonghua shuju, rpt. 1956, 6 vols.

Erya 爾雅: Anon. See *Erya Han zhu* 漢注, ed. Zang Yong 臧庸, in *Wenjing tang congshu* 問經堂叢書, in *Baibu congshu jicheng* 百部叢書集成. vol. 38. Taipei: Yiwen Press, 1968.

Fayan 法言. Yang Xiong 揚雄: See FY.

Fangyan 方言. Yang Xiong,. See *Fangyanjiao jian* 方言校箋. Beijing: Franco-chinoise *tong jian cong kan* 中法漢學研究所通檢叢刊, no. 14; otherwise, see *Siku quanshu* [e-Siku], with annotations by Guo Pu 郭璞.

FY: See *Fayan zhu* 注, ed. Han Jing 韓敬. 1992. Beijing: Zhonghua shuju.

Fengsu tongyi 風俗通義. Ying Shao 應卲. See *Fengsu tongyi zhuzi suoyin* 風俗通義逐子索引. Hong Kong: Commercial Press, 1996.

Han Feizi 韓非子: See *Han Feizi zhuzi suoyin* 韓非子逐字索引. Hong Kong: Commercial Press, 2000.

Han guan jiu yi 漢官: See *Han guan liuzhong zhuzi suoyin* 漢官六種逐字索引. Hong Kong: Commercial Press, 1993.

Hanshu 漢書: See HS.

HHS: *Hou Hanshu* 後漢書. Fan Ye 范曄, et al. See the 1965 Beijing: Zhonghua shuju ed., 12 vols.

HNZ: Liu An 劉安. *Huainan zi* 淮南子. See Liu Wendian 劉文典. *Huainan Honglie jijie* 淮南鴻烈集解. 1926, rpt. Beijing: Zhonghua shuju, 1989. 2 vols.

Horace, *Arts Poetica.* Ref. to standard paragraphing.

HS: Ban Gu 班固, et al., *Hanshu* 漢書. See the 1962 Beijing, Zhonghua shuju ed., 8 vols.

HSWZ: Han Ying 韓嬰 . *Hanshi waizhuan* 韓氏外傳. See the standard paragraphs preserved in the Harvard-Yenching Sinological Institute series. Translations are based on Han Ying, *Han shih wai chuan: Han Ying's Illustrations of the Didactic Application of the Classic of Songs*, trans. by James Robert Hightower. 1952. Cambridge, Mass.: Harvard University Press.

Huayang guozhi 華陽國志. Chang Qu 常璩. See *Huayang guozhi,* ed. Ren Naiqiang 任乃強. Chengdu: Ba Shu shushe, rpt. 1984.

Isocrates, *Evagoras.* See the standard paragraphs in the Loeb Classics.

Jinshu 晉書. Fang Xuanling 房玄齡. See the Beijing, Zhonghua shuju ed. of 1974, 10 vols.

Li Deyu 李德裕 (787-850). See *Li Deyu wenji jiao jian* 李德裕文集校箋, ed. Fu Xuancong 傅璇琮 and Zhou Jianguo 周建國. Shijiazhuang: Hebei jiaoyu rpt. of 2000.

Lidai minghua ji 歷代名畫記. Zhang Yanyuan 張彥遠. 1954, rpt. Taipei: Taiwan Commercial Press, 1971. See also *Some T'ang and Pre-T'ang Texts on Chinese Painting*, trans. William Reynolds Beal Acker. Leiden: E.J. Brill, 1974. 2 vols.

Liji 禮記: See *Liji zhuzi suoyin* 禮記逐字索引. Hong Kong: Commercial Press, 1992.

Liangshu 梁書. Yao Silian 姚思廉. See the 1973 Beijing: Zhonghua shuju ed., 2 vols.

Liezi 列子: See *Liezi zhu zi suo yin* 列子逐字索引. Hong Kong: Commercial Press, 1996.

Lu Zhaolin 盧照鄰 (638-84). See *Lu Zhaolin ji jiao zhu* 盧照鄰集校注. Beijing: Zhonghua shuju, 1998.

LSCQ: *Lüshi chunqiu* 呂氏春秋. See the *Lüshi chunqiu zhuzi suoyin* 呂氏春秋逐字索引. Hong Kong: Commercial Press, 1994.

Lunheng 論衡. Wang Chong 王充. See the *Lunheng zhuzi suoyin* 論衡逐字索引. Hong Kong: Commercial Press, 1966.

Meng qiu 蒙求. Li Han 李瀚. See *Meng Ch'iu: Famous Episodes from Chinese History and Legend*, trans. Burton Watson. Tokyo: Kodansha International, 1979.

Mozi 墨子: See the *Mozi yinde* 墨子引得. Beiping: Harvard-Yenching Institute, 1948 (Harvard-Yenching Sinological Institute series no. 21).

Nan Qi shu 南齊書. Xiao Zixian 蕭子顯. See the Beijing, Zhonghua shuju ed. of 1972, 3 vols.

Qijia Hou Han shu: See Wang Wentai, under Secondary Sources.

Qian Hanji 前漢記. Xun Yue 荀悅. See *Siku quanshu* [e-Siku], vol. 30.

Quan Han wen 全漢文: See Yan Kejun.

Quan Hou Han wen 全後漢文: See Yan Kejun.

Quan Hou Wei wen 全後魏文: See Yan Kejun.

Quan Hou Zhou wen 全後周文: See Yan Kejun.

Quan Jin wen 全晉文: See Yan Kejun.

Sanfu huangtu jiaozheng 三辅黄图校证. Chen Zhi 陈直. Xian: Shaanxi renmin, 1980.

Sanguo zhi 三國志. Chen Shou 陳壽. See the Beijing: Zhonghua shuju ed. of 1959, 5 vols.

Shangshu tongjian 尚書通檢, ed. Gu Jiegang 顧頡剛. Taipei: Chinese Materials and Research Aids Service Center, Inc., 1966.

Shitong 史通. Liu Zhiji 劉知幾. See *Shitong tongshi* 史通通釋, ed. Pu Qilong 浦起龍. Taipei: Yiwen, 1974.

Shuoyuan 說苑. Liu Xiang 劉向. See *Shuo yuan zhu zi suo yin* 說苑逐字索引. Hong Kong: Commercial Press, 1992.

Shuwang benji 蜀王本記: See *Jingdian jilin* 經典集林, vol. 1, *juan* 14, in *Baibu congshu jicheng* 百部叢書集成 no. 38, ed. Hong Yixuan 洪頤煊 (Taipei: Yiwen, 1968).

Siku quanshu 四庫全書 [e-Siku version], based on the Wenyuange version of 1798.

SJ: *Shiji,* comp. by Sima Tan 司馬談, Sima Qian 司馬遷 et al. See the Beijing, Zhonghua shuju, ed. of 1972, 12 vols.

Suishu 隋書. Wei Zheng 魏徵. See the Beijing, Zhonghua shuju ed. of 1973, 3 vols.

Taixuan jing 太玄. Yang Xiong 揚雄. See *Taixuan jing zhu zi suo yin* 太玄逐字索引. Hong Kong: Commercial Press, 1966 Refs. also to Michael Nylan, *The Canon of Supreme Mystery, a Translation with Commentary.* Albany, N.Y.: State University of New York Press.

Tao Qian 陶潛: See *Tao Yuanming ji jianzhu* 陶元明集箋注, Yuan Xingpei 袁行霈. Shanghai: Shanghai guji chubanshe, 2003. For translations, cf. Hightower 1970.

Tongzhi: Zheng Qiao 鄭樵 (1104-62). *Tongzhi* 通志. See *Tongzhi er shi lue* 通志二十略, ed.Wang Shumin 王樹民. Beijing: Zhonghua shuju, 1995, 2 vols., containing "On Collating" (*jiao chou lue* 校讎略), vol. 2, 20.1803-1824; and "Charts and Records" (Tupu 圖譜), vol. 2, 21.1825-26.

TPYL: *Taiping yulan* 太平御覽. Li Fang 李昉, et al., compilers (984). See *Taiping yulan*, in *Siku quanshu* [e-Siku].

Weishu 魏書: Wei Shou 魏收. See the Beijing Zhonghua shuju ed. of 1974, 5 vols.

Wenxin diaolong 文心雕龍. Liu Xie 劉勰. See the *Wenxin diaolong zhuzi suoyin* 文心雕龍逐字索引. Hong Kong: Chinese University Press, 2001. Cf. Vincent Shih, *The Literary Mind and the Carving of Dragons.* 1970. Taipei: Chung Hwa Books.

Wenxuan 文選. Xiao Tong 蕭統, Li Shan 李善, annot. See the *Wenxuan zhu* 註, in *Siku quanshu* [e-Siku]. For translations, see David R. Knechtges, *Wen xuan, or, Selections of Refined Literature.* Princeton: Princeton University Press, 1982- , 3 vols. to date.

Xie Lingyun 謝靈運. See *Xie Lingyun zhuzi suoyin* 集文心雕龍逐字索引. Hong Kong: Chinese University Press, 1999. For translations, see Frodsham, in Secondary Sources.

Xijing zaji 西京雜記. tradit. Liu Xin 劉歆. See *Han Wei Liuchao biji xiao shuo ta guan* 漢魏六朝筆記小說大觀. Shanghai: Shanghai guiji chubanshe, 1999; cf. Beijing : Zhonghua shuju ed. of 1985.

Xinlun 新論. Huan Tan 桓譚: See Timotheus Pokora, trans., *Hsin-lun (New Treatise) and Other Writings by Huan T'an (43 B.C. -28 A.D.).* 1975. Ann Arbor: Center for Chinese Studies, Univ. of Michigan. See also Kong Pingzhong; TPYL.

Xunzi 荀子: See *Xunzi yinde* 荀子引得. Harvard-Yenching Sinological Index Series, supplement no. 22. Taipei, 1966. See also John Knoblock, *Xunzi: ATranslation and Study of the Complete Works.* Stanford: Stanford University Press, 1988-94, 3 vols.

Yan Kejun 嚴可均. 1961. *Quan shanggu sandai Qin Han Sanguo Liuchao wen* 全上古三代秦漢三國六朝文. Taipei: World Books, 9 vols.

Yanshi jiaxun 顏氏家訓, by Yan Zhitui 颜之推. See Zhuang Yunming 庄輝明 and Zhang Yihe 章義和. 1999. *Yanshi jiaxun yizhu* 顏氏家訓譯注.. Tianjin: Tianjin guji chubanshe. Ref. also to *Family Instructions for the Yen Clan*, trans. Teng Ssu-yü. Leiden: E.J. Brill, 1968.

Yan tie lun 鹽鐵論. tradit. Huan Kuan 桓寬. See *Yan tie lun zhuzi suoyin* 鹽鐵論逐字索引. Hong Kong: Commercial Press, 1994.

Yilin 易林. Jiao Yanshou 焦延壽. See the *Jiaoshi Yilin zhuzi suoyin* 焦氏易林逐字索引. Hong Kong: Commercial Press, 1995.

Yiwen leiju 藝文類聚. Ouyang Xun 歐陽詢, et al. See Beijing, Zhonghua shuju ed. of 1965, 2 vols

Yunmeng Shuihudi Qinmu 云梦睡虎地秦墓. Beijing: Wenwu chubanshe, 1981.

Zhanguo ce 戰國策. See the *Zhanguo ce zhuzi suoyin* 戰國策逐子索引. Hong Kong: Commercial Press, 1992.

Zhang Yi 張揖, *Guangya biao* 上廣雅表, *Huang Qing jing jie* 皇清經解, vol. 667A.

Zheng Qiao: See *Tongzhi.*

Zhouli 周禮. See *Zhouli zhushu* 周禮注疏, Zheng Xuan 鄭玄 commentary, in *Siku quanshu* [e-Siku].

Zhuangzi 莊子. See *Zhuangzi yinde* 莊子引得. Harvard-Yenching Sinological Index Series, supplement no. 20. rpt. Taipei, 1956.

SECONDARY SOURCES

Acker: See *Lidai minghua ji.*

Arbuckle, Gary. 1995. "Inevitable Treason: Dong Zhongshu's Theory of Historical Cycles and the Devalidation of the Han Mandate." *Journal of the American Oriental Society* 115: 585-97.

Ashmore, Robert. 2010. *The Transport of Reading: Text and the Understanding in the World of Tao Qian (365-427).* Cambridge, Mass.: Harvard East Asian Monographs.

Bagley, Robert W. 2004. "Anyang Writing and the Origin of the Chinese Writing System." In *The First Writing: Script Invention as History and Process*, ed. Stephen D. Houston. Cambridge: Cambridge University Press, 190-237.

Bauer, Wolfgang. 1976. *China and the Search for Happiness: Recurring Themes in Four Thousand Years of Chinese Cultural History.* New York: Seabury Press.

Beard, Mary. 2009. "Scrolling Down the Ages," *The New York Times Book Review* (April 19), 27.

Beecroft, Alexander J. unpublished ms. entitled *Scenes of Authorship: Patterns of Literary Circulation in Early Greece and China.*

Berkowitz, Alan J. 2000. *Patterns of Disengagement: The Practice and Portrayal of Reclusion in Early Medieval China.* Stanford: Stanford University Press.

Berry, Mary Elizabeth. 2006. *Japan in Print: Information and Nation in the Early Modern Period.* Berkeley: University of California Press.

Bielenstein, Hans. 1954-67. "The Restoration of the Han Dynasty, with Prolegomena on the Historiography of the *Hou Han shu.* " *Bulletin of the Museum of Far Eastern Antiquities* 26: 1-209; 31: 1-286; 39: 1-198, 3 vols.

Bottéro, Françoise. 2003. "Les <Manuels de caractères> à l'époque des Han Occidentaux." In *Éducation et Instruction en Chine*, vol. 1 (L'éducation élémentaire), ed. Christine Nguyen Tri, Catherine Despeux. Paris: Éditions Peeters, 99-120.

Cameron, Alan. 1995. *Callimachus and his Critics*. Princeton: Princeton University Press.

Campany, Robert Ford. 1966. *Strange Writing: Anomaly Accounts in Early Medieval China*. Albany, N.Y.: State University of New York Press.

Carr, Michael Edward. 1979. "A Linguistic Study of the Flora and Fauna Sections of the *Ehr-ya*." Ph.D. thesis, University of Arizona.

Carey, Benedict. 2009. "A Dream Interpretation: Tune-ups for the Brain." *The New York Times*, Nov. 9.

Chen, Jack W. 2009. "On the Act and Representation of Reading in Medieval China." *Journal of the American Oriental Society* 129.1: 57-72.

Chen Li 陳立. 1936. *Gongyang yishu* 公羊義疏. Shanghai: Guoxue jiben congshu; rpt., Taipei: Taiwan Zhonghua shuju.

Cherniack, Susan. 1994. "Book Culture and Textual Transmission in Sung China." *Harvard Journal of Asiatic Studies* 54: 5-126.

Chittick, Andrew. 2003. "The Life and Legacy of Liu Biao: Governor, Warlord, and Imperial Pretender in Late Han China." *Journal of Asian History* 37.2: 155–86.

Chung, Eva. 1982. "A Study of the *Shu* (Letters) of the Han Dynasty (206 B.C.-A.D. 220). Ph.D. thesis, University of Washington.

Coblin, Weldon South. 1972. "An Introductory Study of the Textual and Linguistic Problems in *Erh-ya*." Ph.D. thesis, University of Washington

Colvin, Andrew. 2001. "Patterns of Coherence in the *Fayan* of Yang Xiong." Ph.D. thesis, University of Hawai'i.

Cullen, Christopher. 2010. "Numbers, Numeracy, and the Cosmos." In *China's Early Empires: A Reappraisal*, ed. Michael Nylan and Michael Loewe. Cambridge: Cambridge University Press, 323-38.

Davidson, James N. 1997. *Courtesans and Fishcakes*. London: St. Martin's Press.

Declerq, Dominic. 1998. *Writing Against the State: Political Rhetoric in Third and Fourth Century China*. Leiden: Brill

DeWoskin, Kenneth. 1982. *A Song for One or Two: Music and the Concept of Art in Early China.* Ann Arbor: Center for Chinese Studies, University of Michigan.

Drège, Jean-Pierre. 1991. *Les Bibliothèques en Chine au temps des manuscrits (jusqu'au Xe siècle).* Paris: École Française d'Extême-Orient.

Dubs: Ban Gu. 1983. *The History of the Former Han Dynasty*, trans. Homer H. Dubs. Baltimore, Waverly Press, 3 vols.

Dudbridge, Glen. 2000. *Lost Books of Medieval China.* London: British Library.

Dull, Jack L. 1966. "A Historical Introduction to the Apocryphal (Ch'an-weï) Texts of the Han Dynasty." Ph.D. thesis, University of Washington.

Durrant, Stephen W. 1995. *Cloudy Mirror: Tension and Conflict in the Writings of Sima Qian.* Albany, N.Y.: State University of New York Press.

Early Chinese Texts: A Bibliographical Guide, ed. Michael Loewe. Berkeley: Society for the Study of Early China Monographs, 1993

Egan, Ronald

______ lecture, unpublished ms. "A New Reading of Li Qingzhao's 'Afterword to *Records of Metal and Stone*,'' given for the Institute for Chinese Studies, Oxford University (May 31, 2004).

______ 2006. *The Problem of Beauty: Aesthetic Thought and Pursuits in Northern Song Dynasty China.* Cambridge, Mass.: Harvard University Asia Center.

Farmer, Michael J. 2000. "Art, Education, and Power: Illustrations in the Stone Chamber of Wen Weng." *T'oung pao* 86: 100-35.

Farquhar, Judith. 1994. "Eating Chinese Medicine." *Cultural Anthropology* 9:4 (Nov.): 471-97.

Feeney, Dennis. 2007. *Caesar's Calendar: Ancient Time and the Beginnings of History.* Berkeley: University of California Press

Finley, M.I. 1975. *The Use and Abuse of History.* London: Chatto and Windus.

Fischer, Steven Roger. 2003. *A History of Reading.* London: Reaktion Books.

Frodsham, J.D. 1967. *The Murmuring Stream: the Life and Works of the Chinese Nature Poet, Hsieh Ling-yün (385-433), Duke of K'ang-Lo.* Kuala Lumpur: University of Malaysia Press, 2 vols.

Fu Yuzhang 傅玉璋. 2008. *Zhongguo gudai shixue shi* 中國古代史學史. Hefei: Anhwei daxue.

Fukui Shigemasa 福井重雅. 2003. *Kandai Jukyō no shiteki kenkyū: Jukyō no kangakuka o meguru teisetsu no saikentō* 漢代儒教の史的研究:儒教の官學化をめぐる定說の再檢討. Tokyo: Kyūko Shoin.

Galambos, Imre. 2006. *Orthography of Early Chinese Writing: Evidence from Newly Excavated Manuscripts.* London: British Library.

Geaney, Jane.

_____ 2002. *On the Epistemology of the Senses in Early Chinese Thought.* Albany, N.Y.: State University of New York Press.

_____ 2010. "Grounding 'Language' in the Senses: What the Eyes and Ears Reveal about Ming 名 in Early Chinese Texts." *Philosophy East and West* 60.2: 113-42.

Gentz, Joachim, "Language of Heaven, Exegetical Skepticism, and the Re-Insertion of Religious Concepts in the *Gongyang* Tradition." In Lagerwey, 813-38.

Giele, Enno. 2005. "Signatures in Early Imperial China." *Asiatische Studien/Études Asiatiques* 59.1: 353-87.

Gong Kechang. 1997. *Studies on the Han Fu*, trans. David R. Knechtges, et al. New Haven: American Oriental Society.

Gowers, Emily. 2009. "A Net for Eggheads." *Times Literary Supplement*, July 10: 13.

Greatrex, Roger. 1994. "An Early Western Han Synonymicon: the Fuyang copy of the *Cang Jie pian.*" In *Outstretched Leaves on his Bamboo Staff: Studies in Honour of Göran Malmqvist on his 70th Birthday.* Stockholm: The Association of Oriental Studies, 97-113.

Gu Ming Dong. 2005. *Chinese Theories of Reading and Writing.* Albany, N.Y.: State University of New York Press.

Guan Xihua 管錫華. 2002. *Zhongguo gudai biaodian fuhao fazhan shi* 中國古代標點符號發展史. Chengdu: Ba Shu shushe.

Gunderson, Erik. 2009. *Nox Philologiae: Aulus Gellius and the Fantasy of the Roman Library* Madison: University of Wisconsin Press.

Hadot, Pierre. 2009. *The Present Alone is our Happiness.* Stanford: Stanford University Press.

Harrist, Robert E. 2008. *The Landscape of Words: Stone Inscriptions from Early and Medieval China.* Seattle: University of Washington Press.

He Lingxu 賀淩虛. 1988. *Xi Han zheng zhi si xiang lun ji* 西漢政治思想論集. Taipei: Wunan tushu chuban gongsi.

Henry, Eric. 1999. "'Junzi yue' versus 'Zhongni yue' in *Zuozhuan.*" *Harvard Journal of Asiatic Studies* 59: 125-61.

Hervouet, Yves. 1994. *Un poète de cour sous les Han: Sseu-ma Siang-jou.* Paris: Presses universitaires de France.

Hightower, James Robert. 1970. *The Poetry of T'ao Ch'ien*. Oxford: Clarendon Press.

Hsing I-t'ien 邢義田. 2010. "*Handai Cang Jie, Jijiu, bati he shishu wenti: zai lun Qin Han guanli rehe xuexi wenzi*" 漢代倉頡, 急就, 八體和史書問題: 再論秦漢官吏如何學習文字.In *Paleography and_Early Chinese History* 古文字與古代史, no. 2 (Dec), ed. Li Zong-kun 李宗焜 (Symposium Series of the Institute of History and Philology, Academia Sinica, Taipei, 429-70.

Hsü Fu-kuan 徐復觀 1975. *Liang Han sixiang shi* 兩漢思想史. Hong Kong: Chinese University of Hong Kong. 2 vols.

_____ 1966. *Zhongguo yishu jingshen* 中國藝術精神. Taizhong: Sili Donghai daxue.

Hua Xuecheng 華學誠. 2006. *Yang Xiong Fang yan jiaoshi huizheng* 揚雄方言校釋匯證. Beijing: Zhonghua shuju.

Huang, Harrison. 2010. "Excursion, Estates, and the Kingly Gaze: the Landscape Poetry of Xie Lingyun." Ph.D. thesis, University of California, Berkeley.

Huizinga, Johan. 1943. *Homo Ludens: a Study of the Play-element in Culture*. London: Routledge, rpt. of 2000.

Inglis, Alister D. 2006. *Hong Mai's Record of the Listener and its Song Dynasty Context.* Albany, N.Y.: State University of New York Press.

Jiang Xia'an 江俠庵. 1931. *Xian Qin jingji kao* 先秦經籍考. Shanghai: Commerical Press.

Ji Xusheng 季旭昇. 2002. *Shuowen xinzheng* 說文新證. Taipei: Commercial Press.

Jiao Guimei 焦桂美. 2009. *Nan Bei chao jing xue shi* 南北朝经学史. Shanghai: Shanghai guji chubanshe.

Jin Ke 金柯. 2001. "Lun Hanmo Jingzhou wenxue" 論漢末荊州文學. *Jinggangshan shifan xueyuan xuebao* (Zhexue shehui kexue) 22: 50–54.

Jin Renyi 金仁義. 2002. "Liu Biao yu Jingzhou xuepai" 劉表與荊州學派.*Chizhou shizhuan xuebao* 16.1: 71–74.

Kern, Martin. 2003. "Western Han Aesthetics and the Genesis of the *Fu*." *Harvard Journal of Asiatic Studies* 63: 383-437.

Kalinowski, Marc. 2003. "La production des manuscrits dans la Chine ancienne: Une approche codicologique de la bibliothèque de Mawangdui." *Asiatische Studien/Etudes Asiatiques* 57: 849-80.

Knechtges, David R1976. *Han Rhapsody: a Study of the fu of Yang Hsiung, 53 B.C.-A.D. 18*. Cambridge: Cambridge University Press.

______ 1977. "The Liu Hsin/Yang Hsiung Correspondence on the *Fang yen*." *Monumenta* Serica 33: 309-25.

______ 1978. "Uncovering the Sauce Jar: a Literary Interpretation of Yang Hsiung's 'Chü Ch'in mei Hsin'." In *Ancient China: Studies in Early Civilization*. ed. David T. Roy and Tsuen-hsuin Tsien. Hong Kong: Chinese University Press, 229-52.

_____ 1982. *The Han shu Biography of Yang Xiong (53 B.C.-A.D. 18*). Tempe: Center for Asian Studies, Arizona State University.

_____ unpublished essay. "Secrets of the Western Han Court Exposed: Anecdotes in the *Xijing zaji*."

_____ unpublished essay. "A Western Jin Poem on Pasta." Forthcoming in *Early Medieval China*.

Kong Deming 孔德明. 2010. "Lun Qin dai daobili dui Han fu chuangzao de yingxiang" 論秦代刀筆吏對漢賦創造的影響. *Shanbei shida xuebao (Shehui kexue ban)* 山北師大學報 (社會科學版), 47.4: 35-40.

Kong Pingzhong 孔平仲. 1990. *Heng huan Xin lun* 珩璜新论. Shanghai: Shanghai shudian.

Konstan, David. 2006. *The Emotions of the Ancient Greeks*. Toronto: University of Toronto Press.

Kroll, Paul W. 2010. "Literary Criticism and Personal Character in Poetry, ca. 100-300 CE." In *China's Early Empires: A Reappraisal,* ed. Michael Nylan and Michael Loewe. 2010. Cambridge: Cambridge University Press, 517-33.

Lagerwey: *Early Chinese Religion, Part One: Shang through Han (1250 BC-AD 220),* ed. John Lagerwey and Marc Kalinowski. Leiden: Brill, 2008.

Lee, Brigitta. 2007. "Imitation, Remembrance and the Formation of the Poetic Past in Early Medieval China." Ph.D. thesis, Princeton University.

Letters: See Knechtges 1977.

Lei Hanqing 雷漢卿. 2000. *Shuowen shibu zi yu shenling jisi kao* 說文示部字與神靈祭祀考. Chengdu: Ba-Shu shushe.

Lewis, Mark Edward. 1999. *Writing and Authority in Early China.* Albany, N.Y.: State University of New York Press.

L'Haridon, Béatrice. 2006. "La recherche du modèle dans les dialogues du *Fayan* de Yang Xiong (53 av. J.-C.-18 apr. J.C.): Écriture, éthique, and réflexion historique à la fin des Han occidentaux." Ph.D. thesis, Institute National des Langues and Civilisations orientales. 2 vols.

______ 2010. *Maîtres Motes* 揚雄法言. Paris: Les Belles Lettres.

______ 2011?). "Zizhang duo ai, ai qi ye: Yang Xiong 'Fayan' zhongdui 'Shiji' de lunshu yu chuancheng yi Handai Rujia de wentie wei li" 子長多愛, 愛奇也: 揚雄法言中對的史記的論述與傳承以漢代儒家的問題為例. Forthcoming in *Shiji xue yu shijie Hanxue* 史記學與世界漢學. Taipei: Tangshan 唐山 chubanshe.

Li Qing 李卿. 2003. *Qin Han Wei Jin Nanbei chao shiqi jiazu zongzu guanxi yanjiu* 秦漢魏晉南北朝時期家族宗族關係研究. Shanghai: Renmin chubanshe.

Li Wai-yee. 1994. "The Idea of Authority in the *Shih chi* (Records of the Historian). *Harvard Journal of Asiatic Studies* 54: 345-505.

Lin Yixun 林翼勳. 2008. *Su Shi shi yanjiu* 蘇軾詩研究. Hong Kong: Zhong-Hang yuwen jiaoyu xuehui. 3 vols.

Li Zhen'ai 林貞愛. 2001. *Yang Xiong jijiao zhu* 揚雄集校注. Chengdu: Sichuan daxue chubanshe.

Lin Hansheng 林寒生. 2001. "Erya Han zhu di xueshu jiazhi" 爾雅漢注的學術價值. *Xiamen daxue xuebao (Zhexue shehui kexue)* 厦門大學學報, 哲學社會科學 147: 156-60.

Little, Stephen, et al. 2000. *Taoism and the Arts of China.* Chicago: Art Institute.

Liu Moshu 劉墨書. 2006. "Sanguo shiqi Jingzhou diqu rencai yu zhengju de guanxi" 三國時期荊州人才政局的關係. *Changchun daxue xuebao* 16.6: 96–99.

Liu Rulin 劉汝霖. 1935. *Han Jin xueshu biannian* 漢晉學術編年. Shanghai: Commercial Press. 2 vols.

Loewe, Michael. 1974. *Crisis and Conflict in Han China, 104 B. C. to A. D. 9.* London: George Allen & Unwin, Ltd.

_____ 1993. Ed., *Early Chinese Texts: A Bibliographical Guide.* Berkeley: Society for the Study of Early China.

_____ *A Biographical Dictionary of the Qin, Former Han, and Xin Periods (221 BC-AD 23)* Leiden: Brill.

Lu, Jiyuan. 2007. *The Ethics of Aristotle and Confucius: Mirrors of Value.* London: Routledge.

Lü Simian 吕思勉. 1982. *Lü Simian dushi zhaji* 吕思勉读史札记. Shanghai: Shanghai guji chubanshe.

Ma Guohan 馬國翰. 1883. *Yuhan shanfang ji yishu* 玉函山房輯佚書. Changsha: Langhuan guan. 6 vols.

Ma Jigao 马积高. 1987. *Fu shi* 赋史. Shanghai: Shanghai guji chubanshe..

Mair, Victor H. 1988. *Mei Cherng's "Seven Stimuli" and Wang Bor's "Pavilion of King Terng": Chinese Poems for Princes.* Lewiston, N.Y: Edwin Mellen Press.

_____ 1994. Review, of *Canon of Supreme Mystery. Sino-Platonic Papers* (July): 105-6.

_____ 1997. Review, of the *Canon of Supreme Mystery*, trans. Michael Nylan. *Chinese Science* 14: 147-52.

Matsukawa Kenji 松川健二. 1994. *Rongo no shisōshi* 論語の思想史. Tokyo: Kyūko Shoin. [Chinese translation by Lin Qingzhang 林慶彰 et al. Taipei: Wanchuan, 2006.]

McDermott, Joseph. 2006. *A Social History of the Chinese Book.* Hong Kong: Hong Kong University Press.

Mei Yi-pao. 1929. *The Ethical and Political Works of Motse.* London: Probsthain.

Meyer, Dirk. 2008. "Meaning Construction in Late Warring States Philosophic Discourse." Ph.D. thesis, University of Leiden.

Mittag, Achim. 1983. "Change in *Shijing* Exegesis: Some Notes on the Rediscovery of the *Odes* in the Song Period." *T'oung pao* 79: 197-224.

Naquin, Susan. 2008. Review, of Cynthia Brokaw, *Commerce of Culture: The Sibao Trade in the Qing. Harvard Journal of Asiatic Studies* 68: 203-12.

Nugent, Christopher. 2007. "Literary Collections in Tang Dynasty China." *T'oung pao* 93: 1-52.

Nylan, Michael 戴梅可 1982. "Ying Shao's *Feng su t'ung yi*: An Exploration of Problems in Han Dynasty Political, Philosophical, and Social Unity." Ph.D. thesis, Princeton University.

_____ 1993. *The Canon of the Supreme Mystery*: See *Taixuan jing*, in Primary Sources.

_____ 1994. "The *chin wen/ku wen* (New Text/Old Text) Controversy in Han." *T'oung pao* 80: 83-145.

_____ 1995. "The *ku wen Documents* in Han Times." *T'oung pao* 81: 1-27.

_____ 1999. "Calligraphy: The Sacred Test and Text of Culture." In *Calligraphy and Context*, ed. Cary Liu and Dora Ching. Princeton: The Art Museum, Princeton University, 1999, 1-42.

_____ 2001. "Textual Authority in Pre-Han and Han." *Early China* 25: 1-54.

_____ 2001b. "Legacies of the Sichuan Plain." In *Ancient Sichuan: Treasures from a Lost Civilization*, ed. Robert W. Bagley. Seattle and Princeton: Seattle Art Museum and Princeton University Press, 307-328.

_____ 2004. "The Politics of Pleasure." *Asia Major*, 3rd ser. 14.1 (2001) [actual publication date 2004]: 73-124.

_____ 2007. with Harrison Huang, "Mencius on Pleasure." In *Polishing the Chinese Mirror: Essays in Honor of Henry Rosemont*, ed. Marthe Chandler and Ronnie Littlejohn. La Salle, Ill.: Association of Chinese Philosophers of America and Open Court, 1-26.

_____ 2008. "Classics without Canonization: Reflections on Classical Learning and Authority in Qin (221-210 BC) and Han (206 BC-AD 220). In Lagerwey, 721-77.

_____ 2008b. "Beliefs about Seeing: Optics and Moral Technologies in Early China." *Asia Major* 3rd ser. 21:1 89-132.

_____ forthcoming-a. *Pleasure Theory in Early China.*

_____ forthcoming-b. *Exemplary Figures, A Translation of Yang Xiong's* Fayan. Forthcoming from the University of Washington Press, 2011.

_____ forthcoming-c. "Yang Xiong's 揚雄 Final *Fayan* 法言 Chapter, Rhetoric to What End and for Whom?" To appear in a volume on rhetoric edited by Garret Olberding.

_____ forthcoming-d. "A Revisionist History of Han Ideas of Qin." To appear in a volume to be edited by Yuri Pines, Gideon Shelach, and Andrew Plaks.

Ōkushi Atsuhiro 大櫛敦弘. 1985. "Kandai no nake-ke no san ni kansuru kōsatsu" 漢代の中家の產に關する一考察. *Shigaku zasshi* 史學雜誌 94.7:40-62 (1172-94).

Owen, Stephen1986. *Remembrances: The Experience of the Past in Classical Chinese Literature.* Cambridge, Mass.: Harvard University Press.

_____ 1992. *Readings in Chinese Literary Thought.* Cambridge, Mass.: Council on East Asian Studies, Harvard University.

_____ 2006. *The Making of Early Chinese Classical Poetry.* Cambridge, Mass.: Harvard University Asia Center.

Pan Meiyue 潘美月. 1980. *Songdai cangshu jia kao* 宋代藏書家考. Taipei: Xuehai chubanshe.

Peterson, Willard J. 1989. Review, of *Chinese Ideas about Nature and Society, Studies in Honour of Derk Bodde. Journal of Asian Studies* 48: 365-67.

Pines, Yuri. 2002. "Friends or Foes: Changing Concepts of Ruler-Minister Relations and the Notion of Loyalty in Pre-Imperial China." *Monumenta Serica* 50: 35-74.

Pokora, Timotheus. 1963. "The Life of Huan T'an." *Archiv Orientalni* 31: 31-33.

Poo Mu-chou 蒲慕州. 2010. "Xian Qin Liang Han de zungu siwei yu zhengzhi quanwei 先秦兩漢的尊古思維與政治權威. Unpublished conference paper, from International Conference on Institutions and Social Order in the Han Empire, May 5-7, Chinese University of Hong Kong.

Queen, Sarah A. 2001. "Inventories of the Past: Rethinking the 'School' Affiliation of the *Huainanzi*." *Asia Major* 3rd ser. 14: 51-72.

Qian Yi 錢繹. 1984. *Fangyan jianshu* 方言箋疏. Shanghai: Shanghai guji.

Ricoeur, Paul. 1981. "The Task of Hermeneutics." In idem, *Hermeneutics and the Human Sciences*, trans. John Thompson. Cambridge: Cambridge University Press, 43-62.

Riegel, Jeffrey. 1997. "Eros, Introversion, and the Beginnings of *Shijing* Commentary." *Harvard Journal of Asiatic Studies* 57: 143-77.

Rosthorn, A. von. 1975. "The Erh-ya and other Synonymicons." *Journal of the Chinese Language Teachers Association* 10:3: 137-45 [an English summary of idem, 1942 "Das Er-ya und andere Synonymiken," *Zeitschrif für die Kunde des Morgenlandes* 49: 126–144].

Sailey, Jay: See *Baopuzi* above.

Sebald, W. G. 2003. *On the Natural History of Destruction*, trans. Anthea Bell. New York: Random House.

Serruys, Paul L-M. 1959. *The Chinese Dialects of Han Time According to Fang yen.* Berkeley: University of California Press.

Shaughnessy, Edward L. 1997. "Military Histories of Early China: A Review Article." *Early China* 21: 159-82.

Sukhu, Gopal. 2005-6. "Yao, Shun, and Prefiguration: The Origins and Ideology of the Han Imperial Genealogy." *Early China* 30: 91-153.

Tang Chunsheng 唐春生. 2001. "Liu Biao shiqi binan Jingzhou de beifang mingshi" 劉表時期避難荊州的北方名士. *Hunan daxue xuebao* 15.2: 23–26.

Taniguchi Hiroshi 谷口洋. 2010. "Fu ni jijo o tsukeru koto: RyōKan no majiwari ni okeru sakusha no mezame" 賦に自序をつけること: 兩漢の交における作者 のめざめ. *Tōhōgaku* 東方學 119: 22-39.

Thern, K. L. 1966. *Postface to the Shuo wen chieh tzu: The First Comprehensive Chinese Dictionary*. Ann Arbor: Wisconsin China Series.

Tian Xiaofei. 2005. *Tao Yuanming and Manuscript Culture: The Record of a Dusty Table*. Seattle: University of Washington Press.

Tsien, Tsuen-hsuin. 2004. *Written on Bamboo and Silk: The Beginnings of Chinese Books and Inscriptions*, 2nd ed. Chicago: University of Chicago Press.

Tsuruma Kayazuki 鶴間和幸. 1978. "Kandai gōku no chiiki teki seikaku" 漢代豪族 の地域的性格. *Shigaku zasshi* 87:12: 1-38.

van Ess, Hans. unpublished ms. "The Uncrowned King Reconsidered: Variations on a Theme of the Chinese Past."

Vankeerberghen, Griet. 2010. "Texts in the *Shiji*" In *China's Early Empires: A Reappraisal,* ed. Michael Nylan and Michael Loewe. Cambridge: Cambridge University Press, 461-79.

Vendler, Helen. 1997. *The Art of Shakespeare's* Sonnets. Cambridge, Mass.: Harvard University Press.

Vervoorn, Aat. 1990. *Men of the Cliffs and Caves: The Development of the Chinese Eremitic Tradition to the End of the Han Dynasty*. Shatin, Hong Kong: Chinese University Press.

Veyne, Paul. 1988. *Did the Greeks Believe in Their Myths? An Essay on the Constitutive Imagination*, trans. Paula Wissing. Chicago: University of Chicago Press.

Wagner, Rudolf G. 2000. *Craft of a Chinese Commentator: Wang Bi on the Laozi*. Albany, N.Y.: State University of New York Press.

Wang Guowei 王國維. 2004. *Jiandu jianshu kaojiao zhu* 簡牘检署考校注, with annotations by Hu Pingsheng 胡平生 and Ma Yuehua 馬月華. Shanghai: Shanghai guji.

Wang Ping. 2010. "Between Reluctant Revelation and Disinterested Disclosure: Reading Xiao Tong's Preface to *Tao Yuanming ji*." *Asia Major* 3rd ser. 23.1: 201-22.

Wang Wentai 汪文臺. 1972. *Qijia Hou Hanshu* 七家後漢書. Taipei: n. p.

Wang Xianqian 王先謙. 1900. *Hanshu buzhu* 漢書補注. Changsha: Xushou tang; rpt. Taipei: Yiwen, 1955.

Wang Xiaoyi 王曉毅. 1994. "Jingzhou guanxue yu Sanguo sixiang wenhua" 荊州官學與三國思想文化. *Kongzi yanjiu* 孔子研究 1: 44–49.

Wang Yongping 王永平. 2005. *Zhonggu shiren qianyi yu wenhua jiaoliu* 中古士人遷移與文化交流. Beijing: Shehui kexue wenxian chubanshe.

Wilson, Thomas A. 1995. *The Genealogy of the Way: The Construction and Uses of the Confucian Tradition in Late Imperial China.* Stanford: Stanford University Press.

Wu Fusheng. 2007. "Han Epideictic Rhapsody: AProduct and Critique of Imperial Patronage." *Monumenta Serica* 55: 23-59.

Wu Xiaorun 吴小如, Wu Tongbin 吴同宾. 1982. *Zhongguo wenshi gongju ziliao shu juyao* 中国文史工具资料书举要. Beijing: Zhonghua shuju.

Xu Chaohua 徐朝華. 1987. *Er ya jin zhu* 爾雅今注. Tianjin: Nankai daxue chubanshe.

Xu Fuguan: See Hsü Fu-kuan.

Yan Lingfeng 嚴靈峰. 1975-79. *Zhou Qin Han Wei zhu zi zhi jian shu mu* 周秦漢魏諸子知見書目. Taipei: Zhengzhong shuju. 6 vols.

Yang Haizheng 杨海峥. 2003. *Han Tang Shi ji yan jiu lun gao* 汉唐史记研究论稿. Ji'nan: Qi Lu shushe.

Yates, Robin D.S. 2007. "Soldiers, Scribes, and Women: Literacy among the Lower Orders in Early China," English draft of a *Wenbo* 文博 essay, dated July 18, 2007.

Yoshikawa Tadao 吉川忠夫. 1983. "Go-Kan ni okeru Keishū no gakujutsu" 後漢における荊州の學術. In *Chūgoku shitaifu kaiyū to chi-iki sahkai tono kankei ni tsuiteno sōgōteki kenkyū* 中國士大夫階級と地域社會との關係についての總合, ed. Tanigawa Michio 谷川道雄. Kyoto: Kyōto daigaku.

_____ 1991. "Scholarship in Ching-chou at the End of the Later Han Dynasty." *Acta Asiatica* 60: 1–24.

Yoshinami Takeshi 好並隆司. 1976. "Kandai kōtei shihai chitsujo no keisei" 漢代皇帝支配の形成. *Tōyōshi kenkyū* 東洋史研究 35.2 (Sept.): 39-70.

Yu, Jiyuan. 2007. *The Ethics of Aristotle and Confucius.* London: Routledge.

Yuan Xingpei: See Tao Qian.

Zang Yong 臧庸. 1968. *Erya Han zhu* 爾雅漢注, ed. Zang Yong 臧庸, in *Wenjing tang congshu* 問經堂叢書, in *Baibu congshu jicheng* 百部叢書集成. vol. 38. Taipei: Yiwen Press, vol. 38.

Zhang Cunliang 张存良 and Wu Hong 吴荭. 2009. *Gansu Shuichang, Suiquanzi Hanmu qun* 甘肅水昌水泉子漢墓群.*Wenwu* 文物 (Oct.): 88-91.

Zhang Shichao 张世超. 2009. "Qi yan shi de qiyuan ji xiangguan wenti jin lun" 七言詩的起源及相關問題今論. *Shanxi daxue xuebao (Zhexue shehui kexue ban)* 山西大學學報 (哲學社會科學報) 32.9 (Nov.): 35-42.

Zhang Shuangdi 張雙棣. 1997. *Huainanzi jiaoshi* 淮南子校釋. Beijing: Beijing daxue.

Zhang Yi 張揖 (5th c.), Wang Niansun 王念孫 (early 18th c.). *Shang Guangya biao* 廣雅疏證, *Huang Qing jing jie* 皇清經解, 2000 rpt. Nanjiang: Jiangsu guji chubanshe.

Zhang Yunhua 張運華. 1992. "Jingzhou zhi xue yu Wei Jin xuanxu" 荊州之學與魏晉玄學.*Xiangtan daxue xuebao* (Shehui kexue ban) 18.4: 44-48.

Zhang Zhenze 張震澤. 1993. *Yang Xiong ji jiaozhu* 楊雄集校注. Shanghai: Shanghai guji.

Zhou Zumo 周祖謨 1984. *Erya jiaojian* 爾雅校箋. Nanjing: Jiangsu jiaoyu chubanshe.

_____ 1993. *Fangyan jiaojian* 方言校箋. Beijing: Zhonghua shuju.

Zhu Qianzhi 朱謙之. 2009. *Xinji ben Huan Tan Xin lun* 新輯本桓譚新論. Beijing: Zhonghua shuju.